The Dunces of Doomsday

10 blunders that gave rise to Radical Islam, Terrorist Regimes, and the threat of an American Hiroshima

Paul L. Williams

WND BOOKS

AN IMPRINT OF CUMBERLAND HOUSE PUBLISHING, INC.
NASHVILLE, TENNESSEE

THE DUNCES OF DOOMSDAY
A WND BOOK
PUBLISHED BY CUMBERLAND HOUSE PUBLISHING, INC.
431 Harding Industrial Drive
Nashville, Tennessee 37211

Cover design by James Duncan Creative, Nashville, Tennessee

Library of Congress Cataloging-in-Publication Data

Williams, Paul L.
    The dunces of doomsday : 10 blunders that gave rise to radical Islam, terrorist regimes, and the threat of an American Hiroshima / Paul L. Williams.
        p.   cm.
    Includes bibliographical references and index.
    ISBN-13: 978-1-58182-529-9 (hardcover : alk. paper)
    ISBN-10: 1-58182-529-3 (hardcover : alk. paper)
    1. Islamic countries—Foreign relations—United States. 2. United States—Foreign relations—Islamic countries. 3. United States—Foreign relations—1945–1989.
4. United States—Foreign relations—1989– . 5. Islamic fundamentalism. 6. Nuclear weapons—Government policy—United States. 7. Terrorism—Religious aspects—Islam. I. Title.
DS35.74.U6W55 2006
327.73017'67—dc22

                                                                    2006004336

Printed in the United States of America

1 2 3 4 5 6 7 8 9 10—09 08 07 06

For Judith Ann Schmitt

my sister, my spiritual adviser, my best friend

Jesus said, ". . . You will know the truth, and the truth will set you free."

JOHN 8:31–32

Contents

Prologue

The Dunce Cap

THE FRANCES WILLARD ELEMENTARY School in Scranton, Pennsylvania, was not a model of progressive education in the 1950s. Students were compelled to march in single file against the wall when they entered or exited the building, the desks were bolted to the floor, and discipline was administered by the paddle. I, as a rather rebellious lad from a line of Irish coal miners, was paddled almost every day from kindergarten to sixth grade. Usually I was compelled to hold out my hand for the teacher to whack with a ruler or Ping-Pong paddle. The pain, as I remember it, was excruciating, and the teachers—all of whom, in my memory, were gray-haired, tightly corseted, grim, and beady-eyed matrons with yellow teeth—would paddle me until tears flowed down my cheeks. The tears, I believe, were viewed as empirical evidence that the punishment had led me into a state of true attrition.

Nobody in Frances Willard spoke out of turn in class. To answer a question or ask permission to go to the lavatory, you had to raise your hand and wait for the teacher to acknowledge you. The requests for visits to the privy were summarily dismissed unless deemed absolutely urgent. In such cases, you were granted an official hall pass that you had to present to a hallway attendant before you could proceed to the boys' or girls' restrooms. There were also rooms for men and women, but the only men in the building were Mr. Lavelle, a funereal figure who served as principal, and Mr. Bartosh, the hunchbacked janitor who, we believed, lived in the basement.

Within this regimented facility, you always knew your place among your classmates. Seating was arranged according to report-card grades. The first two rows were reserved for the best and the brightest, the middle row for the mediocre, and the last three rows for the dullards and dimwits. There was always a disproportionate ratio between the stupid and the smart. The seating arrangement represented my first introduction to social Darwinism. The few boys (always fewer than three) who occupied the first two rows were, in the opinion of those of us who inhabited the last three rows, sissies and brownnosers who deserved to be taunted and tormented whenever encountered after school hours.

In sixth grade my instructor was Miss Sadie O'Malley, the strictest and meanest of the shrew teachers. She always wore cashmere sweaters (she made frequent mention of this fact), even in the spring and early fall, and sported a hairstyle that made her look as though she were wearing a Roman helmet.

In an apparent stride toward modernity, Miss O'Malley initiated a new form of discipline in her classroom. Those who spoke out of turn, failed to complete their homework assignments, giggled at inappropriate times, or uttered stupid remarks were obliged to sit on high stools in front of the class with white cone-shaped dunce caps on their heads.

At first, this new form of punishment was very effective and made everyone in class laugh at the sight of the dunce on display. But a problem soon arose. Bernie Valunis and Henry Smith, without fail, would end up as the daily dunces because they never did their homework. And so the novelty of seeing Bernie and Henry in pointed caps wore off until the spectacle was no longer a matter of high hilarity but of low consequence.

Realizing this flaw in her system, Miss O'Malley came up with new grounds for determining dunces. George Bonna became a dunce for multiplying rather than dividing a math problem. Joe Needham for coming to school with head lice. And Billy Harris for laughing when Miss O'Malley split her skirt while picking up an eraser. I too got to wear the cap for writing a short essay (my first attempt at satire) in which Miss Sadie O'Malley appeared as Miss Sadist of the Galley and my classmates as galley slaves in a ship bound for Devil's Island. It really wasn't very funny, and I, more than any others in my class, truly deserved the punishment.

Years later, as a graduate student of medieval philosophy at Drew

University, I discovered that dunce caps come from thirteenth-century philosopher John Duns Scotus, who (surprisingly) was born in Duns, Scotland. This rather oblique scholar believed that conical hats served to increase the potential for learning. His theory was that knowledge centralizes at the apex and then funnels into the mind of the wearer. He also argued that the caps served to prevent important knowledge from escaping the brain by osmosis and vaporizing into thin air. Of course, none of this makes a great deal of sense. For this reason, the "Duns" caps came to symbolize downright stupidity.

From reading such works as John Ford's *The Sun's Darling* (1624) and Charles Dickens's *The Old Curiosity Shop* (1840), one discovers that the practice of dumb students donning dunce caps was a common practice in merry old England.

I state the above to establish my credentials to write this book. I am one of the few established writers in the United States who has actually worn the cap and been designated publicly as a dunce. An old adage states, "It takes one to know one." Who, then, is better prepared than I to identify fellow dunces?

But the dunces that are the subjects of this book—instead of missing homework assignments and committing classroom errors—have made blunders that have given rise to radical Islam, the war on "terror," the occupation of Iraq, and thousands of terrorist attacks throughout the world. These dunces, by either pigheadedness or venality, have placed the lives of millions of Americans in jeopardy. They deserve, as a reward, to be paraded as fools and scoundrels within these pages.

But the purpose of this work is not the parade. By exposing the follies of past and present policies, we might be able to stand against the enemy in our current war with purpose and resolve. It is an enemy that has threatened Western civilization for nearly fourteen hundred years. An enemy that is highly sophisticated, incredibly cunning, and nuclear-capable. It is an enemy intent upon our destruction.

We have been foolish far too long.

The Dunces of Doomsday

BLUNDER 1

Refusing to Identify the Enemy

I want to speak tonight directly to Muslims throughout the world.
We respect your faith. It's practiced freely by many millions of
Americans and by millions more in countries that America counts
as friends. Its teachings are good and peaceful, and those who
commit evil in the name of Allah blaspheme the name of Allah.
The terrorists are traitors to their own faith, trying, in effect, to hijack Islam itself. The enemy of America is not our many Muslim
friends; it is not our many Arab friends. Our enemy is a radical
network of terrorists, and every government that supports them.
Our war on terror begins with al Qaeda, but it does not end there.
It will not end until every terrorist group of global reach has been
found, stopped and defeated.

President George W. Bush, Address to Congress,
September 20, 2001

THE WAR WITHOUT A NAME

The above statement from President Bush represents a falsehood. The
United States is not engaged in a "war on terror." Terror represents a
military tactic that is often more psychological than real. It represents
neither a definable group of militant adherents nor a body politic with a
standing army. A war on terror, by definition, is a misnomer.

Neither is the United States engaged in a war against "radical
Islam" nor terrorists who are trying "to hijack Islam itself." This is verified by the fact that Wahhabism, the most virulent and radical sect of

Islam, has been the official religion of Arabia since 1932—the year when the Saud family established its dynasty. Within Saudi Arabia, adultery, blasphemy, and witchcraft remain crimes punishable by death, women must wear long black abaya gowns and are prohibited from driving cars and appearing in public, and crucifixions represent an acceptable form of capital punishment.[1] The situation in Saudi Arabia, where virtual servitude for non-Muslim workers still exists, is scarcely different from life in Afghanistan under the Taliban. Yet we are not at war with Saudi Arabia.

What's more, the United States is not engaged in a war against al Qaeda. Al Qaeda is just one Muslim terrorist group among hundreds of others throughout the world. "The Declaration of Jihad Against Jews and Christians" of February 28, 1998 was signed not only by Osama bin Laden but also by Ayman al-Zawahiri on behalf of the Jihad Group in Egypt; Abu-Yasir Rifa'I Ahmad Taha, leader of the Islamic Group (Algeria); Sheikh Mir Hamzah, secretary of the Jamiat-ul-Ulema-e-Pakistan; and Fazul Rahman, leader of the Jihad Movement in Bangladesh. The statement received the endorsement of Asbat al Ansar (Lebanon), Harakat ul-Ansar/Mujahideen (Pakistan), al-Badar (Pakistan), the Armed Islamic Group/GIA (Algeria), the Saafi Group for Proselytism and Combat (Algeria), Talaa al Fath (Vanguards of Conquest), the Groupe Roubaix (Canada/France), Harakat ul Jihad (Pakistan), Jaish Mohammad (Pakistan), Jamiat Ulema-e-Islam (Pakistan), Hezbollah (Lebanon), Hezb ul-Mujahideen (Pakistan), al-Gama'a al-Islamiyya (Egypt), al-Hadith (Pakistan), Hamas (Palestinian Authority), the Islamic Movement of Uzbekistan, al-Jihad Group (Yemen), Laskar e-Toiba (Pakistan), the Lebanese Partisans League, the Libyan Islamic Group, the Moro Islamic Liberation Front (Philippines), the Partisans' Movement (Kasmir), Abu Sayyff (Philippines), Al-Ittihad (Somalia), the Ulema Union of Afghanistan, and others. The United States is at war with all of these organizations, which constitute the World Islamic Front. Al Qaeda represents one head of the hydra. If this head is severed, another will appear.

Nor is America at war with militant Islam. U.S. troops haven't been deployed to Russia to suppress the Chechen rebellion or to the Balkans to quash the slaughter of Christians by ethnic Albanians.

It isn't necessary to hold an advanced degree in military science to realize that the United States cannot win the present war if its government officials are reluctant to name, let alone face, the enemy.

And the United States faces a formidable enemy, an enemy that has threatened Western civilization for fourteen hundred years. This enemy possesses an army of untold millions in countries across the world. It has established sleeper cells in houses of worship and religious centers in every major metropolitan area in the United States. It has amassed nuclear weapons and remains intent upon killing four million American civilians—two million of whom must be children—for the sake of "parity."[2] It is an enemy that the richest and most powerful nation on earth has been unable to suppress, let alone vanquish. It is an army that has caused the collapse of the Soviet Union and has defeated U.S. forces in Somalia and Lebanon.

THE ENEMY REVEALED

The enemy is Islam. Not a fringe group within this body of believers who constitute one-fifth of the world's population. Not "radical" Islam as if such a faction can be separated from "mainstream" Islam. But Islam itself, as expressed by the life and teachings of Muhammad, as witnessed by the sociopolitical and religious movement that the Prophet unleashed against Judeo-Christian civilization, as upheld by contemporary Sunnis and Shi'ites throughout the world.

The following supports proof of this claim:

1. The televised spectacle of Muslims in Afghanistan, Algeria, Egypt, Indonesia, Kuwait, Pakistan, the Philippines, Saudi Arabia, Sudan, Yemen, England, and New Jersey dancing in the streets upon hearing of the attacks on the World Trade Center and the Pentagon.
2. The omnipresent images of Osama bin Laden in shops, stores, stalls and marketplaces across the Islamic world and the fact that Osama is now the favored name for newly born Muslim boys.[3]
3. A classified CIA survey shows that 95 percent of educated Saudis between the ages of twenty-one and forty-five support al Qaeda and jihad.[4]
4. A Gallup Poll affirms that a majority of the world's one billion Muslims have an unfavorable opinion of the United States.[5]

5. A 2005 Pew Global Attitude Poll shows that 60 percent of the population of Jordan and 51 percent of Pakistanis have confidence in bin Laden and only 11 percent of the Jordanians and 46 percent of the Pakistanis oppose suicide bombings against the United States and Western countries—these figures become more alarming when one realizes that the poll was conducted of the general populations of both countries, Muslim and non-Muslim alike.[6]

6. An earlier Pew poll shows that 58 percent of the people in Indonesia and 49 percent of the population of Morocco openly expressed their support of bin Laden.[7]

7. Even in Turkey, where the popularity of bin Laden is lowest, 31 percent favor the bombing and killing of American civilians.[8]

8. Anti-Western statements from prominent imams and Muslim religious leaders in such "pro-Western" countries as Albania, Egypt, Kuwait, Pakistan, and Saudi Arabia.

9. Anti-Western statements by contemporary scholars from all four schools of Islamic thought—Malaki, Hanafi, Hanabali, and Shafii.

The real fringe group within Islam is neither al Qaeda nor any other Muslim terrorist group but rather the Sufis, who preach love between God and humanity, uphold principles of strict asceticism, and live in quiet meditation among monastic settings. The Sufis, who represent less than 5 percent of Islam, have been subjected to centuries of violent persecution and brutal oppression from their fellow Muslims.[9]

Of course, the sweeping statement that "our enemy is mainstream Islam" requires a measure of qualification. It does not mean that Americans should trash local grocers for wearing turbans, prohibit veiled women from entering public buildings, or form militias to lay siege to the fourteen hundred mosques in the United States, knowing that more than 80 percent of them have been established by Wahhabists from Saudi Arabia and remain under the control of the Islamic Society of North America, an organization that is funded by the Saudis as a tool to spread the teachings of Wahhabism.[10]

To be sure, many Muslims in America are good, law-abiding citizens entitled to life, liberty, and the pursuit of happiness. But this awareness should not blind us to the realization that other Muslims in our midst—including students, academicians, government employees, merchants, physicians, lawyers, military officials, media executives, and even FBI, CIA, and Justice Department officials—are intent upon our destruction.

DEBUNKING "ISLAMOPHOBIA"

Still, the statement that the enemy is mainstream Islam smacks of "Islamophobia," a dreadful condition recently diagnosed by Islamic apologists and U.N. officials that runs unchecked among conservatives and so-called Orientalists (Western imperialists who dare espouse anything negative about Islam and the Orient).

An individual afflicted with Islamophobia, according to Kofi Annan, who presided over a 2004 U.N. seminar on this subject, manifests the psychological disorder in the following manner:

1. Attacks the Islamic faith as a problem for world peace.
2. Views Islamic history as a history of violence and suppression.
3. Denies that the majority of Muslims throughout the world are "moderate" in their views.
4. Treats conflicts involving Muslims (such as the situation in Bosnia-Herzegovina a decade ago) as the fault of Muslims alone.
5. Incites militant aggression against Islam as a whole.[11]

Language, as the great philosopher Ernst Cassirer pointed out, molds thought. The coining of the word *Islamophobia* represents an attempt by U.N. officials and leftist critics to make people believe that anyone who views Islam as a militant threat is a nutcase with an irrational phobia. This move represents an effort to reverse logic: to make the American people believe that they are the aggressors in the war against Islam, that they are responsible for the attacks of 9/11, and that they have wronged the Muslim people by their lack of respect for the *shariah* (Islamic law).

But Islamophobia is no more a phobia or irrational fear than Aryanophobia would have been for those who feared the rise of Adolf Hitler or the threat of the Third Reich or Marxophobia would have been for those who feared the spread of Communism and the threat posed by the Soviet Union and Communist China. Islamophobia is a totally justifiable fear and a coherent intellectual position, as is evident by the following:

1. Every conflict within today's world, from Chechnya to Somalia, from Indonesia to the Iraq, from Afghanistan to Argentina, from the Balkans to the Philippines, involves a manifestation of Islam. Moreover, Muslim radicals have attacked U.S. forces and innocent civilians in such diverse places as Kenya, Lebanon, New York, Tanzania, Washington DC, and Yemen.

2. Islamic history, from the birth of the Prophet Muhammad to the rise of al Qaeda, is a history of unredeemed violence and brutal suppression (see the next chapter).

3. The majority of Muslims throughout the world are not "moderate" in their views. Robert Spencer writes: "Whether a moderate Muslim majority exists depends on how you define 'moderate Muslim.' Is it the one who will never engage in terrorist acts? That would make moderates an overwhelming majority of Muslims worldwide. Or is a moderate one who sincerely disapproves of those terrorist acts? That would reduce the number of moderates. Or is a moderate Muslim one who actively speaks out and works against the jihadists? That would lower the number yet again. Or finally is a moderate Muslim one who actively engages the jihadists in a theological battle, trying to convince Muslims that jihad terrorism is wrong on Islamic grounds? That would leave us with a tiny handful."[12] On the same subject, Dr. Ali Suna provided the following testimony to the U.S. Senate Select Committee on Intelligence and the U.S. House Permanent Select Committee on Intelligence: "What is the difference between a moderate Muslim and a terrorist Muslim? As a former Muslim myself, my long and careful analysis leads me to the conclusion that the only difference is the latter wants to start the jihad against the infidels now, while the former thinks it is better to wait until the Muslims are strong and then attack."[13]

4. Few "Occidentalists," even those who suffer from the most acute form of Islamophobia, will encourage the Bush administration to take arms against the Sufis in their monasteries, the peaceful and pro-Western populace of Tunisia (the shining example of hope in the Muslim world), or the grizzled shepherds in Kazakhstan.

5. The United States has not incited warfare against the people of Islam. The people of Islam have declared war on the United States,

as evidenced by the widespread support for Osama bin Laden and the World Islamic Statement of 1998.

REFUSAL TO CALL A SPADE A SPADE

The refusal of the Bush administration to identify the enemy represents the first blunder in the present war. This error has resulted in the refusal of our law enforcement and government officials to engage in ethnic and religious profiling. The full extent of the ridiculousness of the current position was brought to light by CBS correspondent Steve Kroft in the course of an interview with U.S. Transportation Secretary Norman Mineta for *60 Minutes.*

At the start of the interview, Mineta told Kroft that any consideration of race, religion, or nationality must be forbidden in airport security. When Kroft inquired if there were any circumstances in which profiling would make sense, Mineta replied, "Absolutely not." When Kroft questioned if a young Muslim man in a turban should be treated the same as an elderly white woman in a cotton dress, Mineta said, "Basically, I hope so." Kroft then pressed the issue by asking, "If you saw three young Arab men sitting, kneeling, praying, before they boarded a flight, getting on, talking to each other in Arabic, getting on the plane, no reason to stop and ask them any questions?" President Bush's Secretary of Transportation replied, "No reason."[14]

Did you ever wonder why blue-eyed Baptists, freckle-faced kids, and gray-haired old ladies are being frisked and searched at airports while turbaned Muslims pass through security without delay or scrutiny? The answer rests with asinine officials like Mineta.

THE ISLAMIC INFESTATION OF THE FBI

This blunder has caused us to accept our foes as our friends and to grant them positions of power within our country. The FBI, manifesting political correctness above common sense, recruited hundreds of ethnic Arabs and Muslims from terror-related countries to translate documents from terrorist sources. On the morning of 9/11, Sibel Sinez Edmonds, an FBI employee, discovered these translators celebrating the news of the attacks on the World Trade Center and the Pentagon. "It's about time they got a taste of what they've been giving the Middle East," the translators told her. The supervisor of the office was not reprimanded for the behavior of these Arabs when reports reached his superiors. Instead, he was promoted to running the Arabic desk, the key position for discerning al Qaeda plots. And he obtained this position after threatening to sue the bureau for racial discrimination.

The Case of Agent Gamal Abdel Hafiz

The refusal to identify the enemy has caused the FBI to hire as special agents in charge of national security Muslims who were born and raised in terror-related countries. One such agent is Gamal Abdel Hafiz, an Egyptian national who obtained U.S. citizenship in 1990.

As a member of the FBI's elite International Terrorism Squad, Hafiz was assigned to the case of BMI (Bait al-Mal, Inc.), an Islamic bank in Secaucus, New Jersey, with financial ties to Osama bin Laden and other terrorists. In 1999 a BMI accountant informed the FBI that the bank's funds had been used to finance the al Qaeda bombings of the U.S. embassies in Kenya and Tanzania.[15] When Special Agent Hafiz was asked by his superiors to meet with Saliman Biheiri, the president of BMI, and to record the conversation, he expressed outrage and asserted, "A Muslim does not record another Muslim." When pressed on the matter, Hafiz blurted out, "I do not record another Muslim. That is against my religion."[16] Attorney Mark Flessner prosecuted the case against BMI and commented on Hafiz's behavior: "It was surreal. I've never heard it happening in the history of the FBI."[17] Special Agent John B. Vincent, who worked with Hafiz, added: "He [Hafiz] wouldn't have any problems interviewing or recording anyone who wasn't a Muslim, but he couldn't record a Muslim."[18]

Agent Hafiz and the Muslim College Professor

Hafiz also became involved in the investigation of Sami al-Arian, a former professor of computer science at the University of Southern Florida (USF). Al-Arian was the organizer of an American cell of the Palestinian Islamic Jihad and transferred vast sums of money to this terrorist group. In its manifesto, Palestinian Islamic Jihad speaks of the United States as the "Great Satan" and proclaims that the group's objective is the destruction of Israel and the end of all Western influence in the Middle East. The group is responsible for the murder of more than one hundred civilians in Israel and Israeli-occupied territories. The victims include two Americans, twenty-year-old Alisha Flatow and sixteen-year-old Shoshana bin-Yishai.[19]

Al-Arian, along with fellow USF professor Basheer Nafi, created the World Islam Studies Enterprise (WISE), which became a breeding ground for jihadists. Blind sheikh Omar Abel-Rahman and a host of other co-conspirators of the 1993 attack at the World Trade Center were frequent visitors to WISE. By 1996 a ratline was established between New York and central Florida to coordinate terrorist activities. Many prominent jihadists from the Al-Farouq Mosque in Brooklyn and the al-Salam Mosque in Jersey City traveled the ratline. The list includes Ramzi Yousef, the chief strategist of the 1993 attack; Jose Padilla, later indicted for an attempt to blow up the Brooklyn Bridge with a radiological device; Mohammed Atta and the other al Qaeda operatives of 9/11; and Adnan el-Shukrijumah, who has been singled out to serve as the commander of the upcoming American Hiroshima.

Upon receiving notice that he was the target of an FBI probe, al-Arian sought out Special Agent Hafiz at a law-enforcement conference in Washington DC and questioned Hafiz about the details of the case.

When he returned to headquarters, Hafiz informed his FBI colleagues about his encounter with al-Arian. Sensing a unique opportunity to extract information about the workings of Islamic terrorist groups within the United States, Barry Carmody, an FBI veteran of thirty-four years, asked Hafiz to follow up his meeting with al-Arian with a telephone call and to secretly tape-record the conversation. Hafiz was outraged by this suggestion, even though such "bugging" was standard FBI procedure. He exclaimed that he would not record the conversation without al-Arian's knowledge and permission. "That's outrageous!" Carmody replied. "That defeats the whole purpose!"[20]

Indeed, the purpose *was* defeated. Hafiz, by his refusal to tape al-Arian, may have prevented the FBI from obtaining valuable information that could have served to uproot al Qaeda's presence in the United States, to thwart the plans for 9/11, and to obtain vital information concerning the activities of cells of Muslim terrorists throughout the country.

Professor Al-Arian's Plight

The case against al-Arian dragged on for years—thanks to Special Agent Hafiz and USF students and faculty members who rallied to the radical professor's defense. When the board of trustees and university president Judy Genshaft moved to remove al-Arian, the Coalition of Progressive Student Organizations at USF published a letter expressing its outrage at "an act of injustice against a tenured faculty professor" that represents "a violation of academic free speech."[21] The coalition represented members of the Africana Studies Club, Amnesty International, the Campus Greens, the College Democrats, Ciba Viva, Free the Planet, the Free Thinkers, the Muslim Student Alliance, the NAACP, NOW@USF, the Student Environmental Association, Students for International Peace and Justice, the PRIDE Alliance, and the Shanachie.[22] The Free Thinkers group represents an interesting addition to the coalition since no student organization on campus displayed sufficient free thought to decry al-Arian's terrorist ties or his anti-American and anti-Israeli activities—not even when tapes were played from speeches in which al-Arian demanded "Death to Israel" and "damnation" for the United States.

On February 20, 2003, al-Arian was indicted in federal court on fifty counts of international terrorism, including money laundering, racketeering, perjury, obstruction of justice, and travel act violations. On December 14, 2005, a Tampa jury acquitted al-Arian of eight counts, making it clear that raising money for terrorist acts does not make a man a terrorist in a U.S. court of law. Despite the verdict, al-Arian remains behind bars in the Coleman Correctional Facility in Sumter County, Florida, while prosecutors decide whether to retry on the charges that caused a deadlock among the jurors.

The Fate of Agent Hafiz

Al-Arian is in the slammer, at least for the time being, but what of Special Agent Hafiz, who refused to tape conversations with fellow Muslims? Was he drummed out of the FBI in disgrace? Was he charged with dereliction of duty? Was he placed on permanent suspension because of his possible involvement with Islamic terrorism? Of course not! The FBI, no less than the students and faculty at USF, did not want to be branded as Islamophobic. Hafiz, therefore, was promoted to the post of deputy legal attaché in Riyadh, Saudi Arabia.[23]

While serving at the FBI post in Riyadh, Hafiz managed to convert Wilfred Rattigan, the legal attaché and his immediate supervisor, to Islam. The two agents set off to Mecca for a *hajj,* the pilgrimage to the holy city that must be made by all believers at least once during their lifetime.[24]

Within months of Hafiz's arrival in Saudi Arabia, the central headquarters of the FBI in Washington DC began receiving complaints about the failure of the Riyadh office to pursue leads regarding terrorist activities. Bureau chiefs were dispatched to investigate the matter. They discovered that Hafiz had shredded more than two thousand documents relating to al Qaeda and the 9/11 attacks.[25] Several of these documents were not duplicated in FBI computer files, including letters from Saudi officials concerning terror suspects.[26] Hafiz and Rattigan were recalled to the States.

The story of Hafiz has the ending of a fractured fairy tale. Bertie Abdel-Hafiz, his ex-wife, charged that he had faked a burglary at their home in Roanoke, Texas, in order to collect an insurance claim of twenty-five thousand dollars.[27] Hafiz was placed on administrative leave, pending a disciplinary review. During the course of the review, Hafiz failed a lie-detector test by denying that he had filed a bogus claim.[28] Despite this, the FBI, in an extraordinary move, reinstated Hafiz to his former position. Hafiz, when contacted by the press, said that he was "thrilled" to have his job back and to "have this injustice lifted."[29]

Isn't it comforting to know that agents like Hafiz have been placed in positions to protect and defend the people of the United States from Islamic terrorists? For this situation, the American people have to thank FBI director Robert Mueller, who deserves a place of prominence among the pointy-headed subjects of this book.

MUELLER MANDATES MUSLIM SENSITIVITY SESSIONS

In the wake of 9/11, FBI Director Mueller said, "The Bureau is against—has been and will be against—any kind of profiling [of Muslims]."[30] Fortunately for the American people, J. Edgar Hoover didn't feel this way during World War II when he rounded up Nazi sympathizers,

Bund and German-American officials supportive of the Third Reich, and secret agents of the Third Reich.

But Mueller doesn't want to be perceived as a figure of intolerance or a religious bigot. For this reason he mandated that all agents must attend sensitivity training sessions in Islamic customs and practices in order not to offend Muslims with a crude remark or disrespectful gesture. The training was provided by imams, mullahs, and Islamic religious leaders and included lessons in the benevolent nature of the Muslim religion. During the sessions, the agents were not allowed to raise questions about the prophet Muhammad or the teachings of the Koran that might be offensive to their instructors. "The Muslim and Arab leaders Mueller brought in to train us about Islam weren't interested in helping us investigate terrorism," former FBI Special Agent John B. Vincent said. "They all have an agenda of making sure FBI agents don't discriminate against Muslims and Arabs. They even came to Quantico to lecture new agents on how not to pick on them."[31]

Director Mueller himself, in order to purge himself of any impure thoughts concerning Islam, received regular private instruction and sensitivity consultation from Khalid Suffuri, former deputy director of the American Muslim Council (AMC).[32] At Suffuri's request, Mueller served as the keynote speaker at the annual AMC luncheon in Washington DC.

Mueller and the Mullahs

By appearing at this luncheon, the FBI director remained completely unaware that he had stumbled into the enemy's camp. AMC has voiced support for Hamas and Hezbollah, Islamic terrorist groups that are responsible for the murders of hundreds of Israelis and Americans.[33]

Mueller, as the leading counterterrorism official in the country, should have known that the organization was suspect by noting that other speakers at the gathering included members of the Palestine Liberation Organization (PLO) and representatives from the Syrian government, an officially designated "terror-sponsoring nation."[34] Did Mueller take note? Did he suspect that something might be fishy with the AMC? Did he head for the nearest exit door? Of course not! In his address, Mueller instead praised the AMC as "the most mainstream Muslim group in the U.S."[35]

Meet the Mainstream Muslim Group's Director

Several months later, after Mueller's memorable appearance at the luncheon, Abdurahman M. Alamoudi, the director and founder of AMC, was arrested for plotting terrorist acts with Libya and funding terrorist activities. At his trial, federal prosecutors produced tapes in which Alamoudi called for the conquest of America in the name of Allah and complained that the 1998 al Qaeda attacks on U.S. embassies in Kenya and Tanzania were far from effective since they resulted in "killing more Africans than Americans."[36] Alamoudi was found guilty and sentenced to twenty-three years in a federal penitentiary.[37]

After his incarceration, more information came to light regarding Alamoudi, including allegations from the U.S. Treasury Department that the AMC founder had close ties with Osama bin Laden and had raised money for al Qaeda throughout the United States[38]

Mueller wasn't the only Washington official to be fooled by Alamoudi and his mainstream group. Alamoudi took part with President Bush in a prayer service for the victims of 9/11 and arranged a Ramadan fast-breaking dinner for congressional leaders at the behest of President Bill Clinton. The *Washington Post* hailed Alamoudi as "a pillar of the local Muslim community," and his face appeared on the cover of *Silent No More: America's False Images of Islam,* a popular book that lionized "mainstream" Muslim leaders.[39] But Mueller is the country's leading counterterrorism official, and if he doesn't recognize the enemy, then the American people are in serious trouble.

AMERICA RETURNS TO THE QUAGMIRE

Not only has the blunder of refusing to identify the enemy resulted in the failure to profile Muslims as terrorists and to hire Islamic nationals to protect the American people from the next attack, but it also has caused the Bush administration to stumble into the horrific quagmire of Iraq (eerily similar to Vietnam) with the mistaken belief that the Iraqi people are friends of the United States and proponents of Western democracy.

After liberating Iraq from the tyrannical rule of Hussein, spending more than $300 billion in Iraqi aid, and losing more than two thousand soldiers to the so-called insurrectionists, the Bush administration blithely assumed it could handpick candidates to establish a secular government that would be the antithesis of the theocracy in Iran.

The U.S. choice for president of the envisioned democracy was Ayad Allawi, whom the Bush administration had propped up to serve as prime minister of the interim government. Millions were spent to secure Allawi's election. Radio and television ads flooded Iraqi radio and television. Flyers were dispatched to every inhabitant of every town and village. Billboards were erected in the marketplaces of every city. Yet Allawi was trounced in the January 30, 2005, election, receiving less than 18 percent of the vote. The Kurdish Alliance, under Jalal Talabani, and the United Iraqi Alliance, under Abdel Aziz al-Hazim, gathered the remaining 72 percent. Talabani is a Kurdish warlord with a long history of shady deals with Israel, the shah of Iran, Turkey, Britain, and the United States. His tug-of-war with rival warlord Masoud Barzani caused the deaths of tens of thousands of Kurds.[40] He has strong ties to the mullahs in Iran who supported his campaign.

Abdel Aziz al-Hazim is a Shi'ite cleric who spent years as an exile in Iran. He espouses the teachings of Ayatollah Ruhollah Khomeini, the spiritual leader and founder of Iran's Islamic Republic.

In response to the election, President Bush praised the Iraqis "for defying terrorist threats and setting their country on the path of democracy and freedom. And I congratulate every candidate who stood for election and those who will take office once the results are certified."[41]

ELECTION RESULTS FROM IRAQ

In truth, the election results could not have been worse for the Bush White House. "This is a government that will have very good relations with Iran," said Juan Cole, an expert on Iraq and political science professor at the University of Michigan. "The Kurdish victory reinforces this conclusion. Talabani is very close to Tehran. In terms of regional geopolitics, this is not the outcome that the United States was hoping for."[42] Similarly, Rami Khouri, editor of Beirut's *Daily Star* added: "The idea that the United States would get a quick, stable, prosperous, pro-American and pro-Israel Iraq has not happened. Most of the neoconservative assumptions about what would happen have proven false."[43]

Any doubts about the disastrous outcomes of the election for the United States were put to rest when Jalal Talabani, as the new Iraqi president, named Ibrahim al-Jaafari as prime minister. Al-Jaafari served as the leader of the Islamic Dawa Party, which upholds the teachings of Ayatollah Khomeini.

One of the first moves of the new government was to establish close relations with the Shi'ite leaders and mullahs of Iran. On May 17, 2005, Iranian foreign minister Kamal Kharzai arrived in Iraq for a landmark visit to show support for the new government in Baghdad. "Iran's absolutely ready to cooperate with Iraq in all fields, the economy as well as other issues of common interest," Kharzai said.[44] The ties were tightened after the arrival of al-Jaafari and seven senior ministers in Tehran on July 16, 2005, to establish trade agreements between the two countries.

In keeping with these developments, President Talabani expressed his willingness to use Kurdish *peshmerga* (private Badr brigades) and the Shi'ite militia to fight Sunni resistance throughout the country. Civil war is expected to erupt in Iraq as soon as the *peshmerga* and Shi'ite forces arrive in Kirkuk to guard the oil fields.[45]

President Bush's nightmare has come to pass. The elections resulted not in the establishment of a new democracy in Iraq but rather the creation of a paler version of the Islamic republic next door with a patched-together constitution (yet to be ratified) that calls for the imposition of Islamic law on all citizens. Furthermore, the population of Kurds, Sunnis, and Shi'ites is held together only by only its mutual hatred of the United States.

THE IRAQIS EXPRESS THEMSELVES

This hatred has been repeatedly expressed by leading Iraqi clerics. Shi'ite Sheikh Majid al Saadi, the religious leader of Baghdad's Kadhimiye shrine, fumed against the United States in an interview with *Wall Street Journal* reporter Yaroslav Trofimow:

Wasn't it America who supported Hussein in the first place during the worst horrors of the 1980s? And wasn't it Washington that betrayed a U.S.-inspired Shi'ite uprising in 1991? That was our first experience with American promises of democracy. We've realized it's a democracy of mass graves. The Americans say they have come to liberate us. Sure, they've come to liberate Iraqis from their bodies. Everyone who shakes a hand with these invaders should have his hand cut off. Everyone who smiles at the oppressors should enter hell.[46]

Similarly, Sunni Sheikh Qutaiba Ammash, imam of Baghdad's al-Nidaa Mosque, railed: "They [the Governing Council of Iraq] dared to proclaim a national holiday on April 9, to celebrate Baghdad's rape by the invaders. God bless our martyrs and protect our prisoners. Let God destroy the people who support America and America itself."[47]

The hatred became crystallized for the world to see on April 9, 2005—Iraq's so-called liberation day—when more than thirty thousand Iraqis gathered in the center of Baghdad with cries of "Out with the U.S. Occupiers" and "Death to Bush."[48]

President Bush may not have realized it, but a secular government had already existed in Iraq before the U.S.-led invasion. It had been established by Hussein.

THE TERROR WITHIN AMERICA'S MOSQUES

Since the government refuses to acknowledge that the enemy is mainstream Islam, a highly seditious and extremely dangerous situation has been allowed to persist within the majority of the fourteen hundred mosques throughout America. Sheikh Hisham Kabbani, chairman of the Islamic Supreme Council of America, expressed his belief that 80 percent of the mosques in the United States support terrorism, sanction the jihad, and call for the destruction of the United States.[49] Kabbani further testified that Muslim schools, community centers, professional associations, and commercial enterprises share the views of al Qaeda, remain hostile to American culture, and want to replace the U.S. constitutional form of government with an Islamic order.[50]

Representative Peter King of New York, a member of the House Select Committee on Homeland Security, believes that Kabbani's assessment is askew. He insists it is too conservative. According to King, 85 percent of U.S. mosques have been radicalized and the leaders and members of the Islamic houses of worship are not cooperative with law-enforcement officials.[51]

Spiritual Gifts from Saudi Arabia

These findings are not surprising. Saudi Arabia has spent more than ninety billion dollars since 1973 to spread Wahhabi teachings throughout the United States.[52] Osama bin Laden's doctrine is pure Wahhabism, and all members of al Qaeda's high command are committed Wahhabists.

Of the fourteen hundred mosques in America, 90 percent have been built in the last twenty years with Wahhabi funds from Saudi Arabia.[53] The 9/11 hijackers received support and shelter from at least seven U.S. mosques. The *zarat*, or tithes, collected in many of these religious establishments serve no good or charitable cause. They rather go to support al Qaeda, Hamas, Hezbollah, the Palestinian "martyrs," and the *madrassahs* (for training a new generation of jihadists) in Afghanistan and Pakistan.

Some U.S. mosques are incredibly opulent, such as the Dar-al-Hijrah Islamic Center, a six-million-dollar structure replete with minarets, in the posh Washington suburb of Falls Church, Virginia. Others are squalid places in the midst of urban ghettos, such as the Al-Salaam Mosque in Jersey City.

A short list of the more troublesome of these Islamic "houses of worship" is as follows: Ali Dulles Area Muslim Society (known as the ADAMS Center) in Sterling, Virginia; Bridgeview Mosque in Chicago; the Lackawanna Islamic Mosque in Lackawanna, New York, a suburb of Buffalo; the Islamic Center of Orange County; the Islamic Center of San Diego; Ayah Dawah Prayer Center in Laurel, Maryland (twenty minutes from Washington); Masjid al-Noor in Santa Clara, California; Masjid al-Hijrah in Fort Lauderdale, Florida; the Islamic Center of Portland, Oregon; Bilal Islamic Center in Los Angeles; the Islamic Center of Cleveland; and the Masjid As-Salam in Albany, New York.[54] Each mosque deserves a separate chapter. But Brooklyn's Al-Farouq Mosque, for the purposes of this book, is a paradigm.

Welcome to Al-Farouq Mosque

Established in 1976, Al-Farouq Mosque at 554 Atlantic Avenue doesn't look like a house of worship. It looks like a poorly lit, private club in Little Italy, where wiseguys spend time shooting pool, playing cards, or planning a hit. It looks like a dingy, neglected restaurant in Chinatown, where the chop suey is rancid. The only indication that 554 Atlantic Avenue is a mosque comes from the Arabic inscription above the entranceway: *Ashadu an la ilaha illa Llah, wa ashhadu anna Mohammad rasulu Llah* ("There is no God but Allah, and Muhammad is his prophet").

This mosque has been responsible for sending hundreds of recruits to al Qaeda training camps throughout the Middle East.[55] One such recruit was Jamal Ahmed al-Fadl, who worked to secure nuclear weapons and materials for al Qaeda during Osama bin Laden's stay in Sudan.

Al-Farouq mosque first gained public attention on November 5, 1990, when El-Sayyid Nosair, a prominent member, murdered Rabbi Meir Kahane, the founder of the Jewish Defense League, in the ballroom of the Marriott East Side Hotel in midtown Manhattan, where Kahane was speaking. The murder represented the first violent outburst of radical Islam on American soil.

AL QAEDA'S U.S. HEADQUARTERS

Before Kahane's murder, the Brooklyn mosque had been the headquarters of the al-Kifah Refugee Center, a front for al Qaeda, with branches in Atlanta, Boston, and Tucson, along with recruiting stations in twenty-six states.[56]

Founded by Abdullah Azzam, bin Laden's mentor, in 1986, the al-Kifah Refugee Center acted as a CIA front for transferring funds, weapons, and recruits to the anti-Soviet mujahideen in Afghanistan. In exchange for this service, Ronald Reagan's administration began to fork over more than two million dollars a year to the mosque.[57] Not many American Protestant or Catholic churches, let alone Jewish synagogues, received similar largesse from Uncle Sam. Meanwhile, Azzam became a frequent visitor to Brooklyn. In a 1988 videotape he can be seen and heard telling a large crowd of African Americans that "blood and martyrdom are the only way to create a Muslim society."[58]

By 1992 Al-Farouq Mosque became a haven for Arabian veterans from the jihad in Afghanistan who entered the United States with passports arranged by the CIA. A feud eventually erupted between the newcomers and the older African American members, which may have resulted in the murder of Mustafa Shalabi, a fiery imam, on March 1, 1991.[59] The murder has never been solved.

The Blind Man's Vision

Sheikh Omar Abdel Rahman, the revered blind cleric who had provided the religious authorization for the assassination of Egyptian president Anwar Sadat, became the new imam at the mosque.[60] Sheik Omar had migrated to Brooklyn in July 1990, after the consular secretary of the U.S. embassy in Egypt granted him a visa, even though his name appeared at the top of a high-alert watch list. Wadith el-Hage, who arrived in Brooklyn from Tucson the day after Shalabi's murder, became the new leader of the al-Kifah Refugee Center. El-Hage, a naturalized American citizen, later became the personal secretary for Osama bin Laden.[61] Neither of the new leaders at Al-Farouq was intent upon launching an Islamic version of a Billy Graham crusade. They were rather focused on launching a major terrorist attack against the "Great Satan" (the blind Sheikh's pet name for the United States).

The attack came on February 26, 1993, at the World Trade Center, a bombing that killed 6 people and injured 1,042, producing more hospital casualties than any event in U.S. history apart from the Civil War.[62] Three of the terrorists involved in the bombing—Mohammad Salameh, Mahmud Abouhalima, and Nidal Ayyad—were prominent members of the Al-Farouq Mosque. The leader of the attack was Ramzi Yousef, a Kuwaiti radical who had been summoned to Brooklyn by Sheikh Omar to mastermind the bombing.

Yousef arrived at Al-Farouq in August 1992 with an Iraqi passport and the intent to kill a quarter of a million American civilians. The number, Yousef later explained, was not random. It represented the number of Japanese civilians who had been killed by the atomic bombs that were dropped on Hiroshima and Nagasaki near the close of World War II.[63]

Following the 1993 World Trade Center bombing, members of the mosque sought to mount further attacks. Under the blind sheik's guidance, they came up with a plan to bomb the Lincoln and Holland tunnels, the United Nations, the FBI headquarters, and other federal buildings in Lower Manhattan. To create the bombs, they began mixing hundreds of pounds of Scott's Super Turf Builder with 255 gallons of diesel fuel in a safe house in Queens, New York.[64] Neighbors became suspicious by the strange comings and goings of men in robes and turbans. A call was made to FBI headquarters, resulting in a raid on June 23, 1993. Eleven men were collared, including Sheikh Omar, and charged as co-conspirators in a terrorist plot.

From Al-Farouq to Florida

At the ensuing trial, Gulshair el-Shukrijumah, the newly appointed imam at Al-Farouq Mosque, served as Sheikh Omar's interpreter. He also acted as a character witness for Clement Rodney Hampton-El (a.k.a. Dr. Rashid), a member of the congregation.[65] After the trial, Gulshair and his family migrated to Miramar, Florida, where he established (thanks to a few million from the Saudi Embassy) Masjid al-Hijrah, another hard-line Wahhabi mosque.[66]

As the spiritual leader of the Florida mosque, Gulshair counseled al Qaeda dirty-bomb suspect Jose Padilla and his wife[67] and allegedly also met with several of the 9/11 hijackers.

Adnan el-Shukrijumah, Gulshair's son, is proof positive that the apple doesn't fall from the tree. Known as "Jafer the Pilot," Adnan was identified by the FBI as "the next Mohammed Atta" and remains the subject of a worldwide manhunt.[68]

The Al-Farouq Arsenal

Meanwhile, the FBI Joint Terrorism Task Force began surveillance of the Al-Farouq Mosque. They noted that members entered the mosque in the early morning to withdraw crates of weapons and boxes of ammunition and haul them to the Calverton Shooting Range on eastern Long Island. At the Calverton range, the members received training with semiautomatic rifles, shotguns, 9mm- and .367-caliber handguns, and AK-47 assault weapons from Ali Mohamed, a former army sergeant at Fort Bragg and an al Qaeda sleeper agent.[69] This surveillance proved that U.S. mosques were serving as arsenals for jihadists.

In the light of such findings, Neil Hamilton, a senior FBI special agent, asked the Justice Department for permission to wiretap the mosque and the imam's office. A federal judge denied his request on the grounds that 554 Atlantic Avenue in Brooklyn represented a "house of worship."[70]

Brooklyn's Bundles for bin Laden

The story of the little shop of Islamic horror in Brooklyn continued in 2003 with the arrest of Mohammad Ali Hasan al-Moayad, a fund-raiser from Al-Farouq, who personally delivered $20 million to Osama bin Laden and another gift of $3.5 million to the al-Aqsa Society, the financial arm of Hamas. This represented the amount that al-Moayad and other members of the mosque had amassed since December 1999.[71]

Lessons from Al-Farouq

The account of the nefarious activities within the Al-Farouq Mosque, which is simply one radical mosque among 1,260 radical mosques throughout the country, serves to support the following findings:

1. Mosques serve as recruiting agencies for al Qaeda and other terrorist organizations.
2. They raise millions for the jihad against America.
3. They act as shelters for terrorists and sleeper agents.
4. They are protected by U.S. federal courts because of their status as religious institutions.
5. They are extremely well financed by oil-rich Saudis.
6. They act as planning centers for terrorist activities.
7. They warehouse weapons.
8. And they stand as shining examples that the present situation of religious tolerance undermines national security.

POISON FOR THE PRISONS

The first blunder in the misnamed war on terror has also caused law-enforcement officials to turn a blind eye to the recruitment of future jihadists within the country's penal system. Billions from oil-rich Saudis fund the Islamic Prison Foundation, a prison-outreach program. The purpose of the program is to convert large numbers of African American inmates not only to Wahhabism but also to rabid anti-Americanism. Warith Deem Umar, who served as the program's director, said: "The 9/11 hijackers should be honored as martyrs. The United States risks further terrorism attacks because it oppresses Muslims around the world."[72] The Islamic Prison Foundation has been incredibly successful. Fifty percent of American Muslims are African Americans, and many became converts in prison.

A PERSONAL NOTE

Stating the obvious truth that the enemy is Islam is not a simple and straightforward task in today's society. Four years ago I wrote *Al-Qaeda: Brotherhood of Terror* for Alpha Books, currently a division of the Penguin Publishing Group. The book traced the development of al Qaeda from the life of Muhammad and the teachings of the Koran. Before publication, the weak-kneed editors and publishers at Alpha decided to submit the work to representatives from the Islamic community for approval. Such approval, of course, was not forthcoming. One Islamic scholar, after reading the first four chapters, decried the manuscript as a tract "worse than *Mein Kampf*."

My error had been a reliance on secondary sources, including Bernard Lewis, professor emeritus of Near Eastern Studies at Princeton University, and an English translation of the Koran by J. M. Rodman that was not authorized by the Council on American-Islamic Relations (CAIR). Alpha eventually published the work in truncated form, with all the offensive material expunged and statements of the benign nature of the Islamic religion inserted from Islamic apologists. The end result was an eviscerated fish that stank to high heaven. I apologize to anyone who bought it.

Later I read Abdullah Yusuf Ali's approved translation of the Koran (a cumbersome text of 1,759 pages, replete with copious commentary) and the 920-page *Sirat Rasul Allah*, the approved life of Muhammad by Ibn Ishaq. These readings were enlightening. They taught me that the "offensive" and "blasphemous" material that had been gutted from my manuscript by Alpha should be corrected since it did not contain a full exposure of the bloodthirsty exploits of Muhammad and the violent teachings of his barbaric religion. The corrected material forms the gist of the next chapter.

BLUNDER 2

Believing Islam Is a Religion of Peace and Tolerance and That Muhammad Was a Kind and Merciful Prophet

I also want to speak tonight directly to Muslims throughout the world. We respect your faith. It's practiced freely by many millions of Americans, and by millions more in countries that America counts as friends. Its teachings are good and peaceful, and those who commit evil in the name of Allah blaspheme the name of Allah. The terrorists are traitors to their own faith, trying, in effect, to hijack Islam itself. The enemy of America is not our many Muslim friends; it is not our many Arab friends. Our enemy is a radical network of terrorists and every government that supports them.

President George W. Bush, Address to a Joint Session of Congress, September 20, 2001

THE DAY AFTER 9/11, President Bush promulgated the granddaddy of all whoppers by saying, "Islam is a religion of peace."[1] After making this genuflection before the altar of political correctness at the Islamic Center of Washington DC, the president proceeded to present himself as an Islamic scholar with a thorough mastery of Koranic Arabic. "The English translation," he said, "is not as eloquent as the original Arabic, but let me quote from the Koran itself. 'In the long run, evil in the extreme will be the end of those who do evil. For that they rejected the signs of Allah and held them up for ridicule.'"[2]

The fact that President Bush possesses little or no knowledge of Arabic and Islam was apparent by the passage he chose to quote from the

Koran. It does not condemn violence against innocent civilians but rather encourage violence against all those who reject or ridicule the "signs of Allah."

The president went on to say: "When we think of Islam we think of a faith that brings comfort to a billion people around the world. Billions of people find comfort and solace and peace. And that's made brothers and sisters out of every race—out of every race."[3]

But Islam, alone among the world religions, stands in opposition to what C. S. Lewis calls "the Law of General Beneficence."[4] This law, commonly known as the Golden Rule, was expressed by Jesus: "Do to others what you would have them do to you" (Matthew 7:12). The Koran and the Hadith stand in sharp opposition to this teaching by dividing the world into two militant zones: the *Dar as-Salaam* (the House of Peace) and the *Dar al-Harb* (House of War). There can be no lasting peace between these two factions until all men live in submission to the will of Allah.[5] Sorry, Mr. Bush, but Islam has not made brothers and sisters out of every race. It has acted to the contrary.

Islam means *submission*—not peace, not brotherhood, not tolerance. Traditional Islam prohibits Muslims from greeting non-Muslims with the salutation *salam 'alaykum* ("peace be upon you").[6] Peace in this world is reserved solely for believers. Unbelievers, according to the teachings of the Prophet, are to be conquered, converted, suppressed, and subjugated to the humiliating status of *dhimmis* (a word meaning "protected and guilty") or put to death. There are no alternatives. Such is the will of Allah.

THE PRAYER FOR BUSH'S CONVERSION

The president's poorly chosen words were echoed by White House Press Secretary Ari Fleischer, who labeled the terrorist attacks of 9/11 "a perversion of Islam,"[7] and by Secretary of State Colin Powell, who cast the al Qaeda hijackers not only out of Islam but out of "Arabdom" by insisting that their acts "should not be seen as something done by Arabs or Islamics" but "something that was done by terrorists."[8]

Unfortunately, President Bush persisted in his folly of serving as a Muslim apologist. Two months after the attacks, he hosted the first *iftar* dinner at the White House to commemorate the end of Ramadan. The president bowed his head during a prayer offered by an imam who asked Allah to "make us true believers." Since true believers, according to the Koran, are only those who accept the teachings of the prophet Muhammad, the imam was praying that the pointed-headed president and the other government officials in attendance would be converted to Islam so that *shariah* (Islamic law) could be imposed upon the American public.

Bush's misguidedness didn't end with the *iftar* dinner. On the first anniversary of 9/11, he appeared before the Afghanistan Embassy to describe Islam as a "loving faith" that all Americans should respect and honor. "All Americans must recognize that the face of terror is not the true faith of Islam," he said. "Islam is a faith based upon love, not hate."[9] Only an individual totally unaware of the fifty verses in the Koran calling for bloody jihad against all unbelievers could make such a statement.

BILL AND HILLARY: "NOTHING IN ISLAM PROMOTES TERRORISM"

Neither President Bush nor any White House official was trying to dupe or deceive the American people. They were merely mouthing the mendacities that had been passed on to them by former President Bill Clinton and his wife, Hillary, and members of the Clinton cabinet.

Despite such injunctions in the Koran as "slay the idolaters wherever you find them" (9:5), President Clinton maintained there was nothing within Islam "that would divide; that would promote terrorism; that would be destructive of our values."[10]

Clinton went on to hail Islam as a positive force in American society: "We welcome Islam in America. It enriches our country with teachings of discipline, compassion and commitment to family." In a subsequent statement, Clinton reiterated two of these values and changed the third. "America," he said, "is made stronger by the core values of Islam—commitment to family, compassion for the disadvantaged, and respect for difference."[11]

First Lady Hillary, not to be undone by her husband, praised Islam for its "universal values—love of family and community, mutual respect, education, and the deepest yearning of all—to live in peace—values that can strengthen us as people and strengthen the United States as a nation."[12]

Poor Bill and Hillary. Both suffer from severe memory lapses. They probably forgot such Koranic teachings as "take not the Jews and the Christians for your friends" (5:51), "inspire terror in the hearts of unbelievers" (8:2), and "against them make ready your strength to the utmost of your power, including steeds of war, to strike terror into the hearts of the enemies of Allah" (8:60).

MADELEINE ALBRIGHT'S "APPALLING IGNORANCE"

Clinton's secretary of state, Madeleine Albright, ascribed a similar triad of virtue to Muslims by describing Islam as "a faith that honors consultation, cherishes peace, and has as one of its fundamental principles the inherent equality of all who embrace it."[13] Albright added that the American people possess an "appalling ignorance" of Islam.

In truth, the appalling ignorance of Islam was best displayed by the remarks of Albright and the pronouncements of the Clintons. When they were uttering these inanities, Islam stood at the heart of every conflict throughout the world, from Chechnya to Somalia, from Indonesia to the Balkans, from Afghanistan to the Philippines. And Muslim forces already had attacked U.S. forces in such diverse places as Kenya, Lebanon, New York City, Tanzania, and Yemen.

MEET THE PROPHET MUHAMMAD

Who was Muhammad? What were his teachings? And why does Islam pose a threat to world peace and stability? These questions cry out for answers that few American political leaders, directors of intelligence agencies, high-ranking military officials, and ivy-league academics have the intestinal fortitude to provide.

Muhammad was born in Mecca (in what is now Saudi Arabia) circa AD 570. His father, Adullah, was a leading member of the powerful Quraish tribe, but he died several months before the birth of the Prophet. Muhammad was named by his grandfather, Abdul Muttalib. Upon hearing of his son's death, the grandfather went to his daughter-in-law's house, took the baby in his arms, and called him Muhammad, which means "the Praised One."

As was the custom of the Quraish, Amina, Muhammad's mother,

gave her baby to a woman from one of the Bedouin tribes so that he could be nursed in the open air of the desert.[14] When he was finally weaned at the advanced age of six, Muhammad was returned to his mother, who took him to Medina. She died during the return trip to Mecca. The young Muhammad now came under the care of his seventy-six-year-old grandfather, who died two years later. The boy finally lived with his uncle, Abu Talib.

Nothing seemed to be remarkable about Muhammad's early life. He received no schooling and could not read or write. In his later years he was obliged to use an amanuensis to record his teachings.

The Quraish tribe to which Muhammad belonged was responsible for guarding the Kaaba and the sacred black stone of the Arabs. The Kaaba now stands in the center of a great portico—the Masjid al-Haram, or the Great Mosque—in the center of Mecca. This mosque was rebuilt in the 1960s by Mohammad bin Laden, father of Osama. The Kaaba was constructed as a cube measuring thirty-five feet wide and fifty feet high. In its southeast corner, five feet from the ground and just right for kissing, is the precious black stone. The stone is not actually black but rather dark red. It is oval in shape and about seven inches in diameter. One of the only *kafirs* (nonbelievers) known to have seen it was the great adventurer Sir Richard Burton, who entered the holy city in Muslim disguise. Burton accomplished this feat without being hacked to pieces because he spoke flawless Arabian and was well versed in the Koran and Islamic customs and traditions.[15]

According to Arabian tradition, the black stone fell from heaven at the time of Adam—a good indication that it is a meteorite. Muslims believe that the Hebrew prophet Abraham, on a pilgrimage to Mecca with his son Ishmael, built the Kaaba to enclose the stone.

Allah, the Moon God

Within the Kaaba in pre-Muslim time were idols of more than 360 tribal gods.[16] One such god was Hubal, the fertility god of the moon. His image, the crescent moon, was placed on the roof of the Kaaba.[17] Three other tribal gods were Hubal's daughters—al-Uzza, Manah, and al-Lat.[18] One can establish the antiquity of the Arab pantheon by the fact that the Greek historian Herodotus mentions al-Lat as a major Arabian deity.

Hubal was also called al-ilah, meaning "the god." Al-ilah later was shortened to Allah. The Sura contains stories of Meccans praying to Allah while standing before the image of Hubal.[19]

Before Muhammad's birth, his tribe paved the way for monotheism by worshiping Allah as the chief god and by wearing symbols of the crescent moon. Allah came to be viewed as the lord of the sky and the soil to whom tribesmen were obliged to pay a tithe of their crops and to sacrifice the firstborn of their herds. The Quraish worshiped Allah by praying toward Mecca several times a day, making an annual pilgrimage to the Kaaba and walking around the sacred stone seven times, and giving alms to the poor. These practices were in effect long before Muhammad was born.[20]

As the alleged descendants of Abraham and Ishmael, the Quraish were the custodians of the Kaaba. They appointed the priests of the shrine and managed its revenues. No tribe was richer or more powerful.[21]

The Wealthy Widow

But the young Muhammad was neither rich nor powerful. He worked as a camel driver and regularly traveled to Damascus and other cities. But fortune smiled on him. At the age of twenty-five, he married Khadijah, a very wealthy forty-year-old widow.[22] Khadijah bore Muhammad four daughters and two sons—a remarkable feat for a woman who should have been menopausal.[23] The sons died in infancy. The couple also adopted Ali, the orphan son of Abu Talib, Muhammad's uncle, and Zayd, a black slave. Ali later married Muhammad's daughter Fatima and eventually became the fourth caliph, or leader, of Islam. When Ali was assassinated in 661, Islam was divided into two segments: the Sunnis, who recognized the legitimacy of the first four caliphs, and the Shi'ites (or "followers of Ali"), who claim that only descendants of Ali may be rightful rulers of the *ummah* (the community of Muslims).[24]

The Cave and Convulsions

All went well with Muhammad and his elderly bride until 611, when, at the age of forty, he decided to spend a few days in meditation and prayer. In a cave three miles from Mecca, the pivotal moment in the history of Islam occurred. Muhammad beheld a vision, which he related to Mohammad Ibn Ishaq, his chief biographer:

> While I was asleep, with a coverlet of silk brocade whereon was some writing, the angel Gabriel appeared to me and said, "Read!" I said, "I do not read." He pressed me with the coverlet so tightly that I thought I was near death. Then he let me go and said, "Read!" So I read aloud. And he departed from me at last. And I awoke from my sleep, and it was as though these words were written on my heart. I heard a voice from heaven saying, "O Muhammad, you are a messenger of Allah, and I am Gabriel."[25]

Since the encounter was both violent and accompanied by convulsions that sent him into unconsciousness, Muhammad was unsure of the source of his vision. He feared that he might be possessed by the *jinn* (demons) that commonly inhabited the souls of Arab soothsayers. When he returned home, he experienced more and more visions that served to assure him of his calling as a prophet. Often he fell to the ground in a swoon. His fits were accompanied by a sound like the ringing of a bell that caused his entire body to tremble so uncontrollably that he begged Khadijah to cover him with a cloak and to cradle him.[26]

His first convert was his wife, Khadijah. His second was his cousin and foster son, Ali. His third was his servant Zayd. And his fourth was his kinsman Abu Bakr, a prominent Quraish chieftain who eventually became the first caliph of Islam. Muhammad's small group of followers called themselves "those devoted to God" (*al-muslimun*).[27]

Bad for Business

At the Kaaba, Muhammad accosted all merchants, pilgrims, and tribesmen with his doctrine of one god and himself as the true prophet. He spoke of the resurrection of the dead, the final judgment, and the need of the people to submit to the will of Allah. *Submit* was the keyword. *Islam* in Arabic means submission.[28] For those who refused to comply with this directive, Muhammad possessed little tolerance. When his uncle, Abu Lahab, rejected his message, Muhammad cursed him and his wife in a violent rage of anger: "May the hands of Abu Lahab perish!

May he himself perish! Nothing shall his wealth and gains avail him. He shall be burnt in a flaming fire, and his wife, laden with faggots, shall have a rope of fire around her neck!" (Koran 111:1-5).

The merchants in Mecca soon discovered that having the new prophet in the midst of the marketplace was not good for business. The situation grew intolerable until Muhammad and two hundred followers were forced to flee for their lives to Medina on June 22, 622. The flight from Mecca—known as the *hajj*—marks the official beginning of the Islamic calendar.[29] According to Islamic chronology, AD 632, the year of the Prophet's death, is designated as 10 AH, and the year 2006 (to commemorate the publication of this book) is designated as 1384 AH.

In Medina, Muhammad met with immediate success. A band of tribal warriors accepted him as a messenger from God and pledged loyalty to him. In no time at all, the illiterate camel driver became the ruler and judge of a budding theocracy.

Muhammad: The Bandit

To amass riches for his realm, Muhammad ordered his followers to raid the caravans that traveled from Syria to Mecca. These caravans, usually made up of several thousand camels and their attendants, carried spices, china, silk, myrrh, and gold.[30] When the raids were successful, four-fifths of the spoils went to the raiders and one-fifth went to Muhammad. Booty became an integral part of the new religion. An entire *surah* (or chapter) of the Koran is devoted to this subject. Muhammad himself participated in dozens of raids in which his followers killed as many of the travelers as possible and stole as much as they could carry.[31]

In 623 Muhammad assembled his band of three hundred bandits to wait in a desert pass for a Quraish caravan en route to Mecca. The rulers of Mecca learned of the raid and sent an army of nine hundred soldiers to end the exploits of the troublesome prophet. The two forces met at Wadi Bedr, twenty miles from Medina, where Muhammad led his men to a great victory.[32]

Muhammad: The Warrior

After the battle, Muhammad collected the head of Abu Jahl, one of the

Quraish chieftains, as a trophy. The other chieftains, even those who pleaded for their lives, were killed. Their bodies were tossed into a pit, save for the body of Umayya, the fattest of the chieftains. Umayya's body, under the heavy armor, had swollen to such an extent under the desert sun that it fell apart when Muhammad's men tried to move it. The scene filled the Prophet with great exaltation. Before covering the pit, he addressed the dead bodies, "O people of the pit, have you found what God threatened is true? For I have found that what my Lord promised me is true."[33]

Muhammad returned with his triumphant troops to Medina. The victors had captured 150 camels, 10 horses, a considerable amount of merchandise, and 70 Meccans, who were ransomed for 1,000 to 4,000 dirams apiece.[34] The prophet was now a force to be feared.

Bedr was neither Muhammad's first foray into battle nor his last. At the battle of Uhud, he lost his two front teeth, which are now on display in Istanbul.[35] Though toothless, the Prophet still managed to drive his spear through the neck of Ubayy ibn Khalaf, a Quraish chieftain. Islamic scholars say that the Prophet personally attended twenty-seven battles and fought in eight of them.[36]

Muhammad: The Assassin

As the ruler of Medina, Muhammad demanded complete loyalty and utter submission from his subjects. This was evidenced by his response to critics. Abu Afak, an old man of a hundred years who had converted to Judaism, made the mistake of penning a satire about the Prophet's proclivity to divide all of creation between what is "forbidden" and what is "permitted." Muhammad was not amused by the work. He sent a servant to forever silence the old satirist as he lay sleeping in a courtyard.[37]

When Asma, a Medinese poet, wrote some unflattering lines about Muhammad, the Prophet summoned his followers and asked, "Who will rid me of Marwan's daughter [Asma]?" A dutiful servant named Umayr raised his hand and made his way to Asma's house in the dead of the night. Umayr plunged his dagger so deeply within the breast of the poetess that her body was nailed to the sleeping couch.[38] In the mosque the next morning, Umayr told the Prophet what he had done and asked if there would be any evil consequences. "None," Muhammad replied, "a few goats will hardly knock their heads together because of it."[39]

Then there was the case of Kab bin al-Ashraf, the son of a Jewess, who composed "amatory verses of an insulting nature about Muslim women."[40] Muhammad asked, "Who will rid me of the poet?" Mohammad bin Musalama asked permission to deceive the poet into walking into an ambush. "O apostle of God," Musalama pointed out, "we shall have to tell lies." Muhammad replied, "Say what you like, for you are free in this matter."[41] Musalama duped the poet into taking a late-night stroll into the desert where a group of assassins awaited. The poet was hacked to pieces and emasculated.

Following the death of Kab, Muhammad issued the blanket command, "Kill any Jew that falls into your power."[42] The first victim of this pronouncement was Ibn Sunayna, a Jewish merchant who had neither written a word nor committed a transgression. The murderer, Muhayissa, was rebuked by his brother, Huwayyisa, who was not yet a Muslim, for killing an innocent man in cold blood. "By God," Huwayyisa complained, "if Muhammad had ordered you to kill me, would you have killed me?" "Yes, by God," Muhayissa responded, "had he ordered me to cut off your head, I would have done so." Huwayyisa exclaimed, "By God, a religion which brings you to this is marvelous!"[43] Huwayyisa immediately became a believer, thereby crystallizing proof that bloodshed (or the threat of bloodshed) would spread the new faith.

Muhammad and the Jewish Question

The situation with the Jews in Medina worsened until a Muslim woman ventured into a shop in the bazaar of the Qaynqa and Nudair Jewish tribes. When the woman sat in a shop, a Jewish prankster managed to sneak behind her in order to pin her skirt to her upper blouse. When she rose to leave, her bodice and skirt ripped open to expose her breasts and derriere while the prankster and his cronies howled with delight. It was an outrageous joke. But a Muslim slew the offending Jew, whose brothers slew the Muslim. As a result, a riot broke out in the city. Muhammad assembled his troops, rounded up the Qaynqa and Nudair

Jews, and ordered them to depart from the city and to leave all their possessions behind.[44]

Muhammad and Genocide

A third tribe of Jews—the Bani Qurayza—remained in Medina. Later they were accused of providing aid to Muhammad's enemies in Mecca. The Prophet reacted to this accusation by blockading the Bani Qurayza in their quarter of the city and denying them access to food supplies for twenty-five days. The leaders of the Jewish tribe expressed their willingness to surrender under the same terms that had been granted to the Qaynqa and Nudair Jews, namely, the relinquishment of their belongings and safe departure to another city.

Muhammad refused these terms. Instead, he appointed Saad Muadh, one of his most corpulent followers, to act as the arbiter who would decide the fate of the Jews. Muadh ruled that the Jewish men should be beheaded, that the women and children should be sold into slavery, and that all the property of the Jews should be divided among the Muslims. Muhammad accepted the wisdom of this ruling. Nine hundred Jews, according to one account, were beheaded. Another account estimates the figure to have been seven hundred. The carnage started in the morning, went on all day, and continued by torchlight into the night. While the heads were rolling, Muhammad was enjoying the sexual favors of Reihana, the widow of one of the victims, who had been set aside for his pleasure.[45] Trenches were dug around the city for the disposal of the bodies.

The Muslims wanted to have sex with their female Jewish captives. But this did not seem fitting to the Prophet, who had decided that the women should be sold as slaves and not kept as concubines. After much begging and pleading, he relented and ruled that his men could have intercourse with the hapless captives as long as they employed the practice of *azl*, that is, withdrawal before ejaculation.[46]

The slaughter of the Bani Qurayza Jews proved to be extremely profitable. In addition to the revenue for the slaves, the spoils of the pogrom included a rich haul of livestock (camels, goats, sheep, and horses), houses, furniture, jewelry, and money. The Muslims also took from the bodies of the slain Jews a large number of weapons, including fifteen hundred swords and scimitars, an equal number of shields, a thousand spears, and three hundred coats of mail.[47] Muhammad took his customary one-fifth, thereby becoming the wealthiest chieftain in the Arab world.

While they remained in Medina, the Muslims continued to raid caravans and other tribes. On one raid, the Wadil-Qura tribe defeated them. After licking their wounds, the Muslims returned to Wadil-Qura to rout the tribe, sack and pillage the village, and to haul off the survivors as slaves. Zayd, one of Muhammad's adopted sons, captured an old woman who had served as a tribal leader. For amusement, she was tied between two camels. The camels were forced to break into a trot until the old woman was ripped in half.[48] Neither Zayd nor any other Muslims received the slightest censure for their actions.

Similarly, during a raid on Khaybar, a prosperous Jewish tribe, the Muslims demanded from Kinana, the tribal chieftain, the location of a chest of buried treasure. When Kinana claimed not to know anything about a buried treasure, Muhammad ordered, "Torture him until you extract what he has." The Muslims kindled a fire on Kinana's chest "with fleet and steel." When Kinana neared the point of death without providing any information about the treasure, Muhammad decided to have him beheaded by an executioner.[49] In this way, all was not lost. The Prophet may not have discovered the treasure, but he had another head for his collection.

Mecca: The New Qibla

The expulsion and execution of the Jews from Medina represents a significant development in the history of Islam. The city was now purged of all religious dissidents and became a place free from the defilement of unbelievers.

Originally, Muhammad made Jerusalem the *qibla*—the point to which all Muslims must turn for prayer.[50] But the Jews had ridiculed his interpretation of their scriptures and his claim to be the promised Messiah. Muhammad, in turn, accused the Jews of corrupting the teachings of the patriarchs of the Bible, of killing the prophets, and of rejecting the revelation of Allah. In 624 he proclaimed that Mecca, the site of the Kaaba and the sacred stone, represented the new *qibla*.[51]

Mecca now became the focal point of the new faith. With the aid of nomadic Arab tribes, Muhammad led a series of armed raids on Mecca, and in 630 he captured the city with no resistance. He declared a general amnesty for all but a few of his enemies. He destroyed the idols in the Kaaba and proclaimed it a mosque. He spared the Black Stone and sanctioned the practice of kissing it. He also pronounced Mecca to be the holy city of Islam and decreed that no unbeliever should ever set foot on its sacred soil.[52]

The remaining years of the Prophet were spent in triumph as the various Arab tribes became united under the banner of Islam.

Muhammad: Sex Addict

After Muhammad's wife, Khadijah, died in 619, the Prophet amassed eleven wives. He attempted to arrange his schedule around the menstrual cycle of his harem with visits to a different tent on different days and nights of the month. His capacity for sexual congress seemed to be beyond limit. *Sahih Bukhari,* one of the most revered Islamic sources, states: "The Prophet used to visit all his wives in a round, during the day and night and they were eleven in number. I asked Anas, 'Had the Prophet the strength for it?' Anas replied, 'We used to say that the Prophet was given the strength of thirty [men].'"[53]

For in-between treats, the Prophet kept several concubines at his disposal, including Reihana, his Jewish captive. In accordance with Islamic law, Muhammad's wives and mistresses were obliged to satisfy his sexual needs at any time of the day or night, and the Prophet retained the right to enjoy them "from the top of their heads to the bottom of their feet."[54]

Muhammad: Pedophile

All of this may seem well and good, save for the case of Aisha, Muhammad's favorite wife. Aisha was the daughter of Abu Bakr, Muhammad's closest friend and most faithful follower. As soon as the Prophet laid eyes on his friend's daughter, he began dreaming about his union with her. The problem was that Aisha, when Muhammad met her, was a small child of four or five, and he was a middle-aged man of fifty.[55]

Still and all, the Prophet wasted no time in attempting to make his dream a reality. When Aisha turned six, Muhammad asked Abu Bakr for his daughter's hand in marriage. Abu Bakr thought that such a union would be improper—not because Aisha was a mere child but rather because he considered himself Muhammad's brother. The Prophet brushed this objection aside by saying that it was perfectly right in the eyes of Allah for him to marry Aisha. Abu Bakr consented. And Muhammad took the child as his new bride.

When they were married, Muhammad, in his mercy, allowed Aisha to take her toys, including her dolls, with her when she moved into their new tent.[56] The marriage was consummated when Aisha was nine and Muhammad fifty-three. This is verified by several passages from *Sahih Bukhari:*

> [Narrated Aisha]:The Prophet married her when she was 6 years old and he consummated his marriage when she was 9 years old, and then she remained with him for 9 years [until his death].[57]

> Khadijah died three years before the Prophet departed to Medina. He stayed there for two years or so and then married Aisha when she was a girl of 6 years of age, and he consummated the marriage when she was 9.[58]

The three-year waiting period before consummation might not have been caused by Muhammad's concern with violating a child but rather by the fact that Aisha contracted some disease, which caused her to lose her hair (which later grew back).[59]

Aisha became Muhammad's favorite sexual partner.[60] Later she was hailed as the "mother of all believers."[61]

Pedophilia was not only practiced by Muhammad but also sanctioned by the Koran. In its discussion of the waiting period required to determine if a wife is pregnant before divorce, the Koran says, "If you are in doubt concerning those of your wives who have ceased menstruating, know that their waiting period shall be three months. The same shall apply to those who have not yet menstruated" (65:4). In case anyone should think that Muslims have abandoned this practice, one need only turn to Ayatollah Khomeini, the most famous Islamic cleric of the twentieth century, who writes:

A man can have sexual pleasure from a child as young as a baby. However, he should not penetrate; sodomizing the child is OK. If the man penetrates and damages the child, then he should be responsible for her subsistence all her life. This girl, however, does not count as one of his four permanent wives. The man will not be eligible to marry the girl's sister. . . . It is better for a girl to marry in such a time when she would begin menstruation at her husband's house rather than her father's house. Any father marrying his daughter so young will have a permanent place in heaven.[62]

The Prophet's Parting Words

At the age of fifty-eight, Muhammad's health began to fail. He experienced high fevers and suffered states of delirium. In the middle of the night, he often would leave his house, visit a graveyard, pray aloud to the deceased, and congratulate them on being dead.[63]

By age sixty-three, the fevers left him in a state of almost complete enervation. Three days before his death, Muhammad rose from his deathbed, visited the mosque, and saw Abu Bakr leading prayers in his stead.[64] His parting words to his followers were "to drive the unbelievers from the Arabian Peninsula."[65]

THE SWORD OF ISLAM

Muhammad's followers wasted no time in heeding his final command. By 642, ten years after the Prophet's death, the armies of Islam had swept most of the Fertile Crescent, including Persia (Iraq), and had expanded throughout North Africa with the defeat of Egypt (641). By 732 they had conquered Crete, Cyprus, and Rhodes, had pushed on to overrun Spain, and had crossed the Pyrenees into France, where Charles Martel, the "Hammer of the Franks," managed to force them into retreat.[66] The Muslims continued to dominate the Iberian Peninsula for centuries. By 950 the Muslim army had swept east to conquer Syria, Sind (northwest India), Baluchistan, Afghanistan, and Turkistan.

The march was stayed when the Seljuk Turks began to invade Muslim lands in the west at the time of the millennium. The Turks eventually converted to Islam, transformed almost overnight from a barbarian horde to righteous Shi'ite warriors involved in *jihad,* and pressed forward through Asia Minor to Constantinople. In 1092 Pope Urban II sounded the alarm for Christians to join in a holy crusade to ward off the Muslim menace. The crusades continued for the next two hundred years in a struggle that ended in a virtual stalemate.[67]

But the crusades failed to stop the Islamic push toward the West. In 1389, Muslim forces of the newly formed Ottoman Empire entered the Balkans and defeated the Serbs at the battle of Kosovo. In 1453, Constantinople fell before the sword of Islam as thousands of citizens were slaughtered in the streets and fifty thousand women and children (half the city's population) were hauled off as slaves. Throughout the subsequent centuries, the expansion continued as the Ottomans swept through much of the Ukraine. The Turks were at the gates of Vienna when they were stopped by the great Polish king John Sobieski and thirty thousand Polish hussars on a day that marks the high point of Muslim expansion in Europe: September 11, 1683.[68]

What was the goal of this seemingly endless warfare? The answer could be found in the teachings of the Prophet, who commanded his followers "to fight against the people until they testify that none has the right to be worshiped but Allah and that Muhammad is the Messenger of Allah." The large-scale jihads came to an end after 1683, not because the people of Islam had rejected or reformed this doctrine of universal submission, but rather because the Muslim world had grown too weak to continue the struggle.[69]

ISLAM REKINDLED

This situation dramatically changed with the discovery of oil in the Middle East and the sudden reappearance of the hoary head of militant Islam. By 2005 the following events had occurred:

1. Libyan president Muammar Abu Minyar al-Qadhafi attempted to convert all of Chad by fire and sword (napalm and attack helicopter).
2. Idi Amin commenced to Islamize Uganda by mass murder.
3. Ayatollah Khomeini came to power in Iran and within two years executed more than eight thousand people as "enemies of Allah."

4. Afghan Arabs drove the Soviet army from Afghanistan and set up an Islamic republic.
5. An Islamic secessionist movement became active in the Philippines.
6. Muslim rebels in Chechnya battled Russia for independence.
7. Muslim troops waged war against Christian secessionists in Indonesia.
8. Israel was forced out of Lebanon by Hezbollah and out of the West Bank and Gaza by Hamas. The conflict in Lebanon alone resulted in forty thousand civilian deaths.
9. Islamic law was imposed in ten northern states of Nigeria.
10. In Turkey and Algeria, elections brought to power Islamic regimes that were removed by less-than-democratic methods.
11. In the Balkans, Muslims with the help of al Qaeda gained control of Kosovo and initiated a purge of Christian Serbs.
12. Muslim militants in Egypt renewed the persecution of Christian Copts.
13. Cells of Islamic terror have been planted in every country of the Western Hemisphere: South and Central America, the United States, and Canada.
14. Events of Islamic terror erupted in Spain, England, and Holland.
15. Islamic terrorists initiated attacks against the United States abroad and at home.

LESSONS FROM THE PROPHET

President George W. Bush and members of his cabinet should be allowed to step down from their high stools and momentarily remove their dunce caps if they manage to learn the following basic lessons about Islam from the life and teachings of Muhammad:

1. Jihad is a religious duty. It is a means of suppressing the enemies of Islam and of establishing faith in Allah. One of the fifty verses within the Koran that sanctions war against unbelievers, including Christians and Jews, says, "Fight those who believe not in Allah nor the Last Day, nor hold that forbidden which hath been forbidden by Allah and his Messenger, nor acknowledge the religion of Truth, [even if they are] the People of the Book [Christians and Jews],

until they pay the *jizya* with willing submission and feel themselves subdued" (9:29). The *jizya* is a mandatory tax that is imposed on all unbelievers in Islamic countries. In many countries, the *jizya* is so hefty that non-Muslims convert in order to survive. For the United States and Israel, it's going to be a long fight. Holy war cannot end until Islamic law rules the entire world.

2. Martyrdom is the highest good. It is the only means to enter the seventh heaven where every blessed male will be granted seventy-two *houris* (virgins with "dark, beautiful eyes," "swelling breasts," and "modest gaze") as brides. The *houris* will cater to the martyr's every whim for all eternity. The Koran teaches, "Allah hath purchased of the believers their persons and their goods; for theirs, in return is the garden of Paradise: they fight in His cause, and slay and are slain: a promise binding on Him in truth" (9:111). Muhammad, not wanting to lose out on the *houris,* maintained that his fatal illness was not due to natural causes but rather to poisonous goat meat that had been served to him by a treacherous Jewess from Khaibar.[70] In the wake of 9/11, FBI agents found letters in the luggage of the terrorists who had piloted three of the four doomed flights. The letters had been written by Mohammed Atta, who had distributed them to his compatriots during their last meeting in Las Vegas. At the close of one letter, Atta wrote, "Know that the Gardens of Paradise are beautified with its best ornaments and its inhabitants are calling you." After the death of a suicide bomber, members of the terrorist groups hold a joyous celebration and speak of the martyr's death as a "wedding." In one of Atta's suitcases that had failed to make it aboard American Airlines Flight 11, inspectors found a perfectly pressed white wedding suit with a sapphire blue necktie.[71]

3. Muslims engaged in jihad must not show tolerance toward nonbelievers. The Koran states, "Slay the idolaters wherever you find them" (9:5). Even in times of peace, they must not display acceptance of *kafirs*, not even "the People of the Book." The Koran mandates, "Take not Jews or Christians as friends" (5:51). President Bush must accept the fact that the leaders of the Muslim world (including Jalal Talabani and Hamid Karzai) are neither his friends nor his allies.

4. Acts of terrorism—such as killing hostages, demanding ransoms, subjecting captives to torture—are justified by the Prophet's example. Decapitation, however, remains the favored means of instilling fear in the enemy, as al Qaeda has established the practice in Afghanistan and Iraq. The Koran says, "Remember your Lord inspired the angels with the message: 'I am with you: give firmness to Believers: I will inspire terror in the hearts of Unbelievers: you smite them above their necks and smite all their fingertips off them" (8:2).

5. Women are sexual objects. The Koran teaches, "Your women are a tilth for you to cultivate so go to your tilth as ye will" (2:223). It also encourages men to beat their disobedient wives: "Good women are the obedient, guarding in secret that which Allah hath guarded. As for those from whom ye fear rebellion, admonish them and banish them to beds apart, and scourge them" (4:34). On one occasion, Muhammad even struck Aisha, his beloved child bride.[72] Because of their inferior status, the testimony of a woman is only worth half that of a man. The Koran says, "Get two witnesses, out of your own men, and if there are not two men, then a man and two women, such as ye choose, for witnesses, so that if one of them errs, the other can remind her" (2:282). Condoleezza Rice should take note.

6. Muslims must collect booty from their victims. In the letter to his co-conspirators of 9/11, Mohammed Atta writes, "Do not forget to take some booty, even if it be a cup of water with which you drink and offer your brothers to drink, if possible." One can only imagine the scene aboard the airplanes that were seized on 9/11 as the terrorists seized toys from children, handbags, wallets, lipstick, packs of gum from the passengers, and bottles of water from the flight attendants before the planes crashed into the World Trade Center towers, the Pentagon, and the Pennsylvania field. The importance of booty cannot be emphasized enough. It merits an entire *surah* of the Koran.

7. Critics of Islam and the Prophet are to be dispatched in the manner of Abu Afak, Asma, and Kab bin al-Ashraf. In 1993 members of al

Qaeda sought out Dr. Faraq Foda, the author of several books critical of Muhammad. He was shot and killed in the presence of his son.[73] Similarly, members of the terrorist group stabbed Naguib Mahfouz, the first Egyptian to win the Nobel Prize in Literature, because of an alleged insult to the Prophet in his novel *The Children of Galawi*.[74] And there is the case of Theo Van Gogh, who was slaughtered on a street in East Amsterdam for making a film that criticized the teachings of the Prophet concerning women.[75]

8. Muslims believe that the Jews have corrupted the teachings of Allah and must be driven from all holy places, including Jerusalem, the third holy city of Islam, in the same manner that the Prophet drove the Jews from the holy city of Medina. The Prophet did not hesitate to massacre Jews and infidels, and the modern jihadists, as the World Islamic Statement of February 23, 1998, makes clear, are committed to follow his example.[76]

9. Since the Prophet sanctified the land of the two holy cities, the U.S. military presence in Saudi Arabia must be eliminated. This is the basis for Osama bin Laden's "Declaration of War Against the Americans Occupying the Land of the Two Holy Places" that was issued on August 23, 1996.[77]

10. In keeping with the Islamic law of "parity"—"an eye for an eye"— four million Americans must die. This is the figure that has been calculated by Sulaiman Abu Ghaith, a leading al Qaeda operative. Abu Ghaith derived this figure by calculating the number of Muslims who have died at the hands of infidels in Afghanistan, Bosnia, Chechnya, Iraq, Kashmir, Palestine, Somalia, and Sudan.[78] That's the good news. The bad news is that Sheikh Nasir bin Hamid al Fahd, on behalf of his fellow Saudi clerics, has recalculated this figure and maintains that ten million Americans must die in order to balance the scales of justice.[79]

There you have it: Islam in a nutshell. The Muslims act like fanatics because Muhammad was a fanatic. They commit horrific acts because they are adherents of a barbaric and violent religion. They slit throats and chop off heads because they follow the example of the Prophet and heed the teachings of the Koran. Osama bin Laden is not a lunatic example of a fringe group of radical Islam. He is an exemplary Muslim who, according to the tenets of his faith, will merit a place in the highest heaven. The Prophet, no doubt, would be proud of him.

BLUNDER 3

Electing a Peanut Farmer as President

The Carter administration has managed the extraordinary feat of having, at one and the same time, the worst relations with our allies, the worst relations with our adversaries, and the most serious upheavals in the developing world since the end of World War II.

Henry Kissinger, 1979

A man can have sex with animals such as sheep, cows, camels, and so on. However, he should kill the animal after orgasm. He should not sell the meat to the people in the village; however, selling the meat to people in a neighboring village is permissible.

. . . .

Americans are the Great Satan, the wounded snake.

Ayatollah Ruhollah Khomeini

For the first time in the history of our country, the majority of people believe that the next five years will be worse than the past five years.

Jimmy Carter, 1980

The more we declared our fear for [the hostages'] safety and our determination to leave no stone unturned, the greater their value became to Khomeini. We made a mistake by contributing unwittingly to Iran's exploitation of the nation's anxiety by letting it appear that the hostages were the only concern of the U.S. government.

Cyrus Vance, President Carter's Secretary of State

I N 1976 THE AMERICAN people made a terrible mistake that resulted in the rise of the mullahs, the disruption of the balance of power in the Middle East, and the renewal of jihad (that had been dormant for three hundred years) by electing a peanut farmer from Plains, Georgia, as the thirty-ninth president.

The Dunces of Doomsday

At the time, James Earl "Jimmy" Carter Jr. didn't seem to be an awful choice for the executive office. The country was just recovering from the Watergate witch hunt, and President Gerald Ford, although a very sensible leader, lacked not only charisma but also developed an unfortunate tendency to trip over his own feet and fall in public, especially when exiting *Air Force One*.

Carter didn't stumble. He was a graduate from the U.S. Naval Academy at Annapolis, where he obtained a sure-footed military gait.

Jimmy also had served two terms in the Georgia Senate and one term as governor. Sure, his record was undistinguished, but he appeared on the cover of *Time* magazine as a representative of "the New South," and he did manage to have a portrait of Martin Luther King Jr. placed in the Georgia State House (although he, like many Georgian politicians, lacked the intestinal fortitude to appear at King's funeral).[1]

BARNEY FIFE FOR PRESIDENT

During the 1976 presidential campaign, Carter presented himself as a born-again Christian who served as a deacon and Sunday school teacher at the Plains Baptist Church—a Boy Scout leader who would bring "honesty and integrity to the White House." What's more, he told the American people, "I will never lie to you."[2] He said this with a straight face, and the people believed him. A politician who would not lie! This was believable because Carter was not a lawyer. He was a Washington outsider, a down-home hayseed who had struggled to make ends meet, and an all-American, freckle-faced Baptist who espoused conservative values, including the downsizing of the federal government. He seemed real. Carter even admitted to *Playboy* magazine that he had lusted in his heart but had never cheated on his childhood sweetheart, Rosalynn, who herself appeared to have emerged from an old edition of *Good Housekeeping*.[3]

The packaging of Carter had been performed by Atlanta advertising executive Gerald Rafshoon, who had long ago mastered the genteel art of selling a pig in a poke.[4] During the presidential campaign, Carter delivered one speech to white audiences and quite another to blacks.[5] He was purposefully ambiguous on key issues, including abortion.

As soon as Carter assumed the oath of office, the White House was peopled with characters who seemed to emerge from *Li'l Abner*'s Dogpatch, including the family matriarch "Miz" Lillian, Jimmy's Bible-toting sister Ruth, and his beer-guzzling brother Billy (who came to receive a mysterious payment of $2.5 million from the Libyan government[6]).

Determined to end dependency on foreign oil, Carter moved to regulate domestic oil prices. The result was the creation of a price-gouging cartel by OPEC that sent oil prices soaring, caused rampant inflation, and drove the U.S. economy into a deep recession. The misery index, Carter's own invention for determining the well-being of the American people, rose by 50 percent during his four years in office.[7]

Carter carried on the Nixon-Kissinger policy of détente with the Soviet Union long after events had rendered the policy obsolete. By 1976 the first Strategic Arms Limitation agreement (SALT 1), which had been signed in 1972, had resulted in the creation of an arms-control lobby within Washington. The lobby secured the right to examine weapons programs at the research-and-development stage. In this way, the lobbyists could seek to veto any or all programs that might violate the SALT agreement.[8] This might have been well and good, save for the fact that some of the lobbyists were corrupt and used their power to extort large sums of money from military contractors. Others were political pinkos who acted to weaken the military so that acts of "imperial aggression" (such as Vietnam) might never occur again. Carter's policy, which resulted in the SALT 2 agreement, furthered this development by granting lobbyists greater power than the highest-ranking Pentagon officials.[9]

The peanut-brained president went on to relinquish control of the Panama Canal, to oppose the Soviet invasion of Afghanistan by pulling the U.S. team out of the Olympics, and by attempting to normalize relations with Cuba through the opening of "interest sections" (official missions but not embassies) in Washington and Havana. His Cuban policy resulted in the Mariel Boatlift whereby Fidel Castro sent 120,000 refugees—including mental patients and hardened criminals—to Miami, thus transforming the resort city into the crime capital of the United States.[10]

HUMAN RIGHTS = POLITICAL WRONGS

For all of the above, Carter should have been tarred and feathered, but of infinitely greater consequence was his human-rights policy, which was based on a simple-minded understanding of the 1975 Helsinki Accord. Under the terms of this agreement, various countries (the United States, Canada, the Soviet Union, and most of Europe) agreed to end human-rights violations. The original idea behind the accord was to force the Soviet Union to liberalize its internal policy of exiling dissidents in Siberia. Of course, it didn't work. The signing ceremony simply had been a formality. Soviet President Leonid Brezhnev continued to drop dissidents into the deep freeze, along with the altruists who sought to monitor Soviet compliance with the accord.

Carter remained intent on enforcing the terms of the accord not only on the country's worst enemies (the USSR, Communist China, Syria, and Cuba) but also on some of America's best friends and oldest allies. For this reason, he established the Bureau of Human Rights and Humanitarian Affairs within the Department of State. The new bureau was headed by Patricia Derian, a diehard liberal who had worked in Mississippi during the 1960s civil-rights movement. In September 1977 Brazil reacted to Derian's criticisms of its alleged violations of human rights by canceling four defense contracts with the United States, two of which dated back to 1942. Argentina became similarly estranged.[11]

Somoza Gets the Shaft

As the self-appointed champion of human rights, President Carter also played a major part in the overthrow of Nicaraguan president Anastasia Somoza. Viron Baku, Carter's assistant secretary of state, made the surprise announcement: "No negotiation, mediation, or compromise can be achieved any longer with a Somoza government. The solution can only begin with a sharp break from the past."[12]

Yes, Somoza was a dictator, but he was a longtime friend and faithful supporter of the United States. Under his regime, Nicaragua had never cast a vote contrary to that of the United States at the United Nations. What's more, he was battling Communist insurgents from Cuba, Panama, the Soviet Union, and Venezuela who had infiltrated Nicaragua to foment political chaos. Somoza wasn't prosecuting pogroms upon innocent civilians or casting peasants and Indians into prison for failing to salute his Lincoln limousine as it passed through rural towns and villages. He was suppressing a rebellion that had been created by outside agitators.

The "sharp break from the past" came in 1979 when Somoza was deposed by the Sandinistas, a Marxist regime whose policies were infinitely more oppressive for the people of Nicaragua. Within three years they seized all private property, forced the native Indians from their lands, and conducted more than eight thousand political executions.[13] All thanks to U.S. president Jimmy Carter, who didn't lift a finger to save the old regime.

But the real problem with Carter's human-rights policy came with Iran—a problem the president solved by unleashing the demonic forces of Islam and bringing the Western world to the brink of doomsday.

America's Once Closest Ally

America's closest friend and ally in the Muslim world was Iran's Mohammad Reza Pahlavi, who ascended to the Peacock Throne as shah (the Persian title for king) in 1941. He succeeded his father, Reza Pahlavi, who had been deposed by the Allies after he showed support for the Third Reich by allowing hundreds of Nazi agents to operate in Iran.[14]

Such intervention was necessary because of Iran's strategic position (including its fifteen-hundred-mile border with the Soviet Union) and its natural resources. Iran was the first Middle Eastern country to have an oil industry. The English discovered the black gold in 1904. The Anglo-Iranian Oil Company was formed shortly afterward, but Iran only owned 16 percent.[15] This arrangement produced widespread discontent and political protests. In 1951 leftist Mohammed Mossadegh won a popular election and assumed the office of prime minister. In this role, he moved to nationalize the oil company, limit the power of the shah, and to establish close relations with the Soviet Union. In 1952 Mossadegh's government was toppled by a coup engineered by the CIA code-named Operation Ajax. The shah regained his throne, and the United States managed to ward off the further spread of communism in the Middle East.

In appreciation, the shah shared the spoils with the restructuring of Iran's oil industry by means of an international consortium. Anglo-Iranian (now British Petroleum) held 40 percent of the shares in the consortium, five American oil companies held another 40 percent, and the remaining shares were distributed between Royal Dutch/Shell and

Compaignie Francaise de Petroles.[16] As a further display of gratitude, the shah endorsed the Baghdad Pact in 1955, joining Turkey and Iraq in a mini-NATO alliance to ward off communism in the Middle East.

By 1961 Iran had become so oil rich that the shah chose to launch a "white revolution," that is, a revolution without bloodshed. More than one hundred billion dollars was spent on roads, railways, airports, water, dams for power and irrigation, agribusiness, pipelines, steel and petrochemical plants, heavy metallurgy, health, education, and welfare.[17] Back-alley bazaars were transformed into Fifth Avenue shops. Rock 'n' roll blared from radio stations. Movie theaters showed such flicks as *Sex and the Single Girl* with Natalie Wood and Tony Curtis and *Walk on the Wild Side* with Barbara Stanwyck and Jane Fonda. *Peyton Place* and *Rawhide* played on Iranian television. Restaurants served hot dogs and beer. Nightclubs, strip joints, and casinos catered to foreign tourists, foreign contractors, and foreign military advisers.[18] Iranian teenage boys appeared in T-shirts and jeans to congregate on street corners and ogle the newly unveiled Iranian teenage girls, who had abandoned abaya gowns for skirts and tight blouses. The situation was enough to make any self-respecting mullah hot under the turban.

The straw that broke the camel's back came with the shah's ruling that newly elected Iranian officials were free to take their oath of office on whatever holy scripture they preferred—including the Christian Bible.[19] Immediately, clerics began condemning the shah in mosques and seminaries. In response, these critics were tossed in and out of jail, among them the grim-faced, gaunt ringleader, Ayatollah Ruhollah Khomeini.

THE RISE OF THE MAD MULLAH

On June 3, 1963, Khomeini, in the company of other mullahs, issued a declaration at the Feyziyeh mosque: "We have come to the conclusion that this regime is fundamentally opposed to Islam and the existence of a religious class." Cheers from thousands of gatherers greeted the declaration. The ayatollah went on to address the shah:

> Forty-five years of your life have passed. Isn't it time for you to think and reflect a little, to ponder about where all of this is leading you, to learn a

lesson from the experience of your father? I hope to God that you didn't have in mind the religious scholars when you said, "The reactionaries are like impure animals," because if you did, it will be difficult for us to tolerate you much longer. The nation will not allow you to continue is this way."[20]

Khomeini invoked *takfir*, the process of condemning the enemies of Islam, and ruled that the shah was an "apostate," that is, a Muslim who had abandoned the teachings of the Prophet. The penalty of apostasy, Khomeini reminded his followers, was death.[21] He further decreed that the United States, as the corrupter of morality, is "the Great Satan."[22]

Several days later, Khomeini was arrested. His imprisonment caused six days of angry protests in the cities of Mashad, Qom, Shirhaz, Tehran, and throughout the country. Tanks and troops quelled the protests, but the confrontations resulted in six hundred deaths.

The stint in the shah's stinky slammer did nothing to silence Khomeini. Upon his release, the ayatollah picked up where he left off with charges that the shah was intent upon destroying Iran's identity as an Islamic nation.[23] Thousands of seminary students throughout the country flocked to Khomeini's cause, and the demonstrations continued.

By 1964 the shah had endured quite enough of the crazy cleric and exiled Khomeini to Turkey. But Turkey was not to the ayatollah's taste and, after a couple of months among the drug-dealing *bubas,* he relocated to the Shi'ite holy city of Najaf in Iraq, where he continued his campaign against the shah with modern technology. Cassettes of his sermons and lectures were sent to millions of his compatriots in Iran.[24] What's more, Khomeini kept in constant contact with the religious leaders of Iran by telephone, thanks to the direct dialing that the shah had made possible by updating the country's system of mass communication.[25]

Too Much, Too Soon

The shah took little heed of these developments and went on with his modernization efforts. By 1977 four nuclear reactors were started, along with a nationwide rash of factories that produced cars, diesel engines, elevators, bicycles, tractors, machine tools, clothes, aluminum, glucose, and arms.[26]

Problems arose. To create agricultural industries, the shah forced villagers to sell their farmlands. The uprooted peasants were relocated with much resistance to model towns called *shahraks*.[27] The transplanted people decried the loss of their ancestral homes and villages and joined the clerics and Khomeini in decrying modernization. When the mayor of Tehran sent bulldozers to demolish private homes and working-class districts to make way for new thoroughfares, hundreds of displaced citizens took to the streets with placards bearing the picture of the exiled Khomeini and copies of the Koran. The shah responded by rounding up the protesters and placing them in detention cells.[28]

Under normal circumstances, the United States would not have interfered with the shah's policies, especially since he had upgraded the quality of life for his citizens, granted women the right to vote, and opened schools that were open to both sexes—so that the daughter of the lowliest peasant could receive an education and embark upon a career in a free and open marketplace. But in 1977, times were not normal. A peanut farmer sat in the Oval Office and the poor shah, like Nicaraguan president Anastasia Somoza, fell victim to Jimmy Carter's mealymouthed duplicity and talent for good ole Southern hornswoggle.

Visits Between Friends

In November 1977 the shah and Empress Farah Diba visited the White House. There they were greeted by four thousand radical Iranian students wearing masks, brandishing clubs, and waving banners demanding the shah's abdication. The rioters were permitted within a hundred feet of the main entrance to the White House, where they attacked other Iranians and Americans who had gathered to see the royal couple. Only fifteen demonstrators were arrested, and they were quickly released.[29]

On New Year's Eve 1977, President Carter attended a state dinner in Tehran. He toasted the shah: "Iran, because of the great leadership of the shah, is an island of stability in one of the most troubled areas of the world. This is a great tribute to you, Your Majesty, and to your leadership and to the respect and admiration and love which your people give you." But not knowing when to shut up, Carter went on to say that he and the shah shared the same "cause of human rights," adding: "We have no other nation on earth who is closer to us in planning for our mutual military security. We have no other with whom we have closer consultation on regional problems that concern us both. And there is no leader with whom I have a deeper sense of personal gratitude and personal friendship."[30]

The professions of friendship and gratitude were mere verbiage. Upon his return to the Oval Office, Carter conferred with Patricia Derian and decided that the shah should not be toasted but roasted on the cause of human rights. He then informed the shah that he intended to withhold all military aid to Iran unless the shah released three thousand political prisoners (including known terrorists) and permitted free assembly—even for the groups who were intent upon overthrowing the shah's government.[31] The shah, knowing that he would be helpless without U.S. support, reluctantly consented and chaos ensued.

THE ISLAMIC REVOLUTION

On September 8, 1978, more than one hundred thousand protesters gathered in Tehran's Shahyad Square and called for an Islamic government, denounced the shah, and repeated the slogan, "Khomeini is our leader."[32] The shah responded with a declaration of martial law. The next day, at Jaleh Square, in the blue-collar region of Tehran, a crowd refused to disperse. Troops opened fire, and large numbers of demonstrators were killed. The event became known as Black Friday.[33]

Still, the demonstrations continued. In October 1978 the first of many strikes in the public sector took place. By November, workers in the oil industry, the customs department, the post office, government-owned factories, banks, and newspapers were on strike. The economy of one of the world's wealthiest countries was paralyzed.[34]

At the urging of the shah, the Iraqi government informed Ayatollah Khomeini that he would have to leave the country unless he abandoned his political activities—a condition that Khomeini rejected. On October 3 Khomeini left Iraq for Kuwait but was denied entrance at the border. He then headed to Paris, where he took up residence in the suburb of Neauphle-le-Chateau in a house that had been rented for him by Iranian exiles. When he took up residence, the ayatollah immediately ordered the removal of the toilet and the installation of an Islamic squat box.[35]

In the midst of this mayhem, President Carter arranged a meeting in Tehran with the shah and several of his business cronies from Georgia. At the meeting, as reported by former Iranian prime minister Amir Abbas Hoveyda, the businessmen confided that Carter wished the shah to cancel a contract he had awarded to Brown and Root for the construction of a large port at Bandar Mahshahr so that the contract could be re-awarded to the visiting group at 10 percent above the established price. The group would then charge the 10 percent as a management fee and pass the actual construction work back to Brown and Root as previously awarded. The visitors insisted that the project would never come to fruition without the shah's consent to this arrangement. They further said that the shah should be willing to go along with this proposal as a sign of appreciation for any help that might be forthcoming from the Carter administration. The shah, retaining his dignity, declined to submit to this crass attempt at blackmail and extortion.[36]

Carter reportedly became irate at the shah's refusal and was then determined to topple him from the throne. When the rioting in Iran turned violent, the U.S. president refused to authorize the shipment of rubber bullets and tear gas to Iran for mob control.[37]

When the shah renewed his pleas for help, Carter responded by demanding that his esteemed friend and ally sign a fifty-year agreement with the United States to supply oil at the fixed rate of eight dollars a barrel. Realizing that such an agreement would only serve to further inflame the mullahs, the shah had no choice but to decline Carter's terms.[38]

After being rebuffed by the shah, Carter began to express a fondness for Khomeini in the struggle for Iran. The president believed that he, as a good Baptist and Sunday school teacher, would be able to communicate with a fellow "man of religion."[39] Andrew Young, Carter's ambassador to the United Nations, went so far as to call Khomeini a misunderstood "saint."[40] Ramsey Clark, a Carter adviser who served as attorney general under Lyndon B. Johnson, held a press conference to report on a trip to Iran and a visit to Paris during which he met with Khomeini. Clark suggested that the United States should take no steps to aid the shah and insisted that Iran should be permitted to determine its destiny without Western interference.[41]

The Fall of the Shah

The culmination of the Islamic Revolution began on December 2, 1978, when countless thousands of protesters defied the shah's ban on demonstrations and took to the streets of Tehran. Wearing the white shrouds of martyrdom, they waved banners denouncing the shah and the Great Satan and demanding the return of Khomeini. More than seven hundred protesters were killed in the first three days of demonstrations. But the bloodshed did little to quell the unrest. By December 12, two million people were in the streets of Tehran demanding the abdication of the man they had once hailed as *shahanshah* or "king of kings."[42]

The military foundation of the shah's regime quickly crumbled. Conscript troops, recoiling at the constant killing of unarmed students and workers, abandoned their units, joined the protests, and fired on their commanding officers.[43]

The shah left Iran on January 16, 1979, for an "extended vacation."[44] Two weeks later, Ayatollah Khomeini returned to Tehran amid the cheers of millions of supporters. Radical Islam had come to power.

The Reign of Terror

Carter ordered Pentagon officials to tell the shah's top military commanders—about 150 of them—to acquiesce to all demands from the ayatollah and to offer no resistance to the transfer of power. The shah's commanders heeded this advice. All of them were murdered in accordance with Khomeini's first command as the supreme Islamic jurist of the newly dubbed Islamic Republic of Iran.

The bloodbath continued for the next three years. More than twenty thousand pro-Western Iranians and "godless Communists" were convicted in the newly established Islamic courts as "enemies of Allah" and executed by firing squads.[45] Churches and synagogues were razed, cemeteries desecrated, and shrines vandalized and demolished. The judicially murdered included the 102-year-old Kurdish poet Allameh Vahidi and a 9-year-old girl convicted of "attacking revolutionary guards."[46] Women returned to servitude. They lost their rights to attend school, to initiate divorce, and to retain custody of their children. When they appeared in public, women were obliged to wear *hyab* (traditional Islamic) clothing. All American music was outlawed. The movie theaters and nightclubs were shut down. And citizens were arrested for owning satellite dishes that could access Western programs.[47]

As the situation worsened in Iran, President Carter received word that his old friend the shah had accepted his invitation to settle down for a spell within the United States. Carter, displaying his unique brand of Southern hospitality, withdrew the invitation and suggested that the shah, whom he had toasted the previous year as the ruler for whom he had the greatest sense of "personal gratitude" and "personal friendship," would really be better off in the Bahamas.

Several of the shah's friends, including Henry Kissinger and David Rockefeller, expressed outrage at Carter's treatment of the man who had served as "America's greatest ally"—especially when they learned that the shah was seriously ill.[48]

At last, Carter's advisers managed to convince him that his continual refusal to allow the shah to enter the States for medical treatment might undermine his image as "a great humanitarian." The president relented. The shah finally arrived in New York on October 22, 1979, was diagnosed with cancer, and died in Cairo on July 27, 1980.

AMERICA HELD HOSTAGE

On November 4, 1979, Iranian students overran the U.S. embassy in Tehran and seized more than sixty hostages in retaliation for Carter's permission for the shah to enter the United States for medical treatment. Ayatollah Khomeini supported the action and condemned the embassy as a "den of spies." The students voted not to release the hostages until the United States returned the shah for trial, along with billions they claimed had been stolen from the Iranian people.[49]

How did Carter respond to this act of barbaric aggression? Did he call out the marines for a show of American might that would have left the newly created Islamic Republic of Iran in a mound of rubble? Of course not. He opted to impose an embargo on Iranian oil and to freeze Iranian assets.

The ayatollah, out of the goodness of his heart, authorized the release women, African Americans, and non-U.S. citizen hostages, since women and minorities already had suffered "the oppression of American society."[50] He kept the remaining fifty-two hostages in captivity for 444 days.

Carter's position during the hostage crisis was founded on his belief that Uncle Sam had lost his guts in a state of near senility. He expressed this opinion in his famous "malaise speech" of July 15, 1979:

> I want to talk to you right now about a fundamental threat to American democracy. . . . I do not refer to the outward strength of America, a nation that is at peace everywhere in the world with unmatched economic power and military might. The threat is nearly invisible in ordinary ways. It is a crisis of confidence. It is a crisis that strikes at the heart and soul and spirit of our national will. We can see this crisis in the growing doubt about the meaning of our lives and in the loss of unity of purpose for our nation.[51]

This assessment of America's lack of resolve was the only point upon which members of the Carter cabinet agreed. Secretary of State Cyrus Vance said, "To oppose Soviet or Cuban involvement in Africa would be futile." He added, "The fact is that we can no more stop change than Canute could still the waters."[52] Security Adviser Zbigniew Brzezinski insisted that "the world is changing under the influences of forces no government can control." Vietnam, in Brzezinski's opinion, had been "the Waterloo of the WASP elite"—no such military action could ever be undertaken again.[53]

The Desert Debacle

After six months of waiting, the president finally decided to act. It was, after all, an election year, and there was no way that Carter and his clan could remain in the White House with fifty-two red-blooded Americans languishing in Iran.

The rescue attempt that Carter approved was code-named Operation Eagle Claw. The plan was to fly helicopters from aircraft carriers in the Gulf of Oman to a remote area in the Iranian desert, which was code-named Desert One. Six C-130 transport planes would also land in the desert with ninety commandos and a small arsenal of weapons. The helicopters would fly the commandos to a hideout in the mountains.[54]

Meanwhile, U.S. operatives in Tehran were to take trucks that were hidden in a warehouse by Iranian agents and drive them to the mountain hideout and pick up the rescue team. The team would then drive back to Tehran and storm the foreign ministry and the embassy and free the hostages. As soon as this was accomplished, the helicopters would fly into Tehran, land in the city's public squares, and whisk off into the night with the commandos and the captives. The helicopters would fly to an abandoned airstrip where C-141s would be waiting to transport the commandos and captives to a landing field in the Saudi Arabian desert.[55]

The mission began on April 24, 1980. Two of the helicopters landed short of Desert One after being caught in a severe sandstorm. When the C-130s landed, three Iranian vehicles were in the area. The team commander, Col. Charles Beckwith, believed that two were driven by smugglers who would not go to the police to report the arrival of the Americans. The third vehicle was a bus with forty-four passengers. Carter ordered that the forty-four passengers should be placed in one of the transport planes and flown to Egypt until the operation was over.[56]

Meanwhile, the helicopters ran into more problems with the sandstorms. One developed a hydraulic leak that left the rescue team with fewer than the six choppers needed to complete the mission. Beckwith recommended that the operation be aborted. Carter concurred.[57]

But this was not the end of the sorry debacle. As the helicopters were preparing to leave, one kicked up so much sand that a second did not see a C-130 preparing to take off and crashed into it. Eight soldiers were killed and three others severely burned. The next morning, gleeful Iranians broadcast footage of the smoking wreck that stood as vivid testimony to American impotence and incompetence. The ayatollah pronounced that his forces had defeated the Great Satan and issued new threats about punishing the prisoners.[58]

Other Carter Legacies in the Middle East

With the shah gone, the Middle East was destabilized. This led to the Soviet invasion of Afghanistan with eighty thousand troops on Christmas Day 1979 and the establishment of a puppet government in Kabul headed by Soviet dummy Babrak Karmal. Religious teachers and clerics throughout the Arab world began calling upon young men to take up arms in a jihad to liberate their Sunni brothers. One of the first to answer the call was Osama bin Laden, a Saudi engineer from one of the wealthiest families in Arabia, who headed off with thousands of others for training camps in Pakistan. The recruits became known as the "holy warriors," or mujahideen. To aid these rebel bands in their struggle against the Soviets, President Carter provided thirty million dollars in military aid.[59] The directive was signed on July 3, 1979. A precedent for support was set that Carter's successor in the Oval Office would follow.

Another result of the destabilization came with Iraq's invasion of Iran. The action was prompted by Iraqi president Saddam Hussein's belief that the Iranian military was so disorganized and demoralized in the wake of the revolution that it would offer little resistance to a full-scale attack. Hussein hoped to obtain control of the Shatt al-Arab, the main sea outlet of the Tigris and Euphrates rivers and the rich Iranian oil fields. The war lasted nearly nine years at a cost of more than one million lives (on both sides) and billions in damages.[60]

Of course, U.S. officials should have been delighted by this development and the opportunity to sit back and watch the two Muslim nutcases blow themselves to smithereens, if not to the seventh heaven. This solution was a no-brainer. Was it adopted? Of course not! This takes us to the next blunder, a blunder that involved Ronald Reagan, who defeated Carter by a landslide in the election of 1980.

Carter himself was down but not out. During subsequent years he transformed himself from America's worst president to America's worst former president by mollycoddling and hobnobbing with such rabid anti-American dictators as Fidel Castro, Hugo Chavez, and Kim Jong-il.

BLUNDER 4

Playing Both Sides Against the Middle and Giving Hussein the Screws

Americans will never make concessions to terrorists—to do so would only invite more terrorism. Once we head down that path, there would be no end to it, no end to the suffering of innocent people, no end to the bloody ransom all civilized people must pay.

Ronald Reagan, June 18, 1985

It is not surprising to see the contaminated hands of America and Israel emerging from the sleeves of devious people, the ringleaders of Saudi Arabia, and the traitors to the two holy shrines.

Ayatollah Ruhollah Khomeini

FROM AN AMERICAN PERSPECTIVE, it would be impossible to conceive of a better or more providential situation to develop in the midst of the Iranian hostage crisis. On September 2, 1980, Hussein launched an invasion of Iran to put an end to the reign of the Ayatollah Khomeini and to prevent the crazy cleric from exporting his Islamic Revolution throughout the Persian Gulf region with the intent of establishing a "universal Islamic order."[1] Such announced plans scared the proverbial excrement out of the oil-rich Saudi sheiks. Khomeini had become a hero not only among his fellow Shi'ites but among Sunni Arabs as well.

The Islamic Revolution was viewed as the triumph of Islam over the United States and the West and as vivid proof that devout believers could topple regional rulers, including the Saudi dynasty.

The impact of the events in Iran was indeed felt by the Saudis when a group of more than three thousand fanatics under Juhayman al-Utaibi, who proclaimed himself as the *Mahdi,* seized the Grand Mosque and demanded the end of the rule of the royal family, who, in al-Utaibi's opinion, had proven themselves to be apostates by their Western alliances. The rebellion was eventually subdued by a special detachment of French mercenaries, who used stun grenades and chemical weapons to recapture the mosque, and by Saudi forces who mowed down thousands of protesters with machine guns. Once the crisis was over, forty-one of the perpetrators, including Juhayman al-Utaibi, were executed by firing squad in Riyadh.

Egypt was the next country to be rocked by the reverberations emanating from Iran, largely because President Anwar Sadat had invited the deposed shah to take shelter there—an affront to the sentiments of most of the population. Sadat was assassinated on October 6, 1981, as he presided over a military parade. The Egyptians, under Hosni Mubarak, moved quickly to suppress the Islamists, jailing and torturing thousands, including Ayman al-Zawahiri, who came to serve as al Qaeda's second in command.[2]

To squelch the Islamic Revolution and to end the terrorism unleashed by Khomeini, many of the Persian Gulf nations—Bahrain, Kuwait, Oman, Qatar, Saudi Arabia, and the United Arab Emirates—banded together to form the Gulf Cooperation Council and to provide support for Hussein, whom Saudi King Fahd hailed as "the sword of Islam."[3]

The ayatollah himself provoked Iraq's invasion. He had called upon his Shi'ite supporters in Iraq to rebel against Hussein, not because Hussein was a bloodthirsty tyrant who had slaughtered colleagues and rivals (often by his own hand), let alone his mass public hangings of Jews, but rather because the Iraqi ruler was not a "faithful Muslim."[4] The proof of this unfaithfulness was evident in Hussein's failure to impose *shariah* (Islamic law) upon his citizens. There were liquor stores in Baghdad and even butcher shops that sold pork. Unveiled women walked the streets after dark in shameless attire, and crowds lined up at movie theaters to see the latest Hollywood releases. The place, in Khomeini's opinion, needed a thorough purge.

Early in 1980, members of the Iranian-backed rebel group known as the Dawa Party set off a series of explosions in Iraq and attempted to assassinate high-ranking Iraqi officials, including Foreign Minister Tariq Aziz. Hussein outlawed the group, deported thousands of Iranians, and executed Ayatollah Muhammad Baqir al-Sadr, one of the Shi'ite clerics who had led a series of protests against his regime.[5]

Between April and September, Iranian aircraft violated Iraqi airspace on sixty-nine occasions, and clashes broke out at regular intervals along the Iran-Iraq border.

Hussein responded by abrogating his 1975 treaty with Iran and proclaiming the Shatt al-Arab, the major waterway connecting the Persian Gulf with the Iranian ports of Khorramshahr and Abadan and the Iraqi port of Basra, to be "a national river."

The invasion began with attacks on the world's largest oil refinery at Abadan.[6] On the ground, Iraqi forces seized a large swath of territory in southern Iran and besieged Abadan and Khorramshahr. But by June 1981 the tide of the war shifted as the Iranians broke the siege at Abadan and recaptured Khorramshahr. Within a year the Iraqis had been forced out of Iran and spent the remainder of the war on the defensive.

During the summer of 1982 Iran attacked the Iraqi post of Basra and appeared to be on the verge of a breakthrough, but Iraqi forces held and the fighting settled into a war of attrition. Not that Hussein played nice. He warded off the invading Iranians with regular doses of poisonous gas.[7] Left to his own devices, the Iraqi president would have made things infinitely worse for the Iranian ayatollah's army. He began to enrich uranium for use in a strategic nuclear weapons program at his French-built nuclear facility at Tuwaitah near Baghdad. He was only stopped from launching a nuclear holocaust when Israelis bombed the facility on June 7, 1981.[8]

THE WORLD TAKES SIDES

Both Iran and Iraq received foreign aid. Libya, China, and North Korea sent weapons, particularly missiles, to Iran, while Iraq's support came primarily from the Gulf States who viewed the Khomeini and his regime as a threat to their security. Kuwait, Saudi Arabia, and the United Arab Emirates propped up Hussein with billions in loans and grants, while Egypt and Jordan sent arms and supplies. Additional aid came to Iraq in the form of munitions from France, high-tech military expertise from West Germany (some of it illegally), and high-end weapons and more than a thousand military advisers from the Soviet Union.[9] The Soviets were motivated by internal concerns about their Islamic holdings in Central Asia—Kazakhstan, Kyrgyzstan, Tajikistan, Turkmenistan, and Uzbekistan.[10]

At the start of the war, the Reagan administration considered Hussein as the lesser of two evils. Sure the Iraqi president was a man of incredible depravity who came from a family of professional brigands. He had acquired his first gun at the age of ten and had committed his first murder before he turned twelve.[11] But the Iranian ayatollah had labeled the United States the Great Satan, he had exiled the shah, he had confiscated U.S. assets, he had called for the expulsion of all Western interests in the Persian Gulf, and he had held fifty-two American hostages for 444 days. No tyrant, king, or political leader in history had done more to undermine America's reputation as a superpower within the world community.

In 1983, while the conflict was at a standstill, President Reagan sent Donald Rumsfeld as a special envoy to Baghdad to hammer out a covert agreement with Hussein for military aid. The Reagan administration eventually agreed to provide Iraq with billions in agricultural credits and hundreds of millions of dollars in advanced weaponry. This weaponry was transported to Iraq by a circuitous route through Egypt and Saudi Arabia.[12] The administration further equipped the Iraqi army with satellite intelligence, supplemented by AWACs (Airborne Warning and Control Systems) reconnaissance, that could be used to direct chemical and biological weapons against Iranian suicide brigades.[13] In addition, the Reagan administration launched Operation Staunch, a voluntary worldwide arms embargo against Tehran and issued an official condemnation of Iran as a terror-sponsoring nation.

Such measures were understandable. Khomeini deserved to be crushed under someone's heel like a spider. But things turned queasy and quizzical. Helping Iraq win was one thing, but supporting Hussein was quite another. The man, as it turned out, was a verifiable lunatic who began to speak of grandiose plans to expand Iraq's borders to those of the ancient Babylonian empire.[14] Now the Reagan administration faced a host of troublesome questions. What if Hussein won the war? What would be the repercussions for Saudi Arabia and other oil-producing countries in the Persian Gulf? What would be the consequences for Israel (who opted to side with the Iranians)? Was America lending support to a madman who was even worse than Khomeini? How could such a turn of events have come to pass?

The insane situation gave way to an insane solution—a solution motivated by events within the tiny country of Lebanon (slightly smaller than the state of Connecticut). Hezbollah, a group of radical Shi'ites with close ties to Khomeini, joined the Palestine Liberation Organization (PLO) and Syrian troops to oppose the Israeli invasion of 1982. Not knowing when to stay out of trouble, the United States decided to act as an impartial peacekeeper by sending in marines to protect the Beirut airport and dispatching warships to protect the marines. In October 1983 a suicide bomber blew up the marines' barracks, killing 241. This convinced the Reagan administration not to retaliate against the atrocity but to withdraw its forces. The peacekeeping effort was an abysmal failure. But the Muslim terrorists in Lebanon wouldn't allow Uncle Sam to retreat without a good lesson in humiliation. And so Hezbollah began to take U.S. citizens as hostages.[15]

The first hostages to be collared and cast into stinky detention cells were American University in Beirut president David Dodge, journalist Terry Anderson, Presbyterian minister Benjamin Weir, U.S. Embassy diplomat William Buckley, American University in Beirut librarian Peter Kilburn, Catholic priest Martin Jenco, and University of Beirut Medical School administrator David Jacobsen.[16]

These seven captives became an obsessive concern for Reagan. He had been elected, in part, to resolve the hostage situation in Iran, but now he faced a new hostage situation in Lebanon. He was getting pressure from the families of the captives, from POW groups, and from veterans' organizations. More and more magazine articles were being published about the forgotten hostages. And yellow ribbons like those that had been used as reminders of the Iranian hostages were beginning to appear in honor of the Hezbollah hostages in cities, towns, and villages across the country. Reagan was beginning to look as helpless as his predecessor.

A CRAZY PROPOSAL

A solution to the Middle East problem was proposed by National Security Adviser Robert McFarlane, who drafted a National Security Decision Directive (NSDD) in June 1985, setting forth the balmy notion of opening diplomatic relations with Iran by supplying arms. Secretary of Defense Caspar Weinberger reacted by saying that the directive was "too crazy to comment on . . . like inviting [Libyan President] Qadhafi to Washington for a cozy chat."[17] Secretary of State George Shultz issued a similar response.[18] But CIA director William Casey claimed the proposal had merit, even though it undermined Operation Staunch, which the United States had spearheaded since the outbreak of the conflict.[19]

McFarlane was not dismayed by this initial reaction to his screwy scheme. In July he found a new way to press the issue. In a meeting with Israeli foreign minister David Kimche, McFarlane learned that Iran had suggested to Israel an exchange of weapons for the hostages. Specifically, the Iranians were in search of TOW (tube-launched, optically tracked, wire-guided) missiles, and Kimche passed the word to McFarlane that a token transfer of such missiles to Iran would be viewed as a "good-will gesture."[20]

McFarlane contacted both Weinberger and Shultz to inform them of the proposal that would not only place the United States in a favorable position with Iran but also free the seven hostages in Lebanon. In his memorandum to Shultz, McFarlane wrote: "The short term dimension concerns the seven hostages; the long term dimension involves the establishment of a private dialogue with Iranian officials on the broader issues. . . . They sought specifically the delivery from Israel of 100 TOW missiles."[21]

McFarlane received the go-ahead to brief President Reagan on the proposal at a White House meeting on July 18, 1985. The matter received a formal review on August 6 at a meeting attended by President Reagan, Vice President George H. W. Bush, Shultz, Weinberger, and White House chief of staff Donald Regan. Despite objections from Shultz and Weinberger, Reagan approved the proposal, and on August

20, 1985, Israel delivered a pallet of TOW missiles on behalf of the U.S. government to the Islamic Republic of Iran.[22]

To comprehend the enormity of this folly, one should recall that the United States had provided billions in aid, including advanced weaponry, to Iraq. It had made its position clear by the launching of Operation Staunch and an arms embargo against Iran. Now the Reagan administration suddenly decided to provide hundreds of millions of dollars in aid to Iraq as a "good-will gesture." Things don't get much nuttier than this in the realm of world politics. But even this crazy situation became crazier.

Ayatollah Khomeini accepted the gift without so much as a thank-you and did nothing to facilitate the release of one hostage. How did the Reagan administration react to this? Did it realize that McFarlane's proposal was daft to begin with? Did it pledge never again to give the ayatollah any weapon of any kind? Of course not! It rather decided to present the ayatollah with another shipment of TOW missiles, which arrived in Tehran on September 15. This time, the ayatollah responded with the release of one hostage—Presbyterian minister Benjamin Weir, who had been held captive since May 8, 1984.[23]

HAWKS FOR A VULTURE

The release of the minister at the cost of hundreds of millions gave new hope to the Washington officials, who now decided to sell arms on a continuous basis until all the hostages were released. The ayatollah decided that a shipment of HAWK (homing-all-the-way-killer) antiaircraft missiles would be nice to add to his collection, and the Gipper was pleased to provide them. How could Khomeini refuse such a generous offer? The HAWKs were shipped to Iran from Israel in early December 1985, despite objections from Regan, Shultz, Weinberger, and McFarlane's successor as the national security adviser, John Poindexter.[24] Weinberger later testified that he informed President Reagan that sending weapons to Iran was against the law. "I argued strongly that we have an embargo that makes sales to Iran illegal," the defense secretary told investigators, "and that the President couldn't violate it [and] that 'washing' the transaction through Israel wouldn't make it legal."[25]

Despite the shipment of HAWKS, the ayatollah again reneged on the deal, claiming that some missiles were defective and others bore offensive Israeli markings.[26] McFarlane traveled to Iran with military aide Lt. Col. Oliver North to meet with agents of Khomeini and to provide spare parts for the HAWKs. After much pleading and coaxing, a single hostage was released—Catholic priest Martin Jenco.[27]

By the end of 1986 the United States had provided Iran with 2,004 TOW and eighteen HAWK missiles, 240 HAWK spare parts, and sensitive intelligence on Iraq. In early November a third hostage was released—University of Beirut Medical School administrator David Jacobsen. Ironically, the sequence of events supported President Reagan's public stance—ignored in covert practice—that dealing with terrorists only contributes to more terrorism. Secretary of State Schultz later summed up the dealings with the Iranians by saying, "Our guys got taken to the cleaners."[28]

Sure, a minister, a priest, and a school administrator had been released in Lebanon, but not William Buckley, the CIA chief in Beirut, whose kidnapping had been a blow to American security interests in the Middle East. What's more, the release of the three was offset by later Hezbollah kidnappings. Within a matter of months the terrorists had increased the number of Western captives in Lebanon to thirty.

A Tangled Web

For the cache of state-of-the-art weapons, the United States had charged Iran a measly thirty million dollars, but Attorney General Edwin Meese discovered that only twelve million dollars had been deposited in U.S. coffers.[29] Where was the rest of the money? Oliver North explained the discrepancy: the remaining eighteen million dollars had been diverted to the Contras in Nicaragua who were battling the Communist Sandinistas.[30] In this way, Poindexter and other White House officials believed it could be shown that the deals with the ayatollah were meant to serve a good and honorable purpose.

Meanwhile, Khomeini gave the Gipper a kick in the pants for good luck. He arranged for *al-Shiraa*, a Lebanese newspaper, to publish an exposé of the arms-for-hostages transactions.[31] The report sent shock waves throughout the Middle East since the Reagan administration had led the way for an arms embargo against Iran. The Gipper reacted with outrage.

He appeared on television and vehemently denied that such transactions had taken place. A week later, as more news of the clandestine deals came to the surface, he was forced to recant his statement.

Hussein Snaps

How did Hussein react to this betrayal by the United States? Did he go ballistic? Did he plan some kind of retaliation? Of course he did! On May 17, 1987, an Iraqi missile hit the U.S. frigate *Stark* in the Persian Gulf and killed thirty-seven American sailors. Hussein later apologized and suggested that the United States, rather than becoming irate with the Iraqis, should direct its anger against Iran. U.S. gunboats became involved in a series of direct military actions with Iraqi vessels. The United States also allowed Kuwaiti ships to fly American flags, thereby elevating an attack on them to be an attack on U.S. property.[32]

Things got ugly. On July 3, 1988, the USS *Vincennes*, while patrolling the northern portion of the Straits of Hormuz, fired at an aircraft that reportedly failed to respond to the ship's warnings and brought the plane down. As it turned out, the plane was a commercial Iran Air jet carrying 290 passengers. All died in the crash. What's more, the plane was flying well within the commercial air corridor, and when it was shot down, it was turning away from the *Vincennes*. Later investigators discovered that the last electronic emission from the plane was its correct transponder signal, identifying it as a commercial aircraft.[33]

In spring 1988 the Iranians launched a final offensive that succeeded in capturing Halabja, a Kurdish town in northern Iraq. Hussein ordered his air force to bomb the town with poison gas, killing at least five thousand civilian inhabitants.[34] In addition, he sanctioned a massive chemical bombing on the Iranian town of Oshnavieh.[35] Such barbaric measures succeeded. Iraq's chemical weapons and Hussein's willingness to use them not only against his enemies but also against his own people convinced the Khomeini regime that it was time to end the war.

THE STAGE IS SET

On August 20, 1988, a U.N.-sponsored cease-fire took effect, and the long war came to an end at the cost of more than one million dead, two million wounded, and two and a half million refugees. The economic impact on Iraq was devastating. The port facilities at Basra were destroyed, the ambitious urban revitalization programs were abandoned, and austerity measures were enforced. Moreover, Iraq was left with a foreign debt of eighty billion dollars—most of which was owed to the Arab Gulf States, the very states that had hailed Hussein as "the sword of Islam." The Iraqi president had been crossed and double-crossed, and as everyone should have realized, there would be hell to pay.

BLUNDER 5

Spreading Death and Destruction to Protect Saudi Oil

One of the things we would like to do is that we would like to become actively engaged in ending the [Iran-Iraq] war in such a way that it becomes very evident to everybody that the guy who is causing the problem is Hussein. If I were to talk to any other Muslim leader, they wouldn't say Hussein is the problem. They'd say Iran is the problem. . . . What we're talking about is a process by which all of the rest of the Arab world comes quickly to realize that Iran is not a threat to them. Iran is not going to overrun Kuwait. Iran is not going to overthrow the government of Saudi Arabia. That the real problem in preventing peace in the region is Hussein. And we'll have to take care of that.

> *Lt. Col. Oliver North, U.S. Congressional*
> *Iran-Contra Hearings, 1987*

We do not have any defense treaties with Kuwait, and there are no special defense or security commitments to Kuwait.

> *Margaret Tutweiller, U.S. State Department*
> *spokeswoman, July 24, 1990*

President Bush is an intelligent man. He is not going to declare an economic war against Iraq. . . . I admire your extraordinary efforts to rebuild your country. I know you need funds. We understand that, and our opinion is that you should have the opportunity to rebuild your country. But we have no opinion on Arab-Arab conflicts like your border disagreement with Kuwait. [U.S. Secretary of State] James Baker has directed our official spokesmen to emphasize this instruction. . . . When we see the Iraqi point of view that the measures taken by the United Arab Emirates and Kuwait are,

in the final analysis, tantamount to military aggression against
Iraq, then it is reasonable for me to be concerned

April Glaspie, U.S. Ambassador to Iraq,
conversation with Hussein, U.S. State Department
transcripts, July 25, 1990

HUSSEIN WAS OUTRAGED. He had waged war to prevent Ayatollah
Khomeini from exporting his Islamic revolution throughout the
Persian Gulf. It hadn't been easy. The war had been the longest (over
eight years) and one of the costliest (more than one hundred billion
dollars) conflicts of the twentieth century. Moreover, for most of the
struggle, he had been forced to wage a defensive war that ravaged his
nation. Iran had found support not only from Lebanon and Libya but
also from such unlikely places as Communist China and North Korea.
What's more, and against all logic, Khomeini, who had an obsessive hatred of Israel that matched Hussein's, had managed to garner the support of Israel, which provided steady shipments of arms to Iran.

The United States had pledged to support Hussein. It had initiated
an arms embargo against Iran and provided him with agricultural credits, advanced weaponry, and satellite intelligence. But in the end, he had
been betrayed. Just when it seemed he might lose the war, the Reagan
administration changed sides and secretly began selling weapons, including sophisticated missilery, to the ayatollah, the most hated figure
in America. It was mind-boggling!

PAYBACK TIME

Kuwait, Saudi Arabia, and the other Arab states who formed the Gulf
Cooperation Council (GCC) had turned to Hussein as their savior, hail-
ing him as the "sword of Islam" when he vowed to protect their oil
fields from a Shi'ite rebellion. And he had protected them. He had
forced Khomeini to sign a truce by gassing the Iranian troops and a few
of his own cities that the Iranians occupied. And how did the Arab
states reward him for this victory? By demanding payment *with interest*
on the billions they had been granted him to safeguard their oil fields.
They refused to forgive the loans, even though his nation had been dev-
astated in order to protect them.

Moreover, the Arab states turned down his request to increase oil prices so he could reap enough revenue to rebuild his country and become the superpower of the Middle East. Iraq possessed enough oil to make Saudi Arabia look like a dry sump in Texas. It was unfair. Each OPEC member had signed a production quota to maintain the price of oil at eighteen dollars a barrel.[1] But Kuwait and the United Arab Emirates continually exceeded their quota and flooded the market. This had brought the price down to twelve dollars a barrel. Hussein could not compete with that. Every dollar-per-barrel drop cost Iraq one billion dollars in annual revenue.[2]

The position of the other Arab leaders was unconscionable. The destruction of the port of Basra had left Hussein landlocked. Now Iraq was dependent on using pipelines through Turkey and Saudi Arabia to get its oil to the marketplace.[3]

The Kick from Kuwait

Hussein had a litany of other grievances. Kuwait, while Iraq was locked in the war with Iran, had pilfered $2.4 billion in oil from the Rumdia oil field—an Iraq oil field—and still Kuwaiti emir Amir Jabir al-Ahmad al-Jabir al-Sabah refused to absolve even the interest on Iraq's debt.[4]

What's more, Hussein believed, the Kuwaiti emir was foolishly decadent. Iraqi newspapers carried front-page stories concerning al-Sabah's sex life. The stories, although lacking objective verification, alleged that the emir was syphilitic and kept seventy wives and married a virgin every Thursday.[5]

For Hussein, the solution was simple. He would invade Kuwait. This simple acquisition would achieve four objectives: (1) access to the Gulf, (2) eliminate the debt to Kuwait, (3) sufficiently threaten the Saudis and the other Arab states so they would forgive their loans, and (4) obtain funds for reconstruction and for his expansion plans so that Iraq would emerge as the richest and the mightiest nation in the Persian Gulf. It was reasonable and justifiable. After all, he had met with April Glaspie, the U.S. Ambassador to Iraq, on July 25, and she had assured him, "We [the Bush administration] have no opinion on the Arab-Arab conflicts, like your border disagreement with Kuwait."[6]

On August 2, 1990, a half million Iraqi troops invaded and occupied

Kuwait. Emir al-Sabah and members of his government fled to Saudi Arabia for protection. Five days later Iraqi troops moved toward the Saudi border.

Bush Burns

This development caused President George H. W. Bush to cough up his Wheaties. He was fearful that Hussein, who manifested symptoms of paranoiac schizophrenia, would invade Saudi Arabia, roll south to absorb all the oil fields in the Persian Gulf, and realize his dream of creating a resurrected Babylonian Empire.[7] Of course, the Iraqi invasion was no threat to U.S. national security, but it was a threat of enormous economic interest. The Arab Gulf states provided the United States with a steady supply of reasonably cheap oil and reinvested their profits in the American economy by purchasing nearly everything on the market from lumber mills to luxury hotels.

On the day of the invasion, President Bush obtained a U.N. resolution that condemned the invasion and called for the immediate withdrawal of Iraq's forces. Hussein, quite naturally, ignored it. Three days later, the United Nations imposed a trade embargo. Hussein, quite comfortable in Kuwait, remained unmoved. On November 29, the United Nations authorized the use of "all necessary means" to drive the Iraqis out of Kuwait if they had not withdrawn by January 15, 1991. Hussein stayed.[8]

OSAMA'S OFFER

Meanwhile, Osama bin Laden and his holy warriors had returned from Afghanistan after trouncing the Soviet Union, one of the world's two superpowers. As soon as Hussein invaded Kuwait, bin Laden rushed to Prince Sultan Ibn Abdul Aziz Al Saud, the Saudi minister of defense, and handed him a ten-page proposal for the defense of the kingdom. He argued that the heavy engineering equipment used by large construction companies, including his family's firm, could be used to construct fortifications at the border and around the oil fields. Bin Laden also proposed that his hard-core band of hundreds of holy warriors (mujahideen) be incorporated within the Saudi military. Since these warriors had driven the Soviets out of Afghanistan, he believed they were more than capable of expelling Hussein's troops from Kuwait. Prince Sultan listened—bin Laden's father, after all, had been one of the country's richest men—but he refused to take the proposal seriously.[9] Instead, he arranged for bin Laden to meet with Prince Turki bin Faisal ibn Abdul Aziz Al Saud, the chief of intelligence.

Prince Turki also listened politely as bin Laden spoke of his plans to unite the Arabs in a jihad against Hussein and warned against inviting or permitting "infidel" forces into the land of the two holy places. Such an invitation, bin Laden insisted, would be an effrontery to the teachings of the Prophet and would outrage all righteous believers.[10] Prince Turki, as an experienced diplomat, gave the ascetic bin Laden a glad smile and a pat on the back and arranged for him to present his plans to a host of minor officials as a means of placating him before showing him the door.

Naturally, these two Saudi princes deserve a prominent place among the dunces of doomsday (even though they are not U.S. officials). What an offer! If they had accepted, bin Laden and Hussein might have killed each other, sparing the world further terrorist attacks (including 9/11), the invasion of Afghanistan, the occupation of Iraq (under George W. Bush) at the cost of more than two thousand American lives and two hundred billion dollars, and the plans for the American Hiroshima.

FAHD'S FAUX PAS

Saudi king Fahd and the princes had too much to lose to place their fate in an upstart like Osama bin Laden, a billionaire with a stockpile of hundreds of thousands of weapons, including delayed-timing devices for his crates of C-4 plastic explosives, long-range sniper rifles, wire-guided antitank missiles, and more than a thousand shoulder-fired Stinger antiaircraft missiles.[11]

Within a week of the invasion of Kuwait, King Fahd accepted a proposal from President Bush, presented to him by Secretary of Defense Dick Cheney, to defend the kingdom with a coalition of military forces so that the flow of cheap crude oil and Arab millions could continue to pour into the United States. Why would King Fahd reject such an offer?

The Saudis had always depended on military assistance from unbelievers. They were first protected by the British then the Americans, who maintained an air base at Dhahran from 1946 to 1962, and finally by the French, who were called upon to suppress the seizure of the Great Mosque in Mecca from a group of fanatics in 1979.

But this intervention called not for the maintenance of a peacetime air base or the use of foreign troops to crush a rebellion. President Bush's plan, which became known as Operation Desert Shield, involved establishing permanent military installations between the two Islamic holy cities of Mecca and Medina.

U.S. troops began arriving by the second week of August 1990 to construct a base within the nearly deserted eighty-square-mile Prince Sultan air base. At this site in the middle of the desert, the Americans set up temper tents with environmental liners to hold in air-conditioning or heat, along with lights, plugs, and air conditioning units. They also established mess quarters, showers, and toilet facilities. The facility became known as "Al's Garage."[12]

By the end of August, the U.S. Army's Red Horse Squadron began the construction of a second base, sixty miles south of Riyadh, which came to include, at the cost of $14.6 million, a tent city, four kitchens, an air transportation hospital, six K-span structures, munitions storage units, bladder berms, and utility distribution centers.[13]

Throughout the summer and fall of 1990, giant U.S. C-130 transporters landed at various airstrips throughout Saudi Arabia to discharge hundreds of tanks, trucks, artillery transport vehicles, and jeeps. Satellite dishes sprouted from the rooftops of hotels, office buildings, and apartment complexes. Long lines of U.S. troops, including uniformed women, walked the highway between the two holy cities.[14]

AN OUTRAGED UMMAH

What could have been more offensive to the *ummah,* the pious community of believers? Bin Laden and his gang of guerrilla warriors seethed with righteous indignation. Bin Laden wrote: "The Arabian Peninsula has never—since Allah made it flat, created its desert, and encircled it with seas—been stormed by any forces like the Crusader armies now spreading in it like locusts, consuming its riches and destroying its plantations. All of this is happening at a time when nations are attacking Muslims like people fighting over a plate of food."[15]

Bin Laden circulated pamphlets and delivered speeches to decry the "American invasion." Sheikh Safar ibn Abd al-Rahman al Hameli, Sheikh Salman bin Fahd al-Awda, and other clerics and scholars who joined in the heated protest were rounded up and cast into Saudi coolers.[16]

In the fall of 1991 Saudi security police uncovered evidence that linked bin Laden to an attempt to spark an armed rebellion within the kingdom.[17] The royal family had finally had enough of the pious rabble-rouser. Despite pleas from bin Laden's friends and family, the Saudis ordered his exile and froze his financial assets.

Bin Laden departed for Sudan, which proved to be a perfect place to establish his terrorist organization. Sudan had abandoned visa requirements for Arabs and was encouraging Muslim militants from around the world to settle within its borders. By the end of 1991, somewhere between one and two thousand al Qaeda operatives had settled in Sudan and set up scores of training camps for new recruits, the main one being a twenty-acre site near Soba, seven miles south of Khartoum.[18]

BUSH'S BUFFOONERY

Were President Bush and his advisers not aware that the installation of military bases between the holy cities would outrage Muslims there and around the world? This question begs an answer since the U.S. intelligence budget in 1990 exceeded fifty billion dollars, with six billion dollars going to the CIA. A good portion of these funds were squandered by bureaucrats who spent their time updating files, attending meetings, and making calls within their cubicles to other bureaucrats. Would it have been too much to expect just one of these intelligence officials to take the time to contact some experts on Middle Eastern affairs, such as Princeton University's Bernard Lewis, and ask, "Is it a good idea for us to set up permanent military facilities in Saudi Arabia?" The official, no doubt, would have been told: "That's one of the stupidest ideas I've ever heard. If you aren't a Muslim, you can't even take up residence in Saudi Arabia, even if you are a movie star, a retired diplomat, a close friend of King Fahd, or a reclusive billionaire. Only Muslims, by law, can live in the holy land of the Prophet. If you happen to die in Saudi Arabia, the

Arabs won't allow your body to be buried within their sacred soil because you are a *kafir.*[19] Your carcass will be shipped back to the States.[20] But you are talking about deploying thousands of troops to permanent military installations. Anyone who knows anything about Islam and Saudi Arabia will tell you that such measures will result in serious trouble—and by trouble, I mean, a jihad that could go on for centuries."

Of course, the call was never made—expert advice was neither sought nor secured. This is most perplexing since the U.S. public school system had downplayed the importance of history so that greater emphasis would be placed on cultural awareness and comparative religions. Hadn't any official within the Bush administration been obliged to sit through such anthropology or world religion courses? Talk about lack of intelligence within the intelligence community! And George H. W. Bush, prior to occupying the Oval Office, had served a stint as director of the CIA. Small wonder he is seated on a high stool with a pointed cap in the pages of this book.

A WAR WITHOUT REASON

Throughout the fall of 1990, as Operation Desert Shield continued, President Bush and his administration were compelled to conjure up a way of justifying the war to the American people. The Kuwaitis aided in their effort by channeling $11.9 million into an organization called Citizens for a Free Kuwait and hiring Hill and Knowlton, one of the world's largest public relations firms, to portray Hussein as the ultimate boogeyman.[21] On September 12, Hill and Knowlton launched a Kuwait Information Day on twenty college campuses across the country. On Sunday, September 23, churches throughout America held a national day of prayer for the tiny embattled emirate. The next day, the public relations firm celebrated Free Kuwait Day by distributing tens of thousands of bumper stickers and T-shirts along with media kits on Kuwaiti history.[22] Lew Allison, a former news producer for CBS and NBC, prepared two dozen news spots about Kuwait for the national evening news.

These efforts served Bush's purpose. Members of his cabinet warned him that the American people would not support a war that was simply about oil. Secretary of State James Baker had said, "If you're [trying] to get me to say that low gasoline prices are worth American lives, it's not something I'm going to say."[23]

Thanks to Hill and Knowlton, the war was presented as a conflict over tyranny. "The fight isn't about oil," Bush asserted in words that would become his mantra. "The fight is against naked aggression that will not stand."[24]

Thus the American people became persuaded, no, really intent on liberating Kuwait without realizing that Kuwait was not a democratic country that merited liberation. Only sixty-five thousand people out of a population of two million were granted the right to vote—and these citizens were males who could establish their Kuwaiti ancestry back to 1920. Women had no rights whatsoever—not even the right to drive. Executive power rested solely with the emir. Senator Daniel Patrick Moynihan described Kuwait as "a poisonous enemy of the U.S." that was famous for its "singularly nasty" hatred of Jews.[25]

On October 10, Hill and Knowlton gained the right to present evidence against Hussein's regime before the congressional Human Rights Caucus. The chief witness for the public relations firm was a fifteen-year-old Kuwaiti girl who was said to have firsthand knowledge of Iraqi atrocities. Her first name was given as Nayirah. Her last name was withheld allegedly because of fears for the safety of her family members who remained in Kuwait.[26]

Nayirah told an astounding story. She testified that she had served as a volunteer at the al-Addan hospital, where she saw Iraqi soldiers barge into the maternity section, enter a room where fifteen premature infants had been placed in incubators, remove them from the incubators, and leave them on the cold floor to die.[27]

This was precisely the type of visceral story that President Bush was seeking. Over the next five weeks, he repeated the story five times to the national media, asserting that Hussein's troops had performed "outrageous acts of barbarism. . . . I don't think that Adolf Hitler ever participated in anything of that nature."[28]

There was only one problem. Nayirah's story, like similar stories of Iraqi atrocities that were circulated by Hill and Knowlton, wasn't true. Middle East Watch, a New York–based human rights organization, sent investigator Aziz Abu-Hamad to hospitals in Kuwait to verify the story. On January 6, 1991, Abu-Hamad reported that he was unable to find

any doctor or any family who would support the account of babies—
not even one baby—being tossed out of incubators by Iraqi soldiers.[29]

BLOOD FOR OIL

Why was Bush so intent upon sending troops to the Persian Gulf? Part
of the answer might lie in the fact that Bush was a Texas oilman who,
early in his career, had made millions with the drilling of the first off-
shore oil well for Kuwait. Bush left oil for politics in 1966. He wound
up as director of the CIA. In this position, Bush established a close relationship with Saudi and Kuwaiti businessmen, including the head of
Saudi Arabia's most corrupt bank, who began pouring millions into
Bush's home state of Texas. They bought real estate and purchased
planes and airports. They bought a bank in Houston with former Texas
governor John Connolly and developed a skyscraper that came to house
the bank of Secretary of State James Baker's grandfather. In the 1980s,
when oil prices were dropping, a Saudi investor with close ties to the
royal family bailed out a tiny Texas oil company, Harken Energy. One of
the directors of Harken was George W. Bush.[30] The real payoff for
George H. W. Bush came later, when he was associated with the Carlyle
Group and secured incredibly lucrative contracts from the rulers of
Kuwait and Saudi Arabia.

Hill and Knowlton did a great job in selling the war. On January 17,
1991, when Desert Shield became Desert Storm, and nine warships
began firing Tomahawk cruise missiles at early warning radar stations
throughout Iraq, 76 percent of the American people agreed with the
president's decision to go to war; only 22 percent expressed disap-
proval.[31] Bush's approval rating soared to 90 percent.[32] As P. T. Barnum
said more than a century ago, nobody ever went broke by underestimat-
ing the intelligence of the American people.

A ONE-SIDED WAR

The war, as it turned out, wasn't really much of a war. Hussein, quite
naturally, had refused to move out of Kuwait by the appointed time, and
Operation Desert Shield transformed into Operation Desert Storm, an
all-out assault on the Iraqi forces, on January 15, 1991. The aim of

Desert Shield was to show the world through live, twenty-four-hour television coverage on CNN the latest military technology (stealth bombers, cruise missiles, "smart" bombs, and laser guidance systems) that pinpointed targets and minimized civilian casualties.[33] Within a matter of days, the Iraqi air force was destroyed, along with airfields, missile sites, communication centers, more than twenty-six biological- and chemical-weapons plants, and three nuclear-weapons facilities.[34]

By the time the ground offensive got under way on February 24, there wasn't much to fight. Forty out of the forty-two Iraqi divisions had been wiped out; more than 50,000 Iraqi soldiers had been killed; another 175,000 were reported missing or captured. In stark contrast, the coalition casualties were incredibly light: 146 dead (35 by friendly fire), 207 wounded, and 106 missing or captured.[35]

Saddam Hussein, however, managed to exact revenge by wrecking the palaces of the oil-rich Kuwaiti sheikhs and the malls of Kuwait City and by loading 3,216 bars of gold, 63 tons of gold coins, and anything else of economic value into 10,000 luxury vehicles stolen from car dealerships and private residences. Soldiers of the retreating army drove this caravan to Baghdad, where they were sold at public auction for $125 million.

Moreover, as a final gesture of contempt, Hussein released millions of tons of crude oil into the Gulf, which drifted south and polluted a huge area of the sea, the seabed, and the coast. He also set ablaze more than five hundred oil wells in Kuwait, which took two years to extinguish. In this way, Hussein, although he lost the war, managed to gain a prominent place in infamy by creating the largest act of pollution in history.[36]

NEW RESOLUTIONS

On April 3, 1991, the U.N. Security Council adopted Resolution 687, which set forth the terms for the cease-fire. Iraq must (1) reduce its military capabilities, (2) destroy all weapons of mass destruction, (3) submit to weapons inspections by a Special Commission on Disarmament, (4) return all stolen property, and (5) contribute to a fund for war-damage claims. Failure to comply would mean that the economic sanctions would remain in place.[37] These sanctions were imposed on all exports and all imports of non-humanitarian goods. Hussein, true to form, failed to comply, and the sanctions remained in effect until 2003.[38]

The effects of the economic measures were devastating. During the war, the coalition's smart bombs had destroyed the entire civilian infrastructure of the country. Water-purification plants, sewage-treatment facilities, electrical power stations, and irrigation systems were left in ruins. Martti Ahtisaari, the first U.N. official to visit postwar Iraq, presented the following report to the General Assembly:

> It should be said at once that nothing we had seen or read had quite prepared us for this particular form of devastation which has now befallen the country. Most means of modern life have been destroyed. The authorities are as yet scarcely able to measure the dimensions of the calamity, much less respond to its consequences. The recent conflict has wrought near apocalyptic results; Iraq has been relegated to a pre-industrial age. All electrically operated installations have ceased to function. Food cannot be preserved; water cannot be purified; sewage cannot be pumped away. Nine thousand homes are destroyed or damaged beyond repair. The flow of food through the private sector has been reduced to a trickle; many food prices are already beyond the purchasing power of most Iraqi families. The mission recommends that sanctions in respect of food supplies should be immediately removed. Drastic international measures are most urgent. The Iraqi people face further catastrophe, epidemic and famine, if massive life supporting needs are not met. The long summer is only weeks away. Time is short.[39]

Because of the shortage of medical supplies and food, malnutrition and disease, especially among children, increased at an alarming rate. Reports from U.N. agencies showed a fivefold increase in child mortality from 1991 to 1996. By 1998 nearly one million Iraqis, mostly young child and the elderly, had died as a result of the sanctions. Two hundred children under five were dying every day. Nevertheless, U.N. sanctions barred the following items:

agricultural pesticides	ambulances
all electrical equipment	baby food
all building materials	badminton rackets

bandages
blankets
boots
cannulas for intravenous drips
catheters for babies
children's bicycles
children's clothes
chlorine and other water
    purification chemicals
cleaning agents
cobalt sources for x-ray machines
deodorants
dialysis equipment
disposable surgical gloves
drugs for angina
ECG monitors
erasers
glue for textbooks
incubators
leather material for shoes
lipsticks
medical gauze
medical journals
medical swabs
medical syringes
medication for epilepsy
nail polish
nasogastric tubes
notebooks
nylon cloth for filtering flour
oxygen tents

paper
pencil sharpeners
pencils
Ping-Pong balls
polyester and acrylic yarn
rice
rubber tubes
schoolbooks
school handicraft equipment
shampoo
shirts
shoelaces
shroud material
soap
sanitary towels
specific adult clothes
specific granite shipments
specific umbilical catheters
steel plate stethoscopes
suction catheters for blockages
surgical instruments
textile plant equipment
thread for children's clothes
tissues
toilet paper
toothbrushes
toothpaste
various other foodstuffs
wool felt for thermal insulation
x-ray equipment
x-ray film

Near-eradicated diseases such as polio, cholera, and typhoid reappeared in postwar Iraq. Cancer rates soared due to a proliferation of depleted uranium weapons used in the smart bombings. The importing of drugs to treat malignancies was outlawed due to a clause in the resolution that prohibited anything from entering Iraq that might serve a "dual use," that is, anything that might fight disease and serve as a component in a chemical or biological bomb.[40]

In 1993 physicians discovered an entirely new disease. Mothers too malnourished to breastfeed—in a country where obesity was once a problem—and unable to afford powdered milk, began feeding their babies sugared water or tea. Almost all the babies died. The doctors called them "sugar babies."[41]

NOT BAGGING THE BOOGEYMAN

Such suffering was unleashed upon the Iraqis because of President Bush's refusal to allow the U.S.-led coalition troops to remove Hussein from office when this task could have been accomplished with little risk and negligible expense. Didn't Bush realize that Hussein would return to his genocidal tactics? The president, after all, had said that Hussein represented "Hitler revisited." And yet he refused to allow American troops to march into Baghdad to bag the boogeyman. He permitted this madman to remain in control of a war-ravaged country with a population of 21.5 million hapless citizens.

This decision, which appears to defy all logic, was later explained by the president in his book *A World Transformed*:

> Trying to eliminate Hussein would have incurred human and political costs. Apprehending him was probably impossible. We would have been forced to occupy Baghdad and, in effect, rule Iraq. There was no viable "exit strategy" we could see, violating another of our principles. Furthermore, we had been self-consciously trying to set a pattern for handling aggression in the post-Cold War. Going in and occupying Iraq, thus unilaterally exceeding the United Nations' mandate, would have destroyed the precedent of international response to aggression that we hoped to establish. Had we gone the invasion route, the United States could conceivably still be an occupying power in a bitterly hostile land.[42]

Although George H. W. Bush clearly merits his place on the high stool as a dunce, his decision to leave Hussein in power appears to make sense. He realized that any measure to remove the tyrant from power would have resulted in the occupation of Iraq without an exit strategy.

This untenable situation, he believed, would result in untold billions in expense and the loss of thousands of American lives. Too bad George W. Bush never read his father's book. It would have saved the United States from the seemingly endless nightmare that is presently unraveling in Iraq.

The elder Bush, unfortunately, did not leave the White House without making another critical error. This one served to bring the United States to the brink of nuclear Armageddon.

BLUNDER 6

Ignoring the Booming Nuclear Black Market

It is not difficult [to acquire nuclear weapons], not if you have contacts in Russia with other militant groups. They are available for $10 million and $20 million.

Osama bin Laden, November 2001

If you have $30 million, go to the black market in central Asia, contact any disgruntled Soviet scientist, and a lot of smart briefcase bombs are available. They have contacted us, we sent our people to Moscow, to Tashkent, to other central Asian states, and they have negotiated, and we purchased some nuclear suitcase bombs.

Ayman al-Zawahiri, November 2002

THE BEGINNING OF THE end of Planet Earth occurred on September 27, 1991, when President George H. W. Bush proclaimed that the United States would withdraw its nuclear weapons from sites throughout the world if the Soviet Union would follow suit. Soviet president Mikhail Gorbachev readily agreed. A deadline was set. The task was to be completed by the end of May 1992.

The process was greatly facilitated by the Nunn-Lugar Nuclear Threat Reduction Act, which provided the Russians with millions in funding to withdraw their nukes from various sites throughout Eastern Europe and to transport the nukes to arsenals within the fourteen newly created Russian republics.[1]

Withdrawing the tactical nukes in order to place them in secured places seemed to be a great idea—a grand display of *perestroika* ("restructuring")—that no one except a raving right-winger could oppose. Who in his or her right mind could argue that the withdrawals would not serve to make the world a safer place? Who but a miserable curmudgeon could refuse to celebrate this act of mutual trust between two nations that had been locked for decades in a cold war?

But truth be told, it was a horrendous mistake. The Russians began to withdraw their twenty-two thousand nukes when everything within the former Soviet Union was falling apart at the seams. With the closing of the communal plants and factories, unemployment soared to more than 30 percent. Inflation rocketed to 2,000 percent, fueling the rise of more than eight hundred criminal gangs.[2] An average of eighty-four murders took place daily; contract killers carried many out. Such a hit could be arranged with members of the eight *Mafyias* within Moscow for less than two hundred dollars.[3] It was a great time and place to get rid of a nagging mate or a burdensome business partner.

Millions of Russians waited in line for hours to redeem government-issued coupons. There was one line for red beets and cabbage, another for eggs and bread, and yet another for vodka and cigarettes. Butcher shops sold blue chickens that had died of malnutrition and pies made from rancid beef, horsemeat, and roadkill. Smart shoppers soon learned not to buy the pies that were surrounded by dead flies. Almost overnight, the second most powerful nation on earth had been transformed into a third-world country.

Under the new capitalism, male life expectancy fell to fifty-eight years—fifteen to seventeen fewer years than men in Western Europe and the United States.[4] By 1996 the suicide rate had doubled. Along with poverty, inflation, unemployment, starvation, and depression, Russians experienced a sharp drop in the birth rate. From 1991 to 2004 the population declined at the precipitous rate of 1.2 million a year. Population experts believed that the Russian population would fall from 147 million to 114 million by 2050.[5] Mother Russia, in the wake of the fall of communism, was dying.

Yet in 1991 nowhere was the misery and deprivation more apparent than within the military, which by 1996 had shrunk to a feeble force of 1.7 million soldiers. Because of chronic food shortages, many soldiers were forced to resort to begging. From 1991 to 1996 more than ten Russian soldiers died daily from noncombative causes, including suicide and malnutrition. An estimated 110,000 lacked proper housing and were sheltered in hovels. No one in the military, not even a high-ranking general or admiral, was receiving a regular paycheck.[6] Russian army and navy officers began to sell everything within their command. In 1993 there were 6,430 reports of stolen weapons from army arsenals, ranging from assault rifles to tanks.[7]

The most notorious example of such sales concerned Adm. Igor Khmelnov, the commander of the Russian Pacific Fleet. In 1997 reports surfaced that ships were being sold in a scam by which the vessels were decommissioned, declared scrap, and sold to foreign buyers at rock-bottom prices. Russian officials denied these reports for years—until they discovered that a 900-foot-long, 47,000-ton aircraft carrier was no longer in service. After a prolonged investigation, Admiral Khmelnov was charged and convicted of selling sixty-four decommissioned ships, including two aircraft carriers, to South Korea and India and bagging the proceeds for himself. The asking price for the aircraft carriers was a measly $5 million.[8]

THE BOOMING NUCLEAR BLACK MARKET

Only a bonehead could believe that it would be possible to move the twenty-two thousand nuclear weapons from the strategic sites to arsenals throughout Russia without a single loss. When President Bush announced his plans for the nuclear withdrawal, Secretary of Defense Dick Cheney told the press that the recovery and safe transport of 99 percent of the nukes by the Russians would constitute an "excellent" performance. Such a performance, everyone in Washington should have realized, would mean that 220 would be lost or stolen. Clearly, this should have been unacceptable.

What bureaucrat in his or her right mind could expect such an "excellent" performance from the poorly housed, malnourished, unpaid, and economically desperate Russian troops of 1991? The temptation would be too great for an ascetic saint to resist, especially when a kilo of chrominium-50 was selling for $25,000, cesium-137 for $1 million, and lithium for $10 million.[9] And the list of prospective buyers included

Egypt, Iran, Libya, North Korea, Pakistan, Saudi Arabia, and a well-financed group of Muslim terrorists called al Qaeda.

In the first three years after the collapse of the Soviet Union, the black market in nuclear weapons boomed throughout the world. By 1995 German officials were able to document more than seven hundred attempted sales of nuclear weapons and materials. An abridged chronology, as provided by CIA director John Deutch to the U.S. Senate on March 20, 1997, included:

1996

March 17: Tanzanian police arrested one individual and seized a container of radioactive cesium.

March 9: Romanian police arrested two individuals for attempting to sell eighty-two kilograms of radioactive material, including low enriched uranium. (One kilogram equals 2.2 pounds. One thousand grams equals one kilogram, and one gram is equal to about 0.04 ounce, or the weight of a small paperclip.)

March 4: Lithuanian officials determined that one hundred kilograms of radioactive material seized from an armed gang was uranium-238.

February 23: The Belarus Committee for State Security (KGB) seized five kilograms of cesium-133 in glass containers.

February 12: Lithuanian authorities arrested seven people and seized nearly one hundred kilograms of uranium.

February 1: Swiss officials arrested a Swiss citizen of Turkish descent for attempting to sell a sample of enriched uranium. Swiss authorities claimed the sample was part of a larger cache still in Turkey.

January 25: German authorities charged a merchant and his lawyer with crimes stemming from their attempt to sell radioactive cesium that was transported to Germany from Zaire onboard a commercial airliner.

January 21: A German parliamentary commission uncovered German government documents indicating that three smugglers offered to supply eleven kilograms of weapons-grade plutonium of Russian-origin, which they claimed was enough to build three nuclear weapons.

1995

December 28: The Russian federal security service (FSB) arrested nine members of a criminal organization in Novosibirsk and seized a quantity of "enriched" uranium-235 that had been transported to the city by middlemen from Kazakhstan.

December 2: Italian prosecutors arrested Roger D'Onofrio with reported links to the CIA and the Mafia as part of an investigation into smuggled radioactive materials, money laundering, and arms trafficking. The seventy-two-year-old D'Onofrio reportedly has dual Italian and U.S. citizenship and retired from the CIA only two years ago.

November 30: A former Greenpeace president revealed that the organization had been offered a nuclear warhead by a disgruntled former Soviet officer who wanted to highlight lax Russian security.

November 29: Russian security officials recovered four containers of radioactive cesium that had been stolen from an industrial plant in the Urals and arrested the thieves. The containers were similar to those allegedly planted by Chechen rebels in a Moscow park.

November 23: Acting on a tip from Chechen separatist leader Shamil Basayev, Russian television reporters discovered a thirty-two-kilogram container—reportedly holding cesium-137—in a Moscow park.

November 23: A German court sentenced businessman Adolph Jaekle to five and a half years in prison for smuggling weapons-grade plutonium into the country. Investigators made the first in a series of contraband plutonium seizures in Germany when they raided Jaekle's home in the southern town of Tengen in May 1994 and found a lead cylinder containing 6.15 grams of plutonium-239.

November 11: Russian Federal Security Service officials arrested two Lithuanian citizens in Smolensk for smuggling ten kilograms of uranium-238 into Russia. Three Russians also were arrested for attempting to sell the uranium. Both the Lithuanians and the Russians claimed that poverty had induced them to attempt to traffic in smuggled nuclear materials.

November 7: During a car search at the Polish-Czech border, Polish border guards discovered eleven cigarette-pack-size containers filled with strontium-90.

November 7: Iranian press reports indicate law-enforcement authorities arrested five Iranians and seized nine packets of enriched uranium in Tehran and two other cities.

October 25: The cleaning staff at Moscow's Sheremetyevo 2 Airport found a small lead container packed with radioactive substances in the men's restroom. Authorities believed the smuggler lost his nerve and abandoned the material.

October 19: According to *Der Stern*, nuclear-weapons smugglers involved in smuggling Russian-origin plutonium into Germany in August 1994 stored eight to ten kilograms of weapons-grade plutonium in Berlin. The article also implicated highly placed Russians in the smuggling activity.

October 14: Russian Mafia figures were behind the 1993 theft of radioactive beryllium from a Russian nuclear laboratory and a failed attempt to sell the material in the West.

September 1: Bulgarian police broke an international nuclear smuggling ring composed of Russians and Ukrainians. The arrests were the culmination of a yearlong undercover operation.

June 15: Press reports indicated that Romanian authorities had seized 24 kilograms of uranium powder and tablets. In 1994 they arrested twenty-four people for involvement in nuclear smuggling and seized

10.35 kilograms of uranium powder and tablets. From 1989 to 1993 the Romanians reportedly broke up five gangs, arrested fifty people, and seized 230 kilograms of nuclear material.

April 13: Slovak police culminated a long investigation with the discovery of 18.39 kilograms of nuclear material, 17.5 kg of which apparently was U-238, in a car stopped near Poprad in eastern Slovakia.

April 5: Four brass containers weighing two kilos each of radioactive americium-241 and cesium-137 were stolen from a storeroom of isotopes in Wroclaw, Poland.

April 4: Six kilograms of U-235, U-238, radium and palladium were found in a Kiev apartment. Occupants were former army officers, a lieutenant colonel and a warrant officer. The nuclear material reportedly came from Russia.

March 14: Polish police in Bielska-Biala province arrested a man for possession of uranium.

March 8: Italian police arrested Nicola Todesco for murder in a plutonium smuggling case gone awry. The victim did not have the money to pay for a quantity of enriched plutonium smuggled out of Bulgaria.

January 25: Lithuanian border police, using U.S.-supplied radiation detectors, seized two tons of radioactive wolfram hidden in a secret compartment in a truck trailer. Wolfram is tungsten, which has a short half-life. This shipment was probably "infected" by a radioactive contaminant.

1994

December 14: Czech police seized 2.72 kilograms of material—later identified as 87.7 percent enriched U-235—in Prague. This was the largest recorded seizure of such material. Police arrested a Czech nuclear physicist and two citizens of the former Soviet Union. The material was found in the backseat of a car parked in an alley.

December 10: Hungarian border guards seized 1.7 kilograms of uranium and arrested four Slovakians. The material (reactor-fuel-grade uranium) was concealed in a fruit jar.

December 6: *Pravda,* Russia's leading daily newspaper, reported that three staffers of the Institute of Nuclear Physics were convicted of stealing 4.5 kilograms of enriched uranium.

November 10: Hungarian police discovered twenty-six kilograms of radioactive material in the trunk of a car. Three suspects were subsequently arrested.

November: German police seized one milligram of cesium-137 in early November and arrested two suspects.

October 19: Turkish police arrested an Azeri national trying to sell 750 grams of uranium.

October 17: Russian authorities seized twenty-seven kilograms of U-238, an unknown quantity of U-235 and detained twelve members of a criminal gang.

October: Four Indian villagers were arrested attempting to sell 2.5 kilograms of yellowcake uranium (uranium extracted from ore).

October 13: Bulgarian officials seized four lead capsules of radioactive material. The capsules were found on a bus en route to Turkey, and police detained the two bus drivers.

October 10: Romanian authorities arrested seven people and seized seven kilograms of uranium and an unidentified quantity of strontium or cesium.

October 1: Romanian police arrested four people trying to sell more than four kilograms of U-235 and U-238.

October: Russian authorities arrested three men trying to sell sixty-seven kilograms of U-238 in the city of Pskov.

September 28: A container with radioactive substances was found on a street in Tallinn.

September 28: Romanian authorities arrested several individuals attempting to sell 4.55 kilograms of uranium tetrachloride (61.9 percent uranium) for twenty-five thousand dollars per kilogram.

September 28: Slovak officials arrested four Slovaks trying to smuggle almost one kilogram of U-235 into Hungary.

September 11: German police arrested a Zairian national attempting to smuggle 850 grams of uraninite into Germany.

September 7: Russian police arrested three people in Glazov trying to sell one hundred kilograms of uranium-238.

September 5: Bulgarian authorities arrested six Bulgarians in connection with and seized nineteen containers of radioactive material.

September: A Pole was sentenced to three years in prison for trying to sell one kilogram of uranium-235/238 in Germany.

August 30: Thieves broke into a chemical plant in Tambov and stole 4.5 grams of cesium-137.

August 29: Hungarian police arrested two men and seized 4.4 kilograms of material believed to be fuel rods from a reactor in Russia.

August 20: Russian authorities arrested two men attempting to steal 9.5 kilograms of uranium-238 from the Arzamas-16 nuclear-weapons research facility.

August 18: Estonian police arrested a man and seized three kilograms of U-238 he had buried under his garage.

August 18: About one hundred uranium-contaminated drums were stolen from South Africa's Atomic Energy Corporation plant in Pelindaba, Transvaal.

August 12: St. Petersburg police arrested three men trying to sell sixty kilograms of unidentified nuclear material.

August 12: German police in Bremen arrested a German for attempting to sell two grams of plutonium.

August 10: More than 500 grams of nuclear material were seized at the Munich airport. Two men were arrested for possession of 363 grams (12.8 ounces) of weapons-grade plutonium-239.

August: Three kilograms of enriched uranium were seized in August in southwestern Romania.

July 19: Turkish national police arrested seven Turks and seized twelve kilograms of weapons-grade uranium.

July: Russian authorities in Shezninks discovered 5.5 kilograms of uranium-238 that had been stolen from the Chelyabinsk-65 nuclear facility.

July: Police in Timisoara, Romania, arrested five Romanians trying to sell 2.6 kilograms of Russian uranium.

June 13: Police seized of .8 grams of uranium-235 (enriched to 88 percent) in Landshut, Germany.

June: Russian security officials announced the arrest of three Russians in St. Petersburg who tried to sell 3.5 kilograms of HEU (bomb-grade uranium; HEU is an acronym for highly enriched uranium).

June: Russian authorities arrested three officers from the Northern Fleet. The officers were accused of stealing 4.5 kilograms of uranium-238 from their base in November 1993.

June: Police in Pitesti, Romania, arrested three Romanians for trying to sell three kilograms of uranium tablets.

May: German police discovered a small but worrisome quantity of super-grade plutonium in the garage of Adolph Jaekle in Tengen, Germany. Extremely expensive to produce, this rare item came from Arzamas-16, one of Russia's two premiere nuclear weapons laboratories.

1993

November: Two employees of the Zlatoust-36 instrument building plant, a weapons-assembly facility in Chelyabinsk, were arrested for stealing two nuclear warheads, which they had hidden in a residential garage.

November: In a case stemming from an incident in November 1993 in which a Russian naval officer stole four kilograms of 20 percent enriched uranium-235 nuclear fuel rods from the Sevmorput shipyard near Murmansk, a Russian court found the officer guilty but gave him a suspended sentence because he admitted the act. Two accomplices were sentenced to three years at a labor camp. The leading Russian prosecutor in the case noted that "potatoes were guarded better" than the nuclear material at the shipyard. (Note: Uranium enriched with 20 percent or higher uranium-235 is considered weapons-usable material.)

The police thwarted the above-listed sales. That's some comfort. What is not comforting is the fact that such seizures and arrests represent only a fraction of the actual transactions. Nor did the nuclear trafficking come to an end in 1996. Thanks largely to Pakistan's Abdul Qadeer Khan, the sales continued on a much grander scale throughout the next decade.

THE RISE OF THE CHECHENS

In the 1990s the Chechen *Mafyia* became the dominant force in the trafficking of nuclear weapons and materials. Throughout Russian history the Chechens have proved themselves to be not only incredibly dangerous but also totally uncontrollable. Religiously and ethnically, they are Muslim but not Arab. They were descended from the Tartars, the western tide of the Golden Horde of Mongolian warrior Genghis Khan, that had settled in the vastness of the Caucasus Mountains. There they refused to assimilate into Russian culture by speaking their own unique language (*Nakh*) and clinging to the traditions of their various *teips,* or clans. During World War II, Joseph Stalin, upon discovering several Chechen leaders had collaborated with the Germans, stuffed more than five hundred thousand of them into boxcars and shipped them off to Siberia.

After being returned to Chechnya and repatriated by Nikita Khrushchev in the 1950s, Chechen gangs formed the largest criminal organization in the Soviet Union by engaging in kidnapping, extortion, grand-scale theft, drugs, prostitution, contract killing, arms running, and bank fraud. By 1995 more than twelve billion dollars had poured into Chechen accounts in Switzerland and Cyprus.[10]

With the black market in nukes booming, the Chechens became the leading buyers. In March 1993, they secured an unknown quantity of highly enriched uranium from Kazakhstan. More than six kilograms were transported from Groznyy, the mountain capital of Chechnya, to Istanbul, Turkey. Six months later Interpol officials arrested four Turkish businessmen and four Iranian agents and confiscated two and a half kilos of the uranium. The remaining kilos slipped through the proverbial cracks.[11]

In September 1993, when Chechnya launched its war of independence from Russia, Chechen rebels stunned the world by displaying SS-20 missiles during a military parade in Groznyy. The missiles had been stolen from a Soviet arsenal. They possessed a range of ninety-five hundred kilometers (almost six thousand miles) with the capability of launching a nuclear warhead.[12]

In Moscow, the Chechen *Mafyia* began using radioactive isotopes, which could be purchased at rock-bottom prices, to commit hits. The first victim was Vladimir Kaplun, the owner of a meatpacking plant. The Chechens simply planted gamma ray–emitting pellets in Kaplun's office. The businessman died of radiation poisoning within a matter of weeks. At least half a dozen similar cases were reported over the next three years.[13]

In November 1994, Dzokhar Dudayev, the leader of the Chechen rebels, petitioned the United Nations to dispatch peacekeeping forces to protect the weapons of mass destruction within the Chechen arsenal from the Russian troops that had been dispatched to quash the rebellion. U.N. officials, along with the international press, scoffed at the notion that Muslim dissidents from the backwater province of Chechnya could possess, let alone maintain, nuclear weapons. This forced Dudayev to provide vivid proof that the Chechens possessed nuclear capability. On November 23, 1995, Chechen commander Shamil Basayev directed a television crew to a plastic bag that had been planted in Izmailovsky Park near Moscow. The bag contained thirty-two kilograms of cesium-137.[14] CIA director John Deutch, while appearing before the Senate, downplayed the incident, maintaining that the cesium, if wrapped around a conventional explosive and detonated, would have posed only a "minimal health hazard."

Deutch's statement shows how little the CIA knows about radiological material. In the best of circumstances, only the explosion would have killed a few hundred. But the blast would have distributed the cesium participles over several square miles of the metropolitan area around Moscow. Within minutes, the microscopic particles would adhere to everything: skin, clothing, cars, buses, buildings, sidewalks, and the soles of shoes.[15]

A single grain of cesium, if inhaled or ingested, is a bone sucker. It heads straight to the marrow to halt the production of platelets and to cause of mutation of cells. Within days of the blast, Russians exposed to these participles would begin displaying the first symptoms of radiation poisoning: bleeding from the nose and mouth, diarrhea, hair loss, purple fingernails, high fever, and delirium. Several hundred would die within a matter of days or weeks. Their bodies would have to be buried in lead-lined caskets to prevent further contamination.[16] Hundreds of others within a matter of years would develop various forms of malignancy: thyroid cancer, pancreatic cancer, liver cancer, breast cancer, cancer of the reproductive organs, and brain tumors.

The cesium would have other results, though. Decontamination efforts would require that the radioactive particles be removed. But removing cesium participles is no easy task. They cannot be blown or washed away. The cleanup effort would require the dumping of mounds of sand over the exposed soil, the removal of trees and shrubbery, the killing of household pets, and the razing of structures throughout the city.[17] Such would be the effects that CIA Director Deutch, in the manner of Dr. Pangloss, dismissed as "minimal."

The plastic bag in Izmailovsky Park should have caused immediate attention and alarm. The U.N. (if it really did not represent *United Nothing*) should have done *something*. At the very least, the International Atomic Energy Agency should have contacted Dudayev to say that he had the U.N.'s attention and that the organization would very much like to know about other weapons of mass destruction in his possession.

DUDAYEV'S MODEST PROPOSAL

Shortly after this incident, Dudayev notified the U.S. State Department that he possessed tactical nuclear suitcase bombs that he was willing to sell to rogue states (such as Iran) or terrorist agencies (such as al Qaeda) unless the United States recognized Chechnya's independence from Russia. Officials from the National Intelligence Council, an umbrella organization for the U.S. analytical community, supported Dudayev's claim. The officials informed a congressional committee that weapons-grade and weapons-usable nuclear materials—including SADMs (small atomic demolition munitions)—had been stolen from Soviet stockpiles. "Of these thefts," the officials warned, "we assess that undetected smuggling has occurred, although we do not know the extent or the magnitude."[18] Despite this testimony, no high-ranking Washington official sought further verification by arranging a visit with Dudayev and agreeing to negotiate the terms of the sale.

Yet the report of nuclear suitcase bombs in the hands of the Chechens had received further verification from Special Forces Sgt. Jonathon "Jack" Keith Idema, who had been sent by the Pentagon to work with the Lithuanian KGB in the wake of the breakup of the Soviet Union. In 1992 Idema reported that weapons-grade nuclear material had not simply leaked into the black market, it was pouring into the black market, and several suitcase nukes being acquired by the Chechens. His reports were dismissed because he refused to provide the names of his informants to the FBI and CIA. Idema's reluctance was based on his awareness that such information would jeopardize the lives of his Lithuanian friends and confidants.[19]

What's more, the Center for Nonproliferation Studies at the Monterey Institute of International Studies received confirmation from a "senior adviser to Boris Yeltsin" that an unspecified number of suitcase nuclear devices had been manufactured for the KGB but had not been listed on the Soviet nuclear inventory.[20]

BIN LADEN'S BIG PURCHASE

Not being able to deal with the United Nations or the United States, Dudayev sold the suitcases to the next party in line with the deep pockets to pay for them: Osama bin Laden. The al Qaeda head gladly paid thirty million dollars in cash and two tons of choice number-four heroin (a street value of seven hundred million dollars) for twenty nuclear suitcase bombs. As soon as the deal was consummated, bin Laden issued his Declaration of War Against the Americans Occupying the Land of the Two Holy Places (August 23, 1996).

Any doubts that al Qaeda was involved in business transactions with the Chechens should have been put to rest when Russian security police arrested Ayman al-Zawahiri at the Chechen border in December 1996. Zawahiri, with his beard shaved and his hair closely cropped, was traveling under the alias of "Mr. Amin." Two al Qaeda operatives and a Chechen guide accompanied him. At his trial in April 1997, Zawahiri allegedly "lied fluently and prayed frequently." When asked why he was trying to enter Chechnya, Zawahiri said that he "wanted to know the price of leather, medicine, and other goods." Lacking sufficient evidence of any wrongdoing, the judge ordered his release.[21]

Even when news of the sale received headlines in such reputable news outlets as the *Times* (London), the BBC, the *Jerusalem Report, Al-Watan Al-Arabi,* and *Al-Majallah* (the British Saudi weekly), Washington officials opted to treat the account as a matter of little or no consequence.[22] They displayed this same attitude when Hamid Mir, a celebrated Pakistani journalist, testified that he had visited laboratories in Afghanistan where al Qaeda scientists and Russian technicians worked to maintain and upgrade the suitcase nukes.[23]

The lack of interest was even more astonishing in light of the fact that former Russian security council secretary Alexander Lebed, during a closed-door session with a U.S. congressional delegation in 1997, testified that more than eighty-four SADMs had disappeared from Russian arsenals and could be in the hands of Muslim extremists.[24] Lebed was not alone in providing such testimony. His statements were supported by Vladimir Denisov, a former head of the Russian Security Council, who told a U.S. congressional committee that tactical nukes designed to fit within a suitcase had been manufactured by the Soviet Union and that he had received reports that several suitcase nukes were missing and might have been acquired by the Chechen *Mafyia*.[25] Additional corroboration came from Aleksey Yabolov, environmental adviser to Russian president Boris Yeltsin, who maintained that more than seven hundred nuclear suitcase bombs had been produced for the KGB and that the whereabouts of these weapons was anybody's guess.[26]

Congressional officials and members of the national press did not seek further substantiation of these accounts—not even when U.N. weapons inspector Hans Blix expressed his opinion that the accounts of the transaction between the Chechens and al Qaeda were accurate.[27] Instead, they rather expressed doubts that such tactical weapons were ever produced despite the fact that thirty-three hundred such small, portable nukes remained in the U.S. arsenal. Some were designed to fit into ordinary luggage, others to be carried in backpacks, and still others to be fired from recoilless rifles.[28]

Moreover, intelligence officials were aware that bin Laden had begun his search for nuclear weapons and weapons in 1993, during his sojourn in Sudan. Sudan, in fact, had become a pivotal transshipping point for black-market nukes. These goods flowed from Russia to Germany to Sudan to such places as Iran, Libya, and Pakistan.[29] The key al Qaeda agent in charge of the procurement of nuclear weapons was Mamdouh Mahmud Salim, an electrical engineer from Iraq. Salim, who combed the world for loose nukes, was eventually arrested in Germany in 1998 while attempting to buy several kilos of enriched uranium for bin Laden.[30] He was extradited for trial in the United States and remains a "ghost prisoner."

How much nuclear material Salim and other al Qaeda agents were able to procure remains unknown. But their efforts resulted in considerable success since, as the CIA later revealed, bin Laden established a laboratory in Khartoum in 1993 and hired a physicist from the Middle East to work on his project to create nuclear weapons capable of killing millions of Americans.[31] Bin Laden, to his credit, made no secret of his intent. On several occasions, he asserted, "It is the duty of Muslims to possess these weapons."[32]

BUBBA, BOOBS, AND BIG MACS

How could Congress turn a blind eye to developments that threatened the lives and well-being of every American? What actions to ward off the nuclear threat were being taken by the federal government? Was anyone at the helm of the ship of state that had suddenly veered into treacherous straits?

The answer to the last question is positive. Someone was at the helm. Unfortunately, that someone was a clown named Bubba. The American people knew that William Jefferson "Bubba" Clinton was a scoundrel, a cheat, and a liar, but he sure was fun. What other president donned shades to play a sax and act like a Blues Brother on late-night television? Sure the electorate knew he had a string of bimbos with big hair and no brains and that he engaged in business practices that would have put Foghorn Leghorn to shame, but some of his antics were downright hilarious—like when he told smug CBS reporters that he had smoked a joint but never inhaled and then he held Hillary's hand while talking about his lengthy affair with Jennifer Flowers.

Clinton could tell a whooper with a straight face and contort language into meaningless gibberish in the manner of a con man at a carnival. At one point he even managed to confound interrogators by questioning the most basic verb in the English language—the meaning of is. And who could not howl at Bubba's Hanukkah with Monica?

Of course, there were consequences for Clinton's behavior. America, before the world community, no longer could claim to be a righteous and morally decent nation. Bin Laden pointed this out in his Letter to America: "You are a nation that permits acts of immorality and you consider them to be pillars of personal freedom. Who can forget your President Clinton's immoral acts committed in the official Oval Office? After that you did not even bring him to account, other than that he 'made a mistake,' after which everything passed with no punishment. Is there a worse kind of event for which your name will go down in history and be remembered by nations?" To be condemned by bin Laden was bad enough. To be unable to refute his allegations showed that America had reached the nadir of depravity.

While the American people were complacent before Clinton's outrageous behavior, the president himself was complacent before the gathering storm that had been unleashed by bin Laden's fatwa. The fact that Clinton ignored verified accounts that al Qaeda had acquired nuclear weapons was simply an extension of the "don't ask, don't tell" rule he imposed on the matter of gays in the military. It was a policy of inertia arising from the prevailing spirit of *panem et circenes* ("bread and circuses") that characterized Rome at the time of the barbarian invasions.

The blunder of ignoring the nuclear threat—which may remain the greatest blunder in human history—was in keeping with other blunders that were committed by this most contemptible and corrupt of U.S. presidents. When the first terrorist attack on American soil took place on February 26, 1993, with a bombing of the World Trade Center, Clinton opted to treat the matter as a criminal incident that did not require an immediate and forthright response. He even chose not to visit the site of the bombing and also refused to ferret out the perpetrators and planners of the attacks at the Al-Farouq Mosque in Brooklyn and the Al-Salaam Mosque in Jersey City.

In Somalia, Clinton allowed Gen. Mohammad Farrah Aideed, an anti-American warlord with a tribe of warriors, to down a Black Hawk helicopter and to drive away American forces with machetes and machine guns, creating "the worst U.S. military defeat since Vietnam." The Somalis, as it turned out, were aided by bin Laden, who had provided the irregulars with AK-47s and rocket-propelled grenade launchers.

In Sudan, Clinton pressured Hassan Abd Allah al-Turabi, the leader of the ruling National Islamic Front, and President Omar Hassan Ahmed Al-Bashir to oust bin Laden and his army of al Qaeda operatives. The Sudanese officials, eager to end the U.N. sanctions that were choking the country's feeble economy, offered to arrest Osama and turn him over to U.S. authorities. The Sudanese officials wanted to sell cotton and gum arabic in Western markets and needed foreign investors to develop the country's oil and natural gas fields. The offer was made in good faith. In the previous year, Sudan had handed over Carlos the

Jackal to French officials at the Khartoum airport. Collaring bin Laden would have been a relatively simple task. But Clinton declined the offer. He believed that bin Laden and the mujahideen would not be a bother to the free world if exiled to some other place.

The Sudanese invited bin Laden to leave. He chose to go to Afghanistan, telling his former hosts that he "would rather die than live in a European state." On May 18, 1996, bin Laden—with 3 wives, 6 children, and 150 mujahideen—departed Khartoum for Jalalabad. President Clinton believed the matter was resolved. But allowing the most dangerous terrorist on the planet to relocate to an impregnable stronghold in Afghanistan from which he could direct terrorist attacks with near impunity was sheer lunacy.[33]

But few in Washington expressed surprise or outrage at this folly. Clinton may have been a clown, but the economy was booming, and nearly every American could afford to spend some time with Mickey and Donald in Central Florida or Southern California. The failure to capture bin Laden was not an issue in the 1996 presidential campaign, and so Clinton won a second term by a landslide.

AL QAEDA'S NUCLEAR ARSENAL

The enormity of these blunders paled in comparison with Clinton's decision to ignore the reports that bin Laden had gained control of the Afghan poppy fields and was spending millions for his nuclear project. He purchased forty-eight additional suitcase nukes from the Russian Mafia[34] and similar devices from central Asian sources.[35] From Simeon Mogilevich, a Ukrainian arms dealer, bin Laden purchased more than twenty kilos of uranium-236. For one delivery of twelve to fifteen kilos, Mogilevich received a payment of seventy million dollars.[36] The uranium had been enriched to 85 percent—far above the standards for weapons-grade material.[37] He purchased several bars of enriched uranium from Egyptian black-marketer Ibrahim Abd and twenty nuclear warheads from Kazakhstan, Russia, Turkmenistan, and Ukraine.[38] Along the way he acquired enough radioactive material to plant a dirty nuke in every major American city.[39]

The belief that bin Laden simply obtained these weapons to keep in his cave without concern for maintenance and upgrading has its roots in the erroneous and prejudicial notion that he is a backward camel jockey lacking knowledge of sophisticated weaponry rather than a highly trained engineer and one of the most gifted military tacticians in contemporary history.

Bin Laden has been extremely mindful of proper maintenance. As soon as he obtained off-the-shelf nukes from the Chechens, he paid an estimated one hundred million dollars for the assistance of nuclear scientists from China and Russia and the Abdul Qadeer Khan laboratory in Pakistan. From 1996 to 2001, Osama also retained a score of Spetsnaz (Soviet special forces) technicians on his payroll.[40] These technicians had been trained to open and operate the suitcase nukes. To simplify the process of activation, the al Qaeda scientists and technicians devised a way of hot-wiring the small nukes to suicide bombers.[41]

The work on the weapons, for the most part, was conducted within laboratories built in deep tunnels in the Khowst area and in the labyrinthine caves of Kandahar.[42] Within these laboratories, scientists removed the active uranium and plutonium from some weapons so that the nuclear materials could be processed and placed in backpacks for easy transportation and little chance of detection.[43]

In October 2001, Mossad (Israeli intelligence) apprehended an al Qaeda operative as he attempted to enter Israel at a border checkpoint in Ramallah. The terrorist was carrying a plutonium-implosion bomb that could have transformed Israel into a desert wasteland.[44] Positive proof had been provided that al Qaeda possessed nuclear weapons. But few within the land of the free and the home of the brave were paying attention.

BLUNDER 7

Siding with the Enemy

What we are trying to do is to limit his [Milosevic's] ability to win a military victory and engage in ethnic cleansing and slaughter innocent people and to do everything we can do to induce him to take this peace agreement

> *President Bill Clinton,*
> *November 23, 1999*

We must act to save thousands of innocent men, women, and children from humanitarian catastrophe, from death, barbarism, and ethnic cleansing by a brutal dictatorship.

> *British prime minister Tony Blair,*
> *November 22, 1999*

The accusations against me are unscrupulous lies and a treacherous distortion of history.

> *Former Serbian president Slobodan Milosevic,*
> *November 2004*

DISMISSING THE WORLD TRADE CENTER bombing as a criminal act! Refusing to ferret out the terrorists in the Al-Farouq and Al-Salaam mosques! Running from the machete-wielding Muslims in Mogadishu! Ignoring the nuclear menace! Just one of these blunders would have been enough to grant Bill "Bubba" Clinton a prominent place in the Presidential Hall of Shame—let alone his acts of perjury and perversion. But the list of this fathead's fatuity is incredibly longer and includes an act that made the United States an ally of bin Laden in a jihad against a Christian government in the Balkans.

123

The problem in Kosovo began in 1989 when Slobodan Milosevic, president of Serbia and the Free Republic of Yugoslavia, set out to create a greater Serbia by annexing Kosovo. When the Kosovo assembly approved this measure, ethnic Albanians (a sanitized way of saying native Muslims) rebelled. In 1990 Milosevic sent troops into Kosovo to crush the rebellion and restore order. In1992 the ethnic Albanians established their own government in Kosovo—the Republic of Kosovo—with self-proclaimed pacifist Ibrahim Rugova as its president.[1]

With two governments in one small country, the situation quickly became downright ugly. In 1993 Milosevic ordered the arrest of thirty ethnic Albanians for planning an armed uprising. In 1995 a Serbian court sentenced sixty-eight members of Rugova's government to prison for setting up a parallel police force.

BIN LADEN IN THE BALKANS

To aid in their struggle for independence, the ethnic Albanians turned to Osama bin Laden and the mujahideen. Muslim warriors from Chechnya, Egypt, and Saudi Arabia began to arrive in droves in Kosovo. Some were granted press credentials from the Republic of Kosovo (Rugova's rival government) to escape detection from international observers. Others married Bosnian Muslim women and then joined the Bosnian army. By 1995 more than six thousand holy warriors had migrated to the Balkans in preparation for the struggle against the Christian Serbs.[2]

Bin Laden visited the area three times between 1994 and 1996. In the wake of these visits, al Qaeda training camps popped up in Zenica in Bosnia and Malisevo and Mitrovica in Kosovo; elaborate command and control centers were established in Croatia, Macedonia, and Bulgaria; and a central headquarters for the mujahideen was situated in Tropje, Albania, on the property of Sali Berisha, the former Albanian premier.[3]

The head of al Qaeda also provided seven hundred million dollars to establish the Kosovo Liberation Army (KLA). The purpose of this organization was to drive the Christian Serbs from Kosovo, to topple the government of Slobodan Milosevic, to undermine the efforts of Ibrahim Rugova to exact a peaceful solution to the civil war, and to unite the

Muslims of Kosovo, Macedonia, and Albania into the Islamic Republic of Greater Albania.[4]

CLINTON'S NEW MUSLIM FRIENDS

President Clinton, along with Secretary of State Madeleine Albright and Secretary of Defense William Cohen, came to view the KLA as "freedom fighters."[5] CIA director George Tenet and other CIA officials shared this view. In no time, millions of U.S. dollars in aid flowed to the Muslim rebels in the form of military training and field advice.[6] The United States, unbeknown to the American people, was in league with the terrorist group that was intent upon its destruction. Human history, going back to the tree-swinging primates, doesn't get much crazier than this.

By 1998 the KLA became a formidable army of thirty thousand highly trained troops with sophisticated weaponry that included shoulder-launched antitank rocket launchers, mortars, recoilless rifles, and antiaircraft machine guns. From Tropje, the KLA began to conduct hit-and-run terrorist attacks throughout Kosovo. They bombed police stations, killed scores of police officers and government workers, and desecrated Christian cemeteries.[7]

Milosevic responded by burning homes and killing dozens of KLA members in the Drenica region. A full-scale conflict erupted, culminating in the infamous massacre of January 15, 1999, when the bodies of forty-five ethnic Albanians were discovered in a gully in the small village of Racak.[8]

Confronted with this crime, Milosevic insisted that the bodies had been planted by the KLA to implicate the Serbs and to justify Western intervention in the conflict. Milosevic's testimony was supported by investigative journalists from *Le Figaro* and *Le Monde*, who discovered that the bodies had been placed in unnatural positions, that the site of the "massacre" was devoid of cartridges, and that the villagers were unable to identify the victims.[9]

PUTTING THE SCREWS TO SLOBODAN

These findings were overshadowed by outcries within the Clinton administration of genocide and ethic cleansing and claims by CIA director

George Tenet (the same dunderhead who produced the intelligence on Hussein leading to the Iraq War) that more than ten thousand ethnic Albanians had been slaughtered and then buried in mass graves by bloodthirsty Serbs.[10]

Clinton, being a knucklehead, decided to intervene in the struggle. The KLA and Rugova's rival government were asked to sit down with Milosevic to hammer out a settlement. Members of the Clinton administration produced the paperwork and then asked everyone to sign it. Milosevic refused for a very good reason: the settlement called for a referendum on independence for Kosovo. It didn't take an expert in math to realize that such a referendum would produce disastrous results for the Serbs and Christians throughout the Balkans. After all, there were 1.7 million ethnic Albanians (all Muslim) in Kosovo and a mere 200,000 Serbs.[11] Clinton, in fact, was demanding that the Christian government acquiesce to radical Islam and the forces of bin Laden. He was serving the cause of the jihad and acting against the peace and stability of the Western world. But no one in Washington, including the Republican members of the House and Senate, questioned his judgment.

Clinton did not take Milosevic's refusal lightly. He summoned his NATO allies and began a bombing campaign that reduced Kosovo to a heap of rubble. At the start of the campaign, U.S. Secretary of Defense William Cohen announced that 100,000 ethnic Albanians of military age were missing after being taken from columns of families that the Serbs were deporting to Albania and Macedonia. "They may have been murdered," Cohen said.[12] Between March 24 and June 10, 1999, a total of 37,465 missions were flown, destroying 400 Serbian artillery weapons, 270 armored personnel carriers, and causing 1.4 million ethnic Albanians to flee for their lives—the greatest mass migration of refugees since World War II. The cost of the ten weeks of bombings exceeded $1.4 million. Milosevic and the Serbs decided to toss in the towel. The accord of June 21, 1999, ended the air raids, eliminated the presence of the Serbian government in Kosovo, and authorized a NATO force of 1,700 police officers to establish law and order until democratic elections could be held.[13]

But the situation in Kosovo was far beyond the capability of the meager NATO police force. Hashim Thaci, a leader of the KLA, proclaimed himself prime minister of the Kosovo government. Those ethnic Albanians who had fled for safety from the Serbs and the NATO bombings now returned with a vengeance. A pogrom began in the Balkans, and neither the Clinton administration nor the United Nations uttered a word of protest.

THE REAL ETHNIC CLEANSING

More than two hundred Christian churches and monasteries were destroyed. Some—including the Devic Monastery, the Cathedral of St. George, the Church of St. Nicholas, and the Monastery of the Holy Archangels—had been built in the thirteenth and fourteenth centuries.[14] Accounts surfaced of mass executions of Serbian farmers, the murders of scores of priests, and "granny killings"—the drowning of elderly women in bathtubs.[15]

Of the two hundred thousand Serbs who lived in Kosovo before the war, only four hundred remained a month after Kosovo became a NATO protectorate.[16] Most had gathered their possessions and fled for their lives. The Serbs who remained were sequestered in three gloomy apartment buildings, where the international police remained on guard day and night.[17] Hundreds of Wahhabi mosques and schools, thanks to contributions from the Saudis, now appeared in every town and village throughout the country. The back door to Europe had been pried open by bin Laden and the mujahideen for the drug trade and the movement of weapons of mass destruction.

In the aftermath of the war, NATO sent forensic teams from fifteen countries and eight human-rights organizations into Kosovo to find the killing fields and evidence of Milosevic's genocide. Mass murder is difficult to hide. One need only recall the entry of war-crime inspectors into Nazi Germany, Cambodia, and Rwanda to understand that the executions of thousands of people leaves behind massive and undeniable evidence. But the bodies of the ten thousand victims of Milosevic's reign of terror failed to materialize.

One account of Serbian atrocities concerned a mine in Trepca, where seven hundred bodies of ethnic Albanians were reported to have been dumped. A French gendarmerie spelunking team descended half a mile to the bottom of the mine in search of bodies. They found none. Some villagers said that the bodies were burned in a nearby furnace. A second French team inspected the ashes. They found no teeth, no bones, no trace of human remains.[18]

The Spanish team was told to prepare for the worst, as it was going into Kosovo's real killing fields. The team was told to prepare for more than 2,000 autopsies. But no mass graves were discovered, only 187 bodies that had been buried in individual graves. Many had died of natural causes. Juan Lopez Palafox, the chief inspector of the Spanish team, compared Kosovo to Rwanda, saying: "In the former Yugoslavia crimes were committed, some no doubt horrible, but they derived from the war. In Rwanda we saw 450 corpses [at one site] of women and children, one on top of the other, all with their heads broken open."[19]

Clinton's claims, based on flawed intelligence from the CIA, had been wrong. After combing the country, the NATO teams and human-rights organizations uncovered 2,108 bodies, many of which were not victims of war crimes.[20]

But neither the Clinton administration nor the CIA nor NATO would admit they had been in error. Despite the lack of evidence, Milosevic was accused of genocide and crimes against humanity and placed on trial in February 2002 before an international criminal tribunal in The Hague.[21] There was scant chance he would receive a favorable verdict. The United States, in an unprecedented move, demanded and received the right to censor all evidence.[22] The trial, even four years later, is ongoing.

THE BOMBINGS OF THE EMBASSIES

Bin Laden and the mujahideen, however, showed no appreciation for America's help in driving the Serbs out of Kosovo and tossing Slobodan Milosevic in the slammer. Quite to the contrary, on August 7, 1998, just when the Clinton administration entered its controversial relationship with the KLA, Muslim fanatics displayed their ingratitude by bombing the U.S. embassies in Kenya and Tanzania and killing 234 people, 12 of them Americans, and wounding 5,000 more. A tip from a CIA informant thwarted bin Laden's plan to bomb a third embassy—the embassy in Kampala, Uganda.[23]

But the embassy bombings drove Clinton to desperate measures. He had been caught with his pants down and his popularity was plummeting. Calls were being raised for his impeachment. He had to do something to prove that he was not a worse president than Jimmy Carter. On August 17, 1998, Clinton had been forced to testify before a grand jury for four hours about his sexual escapades and to appear on national television to say that he had had an "inappropriate relationship" with a White House intern and that he had misled the American people. Now he would not mislead. He would lead! Clinton would show the world that he was a man of resolve and decision by crushing bin Laden and his mujahideen like bedbugs.

On August 20, Clinton ordered a cruise missile attack on al Qaeda residential and military complexes in Khost, Afghanistan, and the bombing of the al-Shifa Pharmaceutical Plant near Khartoum, which Tenet and the CIA assured him was an al Qaeda laboratory for the production of deadly VX nerve gas.[24] From the Oval Office, the president addressed his fellow countrymen:

> Our mission was clear; to strike at the network of radical groups affiliated with and funded by Osama bin Laden, perhaps the pre-eminent organizer and financier of international terrorism in the world today. . . . Earlier today, the United States carried out simultaneous strikes against terrorist facilities and infrastructures in Afghanistan. It contained key elements of bin Laden's network and infrastructure and has served as the training camp for literally thousands of terrorists around the globe. We have reason to believe that a gathering of key terrorist leaders was to take place there today, thus underscoring the urgency of our actions. Our forces also attacked a factory in Sudan associated with the bin Laden network. The factory was involved in the production of materials for chemical weapons.[25]

The retaliatory attack wasn't a very smart move. Bin Laden, al-Zawahiri, and friends were not in the Khost camps. They were safe and secure within a *madrassah* (Muslim religious school) in Pakistan. Although the missiles struck the camps, the only casualties were local farmers and some low-level militants.[26] The camps themselves had been built of stone, wood, and mud, making it easy for al Qaeda to rebuild them in a matter of days. And the Sudan pharmaceutical plant was not involved in making nerve gas or any other chemical weapon. It produced common, over-the-counter drugs, including ibuprofen.[27]

CLINTON UNITES RADICAL ISLAM

Clinton's attack on al Qaeda was a resounding dud—several of the bombs failed to detonate upon impact. Moreover, the attacks served as a rallying call to Muslims across the world to join in the jihad against the Great Satan. The camps at Khost contained five mosques that provided religious services not only to the mujahideen but also to the local villagers. Four mosques were destroyed, leaving the area littered with burned pages from hundreds of Korans. The pictures of the bombed mosques and the burned pages appeared in newspapers throughout the Middle East. "America has invited death upon itself," Mavi Fazlur Rehman Khalil, head of Harakat ul-Ansar, told a newscaster from Al-jazeera. "If we don't get justice from the world court, we know how to get our own justice."[28]

This sixth major blunder by Clinton in the struggle against Islam only served to enhance bin Laden's reputation as a great and righteous warrior in the tradition of Saladin. Rahimullah Yusufzai, a Pakistani journalist who interviewed bin Laden for ABC News, noted in his weekly column, "In an Islamic world desperately short of genuine heroes, Osama bin Laden has emerged as a new cult figure."[29] Similarly, Hassan Abd Allah al-Turabi, Sudan's leading imam, told reporters from the *Christian Science Monitor:* "Bin Laden lives in a very remote place, but now—ho, ho—you [Americans] have raised him as a hero, the symbol of all anti-West forces in the world. All the Arab and Muslim young people, believe me, look to him as an example." Al-Turabi concluded by saying that Clinton's attacks on the Afghanistan camps would serve to create "100,000 bin Ladens."[30]

Clinton's missile attacks on Afghanistan served a further purpose. They strengthened the bond between al Qaeda and the Taliban. Prior to the bombings, the relationship between bin Laden and Taliban leader Mullah Mohammad Omar had been strained to the limit. Omar, who was seeking international recognition for his newly created government in Afghanistan, did not appreciate bin Laden's repeated calls for violence against Americans.[31] He declared that the fatwas were "null and void" since bin Laden lacked the religious authority to issue them.[32] Moreover, the scruffy Taliban religious leader resented the arrogance of the Arab mujahideen, whose aristocratic attitude toward Pashtun customs and beliefs was becoming intolerable. Tensions became so intense that gunfire broke out between Taliban soldiers and bin Laden's bodyguards.[33] In June 1998 the Taliban struck a deal with Saudi officials to send bin Laden to a Saudi prison in exchange for Saudi support and U.S. recognition. Prince Turki bin Faisal ibn Abdul Aziz Al Saud, head of the Saudi General Intelligence Agency, confided to the Clinton administration that the exchange was "a deal done."[34]

But after the missile attacks against the Afghan camps, Prince Turki returned to Afghanistan to find the one-eyed mullah a changed man. "Mullah Omar was very heated," the prince later recalled. "In a loud voice he denounced all our efforts and praised bin Laden as a worthy and legitimate scholar of Islam. He told me we should not do the infidel's work by taking Osama from them."[35]

Thanks to Clinton's foolish retaliation, the opportunity to separate the Taliban from al Qaeda had been lost and with it the possibility of preventing future acts of terrorism. "Rather than trying to divide and conquer," Larry Goodson, professor of Middle East studies at the U.S. Army War College, said, "we adopted the approach to keep Afghanistan in a box. We were not going to recognize them. We were not going to aid them in significant ways. In fact, we took a very hard line toward the Taliban regime."[36]

Money now poured into al Qaeda's coffers from Islamic "charitable" and "humanitarian" organizations across the world. By 1998 the Global Relief Foundation in Chicago had raised more than five million dollars a year for bin Laden's holy war against the United States.[37] Similarly, the al-Haramain Islamic Foundation in Ashland, Oregon, with prayer houses in Ashland and Springfield, Missouri, managed to solicit more than thirty million dollars a year—money that would go, in large part, to fund the jihad.[38] Millions more came from such American nonprofit, tax-exempt organizations as the Hatikva Center, the Holy Land Foundation for Relief and Development, the al-Wafa Humanitarian Organization, and Benevolence International in Chicago.[39]

THE NIGHT OF POWER

Enriched and emboldened, bin Laden now made plans for a "night of power" on January 3, 2000, the holiest day of Ramadan, with an attack on the USS *Sullivans,* a U.S. warship anchored in the Yemeni harbor of Aden. The attack was a failure. Al Qaeda's small boat had been loaded with boxes of heavy explosives that were to detonate as soon as the boat rammed into the warship, but the small boat sank as soon as it was launched. A few setbacks, however, were only to be expected in the jihad. Bin Laden and his buddies went back to the planning table.

The revised attack took place on October 10, 2000, when the USS *Cole* cruised into Aden harbor for a short "gas and go" stop. As soon as the one-billion-dollar destroyer with a complement of 249 men and 44 women became attached to a floating fuel station, a skiff packed with five hundred pounds of C-4 plastic explosives headed across the harbor toward the *Cole.* U.S. sailors attempted to wave off the two suicide bombers manning the boat. But the bombers were not to be deterred. As soon as the skiff reached the port side of the hull, the terrorists pressed a detonator, blowing an enormous hole in the side of the warship. Seventeen American sailors were killed. It was a glorious victory for al Qaeda. The only disappointment for bin Laden was that the operative who was supposed to film the attack for propaganda purposes fell asleep at his observation post on Steamer Point.[40]

The greatest nation in the world had been attacked by a group of Muslim fanatics in one of the poorest and most radical countries on the Arabian Peninsula. Did Bill Clinton threaten President Ali Abdullah Saleh of Yemen with a U.S. invasion unless the terrorists were rounded up, granted a perfunctory trial, and executed by firing squad? Did he seek to form an international alliance with such countries as China, India, and Russia to crush cells of radical Islamists across the world? Did he adopt firm measures against Muslim groups and organizations within the United States that support the jihad and benefit from tax-exempt status? Such decisive action would require leadership from a person of moral conviction and patriotic ideals. That person was not William Jefferson Clinton.

Several days after the attack on the *Cole,* the president and his cabi-net met in the Oval Office to discuss an appropriate response. Attorney General Janet Reno insisted that any show of force would have to be consistent with international law. She attempted to clarify this by adding that a military strike on al Qaeda camps and compounds in Afghanistan must not represent retaliation but rather an effort to prevent future acts of terrorism.[41] CIA director George Tenet said that a retaliatory strike should only be commissioned after an exhaustive investigation into the incident that could take months, if not years.[42] Secretary of State Madeleine Albright said that a counterstrike against al Qaeda would not be helpful since the administration was attempting to halt the fighting between the Israelis and the Palestinians.[43] Secretary of Defense William Cohen argued that the incident was not sufficient provocation for military action.[44] And so the matter was dismissed as a minor occurrence without grave and certain consequence to national security.

The meeting represented the sorry state of Uncle Sam's health. At the relatively young age of 224, he had lost his teeth, experienced severe constipation, and manifested advanced symptoms of senility.

OSAMA'S ODE

The attack of October 2000 in the port of Yemen was an event of great significance to bin Laden. In his mind, the skiff symbolized al Qaeda and the *Cole* represented the United States. In January 2001 he penned the following poem to commemorate the incident:

> A destroyer: even the brave fear its might.
> It inspires horror in the harbor and in the open sea.
> She sails into the waves.
> Flanked by arrogance, haughtiness, and false power,
> To her doom she moves slowly.
> A dinghy awaits her, riding the waves.[45]

While bin Laden was composing doggerel for his terrorist companions, Clinton was spending his last hours in the White House. He did not devote his time to firing a parting shot at al Qaeda or issuing attack orders on key targets in Kabul and Kandahar. He was signing pardons for his well-connected friends.

BLUNDER 8

Initiating Operation Enduring Forever

It was an interesting day.

President George W. Bush, speaking of 9/11

We have taken a ball of quicksilver and hit it with a hammer.

John Arquilla, counterinsurgency specialist

It seems clear to me heroin is the number one asset of Osama bin Laden. There is a need to update our view of how terrorism is financed. And the view of Osama bin Laden relying on Wahhabi donations from abroad is outdated. And the view of him as one of the world's largest heroin dealers is the more accurate, up-to-date view.

Mark Steven Kirk (R-IL)

We are making these drugs for Satan—Americans and Jews. If we cannot kill them with guns, we will kill them with drugs.

Fatwa of Hezbollah

ROBERT BURNS, AN INFINITELY better poet than Osama bin Laden, wrote that the "best laid schemes o' mice and men gang aft a-gley." So it was with 9/11. Sure, the attacks were an enormous strategic and financial success, resulting in the deaths of 2,292 Americans, widespread urban devastation that resulted in public and private expenses in excess of $16.5 billion, and the loss of 200,000 jobs. And the cost to al Qaeda was less than $500,000. What other military operation in modern history produced more bang for the buck? But the attack had not gone off without a hitch. The plans called for two other events to take place: the assassination of George Bush and the destruction of the White House. But why complain? Three out of five isn't bad—not by any standard within the Pentagon.

A BULLET FOR BUSH

President George W. Bush escaped the hit by a fluke. He had traveled to Sarasota, Florida, the night before to meet with some Republican big spenders at the Colony Beach Resort. He went to bed around 10:00 p.m. and slept well, despite Secret Service confirmation of a report from the Sarasota police concerning threats on his life that had been made by someone from the Middle East.[1]

The president awoke at 6:00 a.m. and laced up his running shoes for a four-mile jog around a nearby golf course.[2] While Bush was taking his morning constitutional, a van carrying a host of Middle Easterners pulled up to the guard station at the Colony and announced that they had arrived to conduct a "poolside" interview with President Bush. They said the interview had been prearranged by the White House and asked for a certain Secret Service agent by name. The guard relayed the message to a security official in the lobby. The official knew nothing about the interview and had never heard of the Secret Service agent whom the Muslim had named as the contact. Still and all, the official didn't want to act in a hasty or dismissive manner. For this reason, he asked the Muslims to contact the president's press relations office in Washington and to return when they had obtained further clearance.

The security official, it is now believed, foiled the assassination attempt. Two days earlier, al Qaeda operatives who adopted the same ruse had murdered Gen. Ahmed Shah Massoud, leader of Afghanistan's Northern Alliance. They presented themselves as journalists from Arabic News International who had come to conduct an interview. As soon as the interview began, a bomb within the video camera exploded, killing Massoud and the journalists.[3] The assassination was timed to remove the Northern Alliance commander from the field of play in the wake of 9/11.[4]

After his early morning jog, George Bush took a quick shower and sat down for breakfast and his daily briefing. While this was taking place, the two Boeing 767-200 jetliners that would crash into the Word Trade Center towers departed from Boston's Logan Airport.[5]

At 9:00 a.m. the president was visiting the Emma Booker Elementary School to promote his No Child Left Behind program. He spent some time reading *My Pet Goat* to a class of second graders. By 9:07 he was informed that America was under attack and that the twin towers of the World Trade Center were in flames. By 9:40 the president was headed for the Sarasota airport to board *Air Force One* when he received notification that a Boeing 757, which had departed from Dulles Airport, had crashed into the west side of the Pentagon.[6]

At 9:55 *Air Force One* took off like a rocket from Sarasota without fighter protection.[7] This lack of security in the midst of momentous crisis defies all explanation. It shows that the leaders in charge (Dick Cheney, Donald Rumsfeld, Colin Powell, et al.) were incapable of protecting the leader of the free world—let alone millions of ordinary American citizens—in the midst of a terrorist attack.

Shortly after takeoff, the president received a call from Vice President Cheney about a "credible threat" to *Air Force One* and that the plane was not safe to land in Washington.[8] What to do? No one knew. For this reason, the president's plane began flying in big, slow circles over Sarasota. Finally, *Air Force One* was directed to Barksdale Air Force Base near Shreveport, Louisiana, where it landed at 11:45 a.m.[9]

Members of the White House were already acting like pointy-headed nincompoops, and the war on terror had yet to begin.

George W. Bush's moment had come. Just before 9/11, his approval rating had languished at 51 percent. But immediately after the attacks it soared to 90 percent, a record high for presidents in the Gallup Poll.[10] When he addressed the nation with the following words on October 9, he was the most respected and admired leader in the world:

> Now this war will not be like the war against Iraq a decade ago with a deliberate liberation of territory and a swift conclusion. It will not look like the air war above Kosovo two years ago, where no ground troops were used and not a single American was lost in combat.
>
> Our response involves far more than instant retaliation and isolated strikes. Americans should not expect one battle, but a lengthy campaign

unlike any other we have ever seen. It may include dramatic strikes visible on TV and covert operations secret even in success.

We will starve terrorists of funding, turn them against one another, drive them from place to place until there is no refuge or rest.

And we will pursue nations that provide aid or safe harbor to terrorism. Every nation in every region now has a decision to make: either you are with us, or you are with the terrorists.

From this day forward, any nation that continues to harbor or support terrorism will be regarded by the United States as a hostile regime. Our nation has been put on notice; we're not immune from attack. We will take measures against terrorism to protect Americans.[11]

THE BEGINNING BLUNDER

With this unofficial declaration of war, the triumphant march of folly continued. The first mistake came with the labeling of the campaign against international Islamic terrorism as Operation Infinite Justice. The label, the Bush administration soon discovered, was offensively incorrect and served to inflame devout Muslims, who held that only Allah could deliver "infinite justice." In Beirut, Sheikh Arif al-Nabulsi, head of South Lebanon's religious scholars, said that the U.S. campaign should be called "Operation Infinite *Injustice*," because the war was intended to establish America's control over the oil-rich Muslim republics in Central Asia that had once been part of the Soviet Union. A hard-line Iranian newspaper maintained that a more appropriate name for the military operation would be "Infinite Imperialism."[12] In response to such statements, the president decided to rename the campaign as "Operation Enduring Freedom" and expressed his deep and sincere apology to anyone he might have offended.[13] Any question about the president's leadership and resolve had been answered by this weak-kneed response to the very forces he intended to oppose.

The Second Misstep

A second mistake was made by Bush's idiotic identification of the Taliban with al Qaeda. On the evening of 9/11, the president addressed the nation and said: "We have to force countries to choose. We will make no distinction between the terrorists who committed these acts and those who harbor them."[14] This statement represented the first expression of the so-called Bush Doctrine, a policy that would commit U.S. troops to a broad-based, long-term, and largely unfocused war against militant Muslim fanaticism whenever and wherever it reared its ugly head. The Taliban, however, was not al Qaeda, and al Qaeda was not the Taliban. But this distinction was automatically dissolved by presidential fiat. Overnight, bin Laden's forces were multiplied tenfold. This new alliance, according to Rohan Gunartna, a Sri Lanka native and principal investigator of the U.N. Terrorism Prevention Branch, could have been prevented if the Bush administration had granted Pakistani president Pervez Musharraf a reasonable amount of time to come to terms with Mullah Omar for the surrender of bin Laden and his high command to a peacekeeping force or a neutral country.[15]

The Third Boner

Yet another mistake came with the crazy assumption that al Qaeda, like the twelfth-century Assassins, represented a radical fringe group within Islam—a religious aberration that was abhorred by the majority of Muslims throughout the world. This blunder was a boneheaded denial of facts and figures. At the start of Operation Enduring Freedom, U.S. intelligence agencies were aware that al Qaeda could boast tens of thousands of operatives and had ties to hundreds of Islamic terrorist groups. A classified CIA survey showed that 95 percent of educated Saudis between the ages of twenty-one and forty-one expressed hatred of the United States and support for bin Laden,[16] and a Gallup poll verified that a substantial majority of the world's Muslims supported al Qaeda's call for jihad.[17]

BOMBS AND BUNDLES

Other mistakes occurred as soon as the military campaign in Afghanistan commenced on October 7, 2001, with a salvo of fifty missiles from three U.S. cruisers and a destroyer in the Arabian Sea. One missile struck one of Mullah Omar's residences in Kandahar, killing his stepfather and his ten-year-old son. Another struck the small village of

Kouram, killing one hundred civilians. A third destroyed a mosque and a residential village near Jalalabad.[18]

Such pitfalls were to be expected. No one could expect a military invasion of hostile territory without a few strategic missteps and civilian casualties. But what wasn't to be expected was the double-mindedness of the offensive. The misguided missiles were symptomatic of a misguided mission. Along with the bombs, the United States dropped bundles of food, clothing, and medical supplies to towns and villages throughout Afghanistan. These bundles were intended to provide clear and certain proof that the United States was not an imperialist nation but a kind and caring country that did not mean to offend the general populace. Of course, enemy forces quickly confiscated many of these bundles. The few that reached the poverty-stricken and war-ridden Afghani peasants failed to serve their intended purpose. Since less than 30 percent of the people could read, most assumed that the bundles that fell from the sky were either CARE packages from fellow Muslims or miraculous gifts from Allah.[19]

Shortly after the start of the invasion, Osama bin Laden appeared on television in Kabul with his favorite sidekick, Ayman al-Zawahiri. Dressed in standard green camouflage jackets, the two sat before a campfire with sticks, appearing like two Muslim boy scouts about to roast some marshmallows. Bin Laden offered the camera a sheepish grin and said: "God has blessed a vanguard group of Muslims, the forefront of Islam, to destroy America. May God bless them and allot them a supreme place in heaven."[20]

But something was screwy from the start of this invasion. The coalition troops expected to encounter the fiercest group of guerrilla fighters in the world, a group that had sent the great Soviet Army packing from the mountains of Afghanistan. But the invasion forces encountered only a modicum of resistance. On November 9 they gained control of the strategic town of Mazar-i-Sharif, which had raised the white flag with barely a whimper. Two days later Taliban in the south and the city of Heart in the west fell with hardly a shot being fired. On November 12, much to the amazement of all, the U.S.-led forces entered Kabul to cheers from a carefully choreographed crowd of onlookers.[21] Where were the mujahideen? Where were the thousands of student warriors who comprised the Taliban? Where were the Muslim freedom fighters who had been called to fight the Great Satan? The invasion turned out to be a cakewalk. The only U.S. casualties during the first six weeks of combat were two airmen who had been killed when the Taliban managed to shoot down their helicopter. And this incident did not occur in Afghanistan but rather in Pakistan, near the Dalbandin air base.[22] None of the cities in Afghanistan had to be conquered by force. They all had been subjected to strategic withdrawal and abandoned.

The coalition forces pressed on to Jalalabad, where, once again, they encountered scant resistance. From the palm trees of this desert city they were able to see Tora Bora, the highest snowcapped peak of Spin Ghar, rising more than thirteen thousand feet above the great White Mountains. This was the final goal of the invasion, the place where bin Laden and his gang had built an "impregnable fortress."

The story of the fortress was based on the testimony of Viktor Kutsenko, a former Soviet army commander who had served in Afghanistan. Kutsenko maintained that the fortress was built 350 yards beneath the solid rock of Tora Bora. Other Russians and members of the Northern Alliance added to the commander's testimony so that the CIA was able to come up with intricate drawings of bin Laden's secret lair. The drawings displayed a vast underground complex with a bakery, a hospital with ultrasound equipment, a hotel for two thousand occupants, a mosque, a hydroelectric plant, a library, an arsenal of weapons of mass destruction, and a service bay for tanks, trucks, and other vehicles. The fortress contained a masterful ventilation system—designed by bin Laden himself—that allowed fresh air to circulate to every nook and cranny of the complex.

News of the lair, replete with drawings, was published in the *New York Times* on November 26 and the *Independent* (London) on November 27.[23] On December 2, Secretary of Defense Donald Rumsfeld appeared on NBC's *Meet the Press* to assure the American people of the existence of the incredible complex that had been created by al Qaeda within Tora Bora. "And there's not one of those," Rumsfeld told Tim Russert. "There are many of those. And they have been used very effectively. And I might add, Afghanistan is not the only country that has gone underground. Any number of countries have gone underground."

Poor Rumsfeld should have bitten his tongue. The great troglodyte lair did not exist. It was a figment of Soviet imagination that had been fueled by a few bottles of bad vodka. Yet the CIA, the Defense Department, and the editors of the nation's leading newspaper had accepted the story as unquestionable fact.

THE BIG BATTLE BEGINS

By the end of November 2001, U.S. B-52 bombers began to pound Tora Bora with "bunker blasters" in an all-out effort to collapse bin Laden's mythical underground kingdom. On the ground, U.S. Special Forces (Delta Force and navy Seals) guided missiles with laser devices to targets by outlining the mouths of caves that might serve as sources of ventilation for the fanciful fortress.[24]

Believing that two thousand al Qaeda troops were sequestered within the secret lair, Gen. Tommy Franks, who ran the U.S. military campaign from Central Command in Florida, decided that it was far too risky to place American soldiers on the ground. High casualties appeared to be inevitable, and the Bush administration didn't want hundreds of soldiers returning home in body bags.

For this reason, the CIA, flush with billions for extra spending, recruited local warlords to join the Northern Alliance in storming the mountain fortress.[25] The U.S. soldiers, for the most part, were merely required to stand by for the cleanup campaign. The United States, unbeknown to its citizens, was hiring—in violation of international law—an army of mercenaries to fight its holy war and preparing them to serve as cannon fodder. The situation was becoming increasingly surreal.

When the ground offensive got under way on December 3, the warlords reported that al Qaeda and the Taliban were displaying fierce resistance. Army intelligence officers fancied hearing over their short-range radios the ghostly voice of bin Laden giving orders to his top lieutenants from his place within the belly of the mountain.[26] The end of the struggle appeared to be a matter of days away.

For this reason, the United States continued to bomb the mountain to smithereens with continuous air strikes. At one point, a so-called daisy cutter—a 6,800-kilogram bomb, the largest conventional weapon in the U.S. arsenal—was dropped on a "strategic" Tora Bora target. Gen. Richard Myers, chairman of the U.S. Joint Chiefs of Staff, told the press: "We think we know in general where bin Laden and some of his senior leadership are hiding. We think it's in this so-called Tora Bora area, and that's why we're focusing so hard on the area right now."[27]

THE ENEMY ON PARADE

By December 11, 2001, U.S. officials reported that the caves and mountainside of Tora Bora were littered with the bodies of Taliban fighters and the terrorists and that al Qaeda's defenses had crumbled beneath the massive air and ground offensive.[28] In a gesture of goodwill, if not compassionate conservatism, the coalition forces offered the trapped enemy forces a chance to surrender. The offer, according to U.S. officials, was turned down, and sporadic outbursts of "fierce fighting" erupted across the steep mountainside. The warlords requested and received more supplies, more equipment, and, of course, more money. Gen. Tommy Franks excitedly confided to CNN that al Qaeda and the Taliban had been placed between "a hammer and an anvil."[29] Yet when newsmen traveled to the front lines, they heard no sounds of gunfire and no signs of enemy resistance.[30]

When a final surrender was reached and the last cave breached, the warlords estimated that the al Qaeda body count was between two and three hundred and that hundreds more had been taken as prisoners. As proof of the great success of the campaign, nineteen emaciated, bedraggled, and toothless prisoners were paraded through the streets of Kandahar on December 17.[31]

The seven Afghan warlords who had been recruited for the operation collected their bags of money and caches of weapons and returned to their tribes. It was a very successful venture for them. For a few weeks of combat, they had received more than three billion dollars from the CIA.[32] The lion's share went to Yunis Khan, the godfather of Jalalabad. He had been recruited for the campaign in early November. No one within the CIA bothered to check into Khan's background or to question his loyalties. Such a check, of course, would have required a measure of real intelligence that the CIA did not possess. Even a most cursory investigation of Khan would have revealed that he was a close friend of Osama bin Laden and that he had issued a well-publicized call for jihad against the U.S. forces in Afghanistan.[33]

THE BACK DOOR LEFT OPEN

What had happened? Where in the world was Osama bin Laden? Where was his high command? Where were the members of his elite, international 055 Brigade? Where were the leaders of the Taliban? How had thousands of terrorists and jihadists vanished into thin air at the summit of Tora Bora? Nothing about the offensive made sense, including the hapless, lice-ridden specimens on display as captives.

Before the invasion, U.S. officials had instructed Pakistani president Musharraf to seal the one-hundred-mile border of lawless countryside between Pakistan and Afghanistan. But Musharraf opted to ignore this instruction. After all, he had done enough just by agreeing to serve as an ally. Of course, he was rewarded for this agreement by the lifting of trade restrictions, which would allow up to $426 million in new imports to flow into the United States every year and bought the Bush administration's pledge of assistance in the conflict with India over Kashmir.[34] But there was no way he was going to enter the autonomous frontier provinces to secure the border. If his troops trespassed there, the mullahs would rise in bloody rebellion against his regime. And so he cannot be blamed for his decision to leave the back door to Pakistan wide open. No one—not even a dunce like President Bush or Secretary of Defense Rumsfeld—could expect Musharraf to commit troops to that area. It would have been political suicide.

Yet the closing of the back door had been the key to Operation Enduring Freedom from the get-go. The bombings and the ground offensive made no sense if the terrorists could just pack up their gear and wander across the border to a safe haven. "The border with Pakistan was the key," according to Pir Baksh Bardiwal, the intelligence chief of the Northern Alliance, "but [the] Americans paid no attention to it. Al Qaeda escaped right out from under their noses."[35]

Bin Laden had made his great escape on or about December 16, 2001. He and his men journeyed on horseback directly south toward Pakistan, through the same mountain passes and smugglers' trails the CIA's convoys had passed through during the Afghan war against the Soviet Union. All along the route, in dozens of villages and towns, the Pashtun tribes lighted campfires to guide the horsemen as they continued through the snow toward the old Pakistani military outpost of Parachinar.[36]

From Parachinar, many of the mujahideen made their way to Peshawar, where they obtained passports from sympathetic officials from Pakistan's passport agency.[37] The group of passport recipients included such notables as Sadd bin Laden, bin Laden's oldest son; Yaaz bin Sifat, a key al Qaeda planner; Mohammad Islam Haani, the mayor of Kabul under the Taliban; Saif Al-Adel, al Qaeda's military commander; Ayman al-Zawahiri, Osama's top lieutenant; and Abu Musab Al-Zarqawi, an up-and-coming star of the jihad. From Peshawar, they traveled through the southernmost provinces of Afghanistan, an area neglected by the coalition forces, to head west to Iran, where they found safe haven.[38]

On December 27, 2001, a gaunt and gray Osama bin Laden, dressed in standard *shalwar kameez* (the long shirt and bloused trousers of the mujahideen) and a camouflage jacket, appeared on Aljazeera like the ghost of Christmas Past to issue the following holiday greeting:

> Three months after the blessed strike against world infidelity, namely, America, and two months after the fierce crusade against Islam, it gives us pleasure to speak about the ramifications of these events. These events have revealed extremely important things to Muslims. It has become clear that the West in general, led by America, bears an unspeakable crusader grudge against Islam. Those who lived these months under the continuous bombardments by the various kinds of U.S. aircraft are well aware of this. Many villagers were wiped out without any guilt. Millions of people were expelled during this very cold winter—and the oppressed ones are men, women, and children.[39]

Along with the hollow victory, Americans received more bad news. While combing the tunnels of an al Qaeda base near Kandahar, U.S. troops discovered low-grade uranium-235 in a lead-lined canister. Although not weapons-grade and unsuitable for use in the construction of a fission bomb, the uranium represented an ideal ingredient for a dirty nuke that could spread radioactive contamination throughout a major metropolitan area. This discovery, along with documents found within a safe house in Kabul that contained plans and drawings for superbombs, provided further evidence that the terrorists had gone nuclear and that the next attack on American soil would be a catastrophic event.[40]

This finding was reinforced by a confidential report from British intelligence concerning two special agents who managed to infiltrate an al Qaeda training camp in Afghanistan by posing as recruits from a London mosque. After completing the training and taking the *bayat* (the oath of allegiance to the mujahideen), the agents were sent to Herat, where they visited a laboratory and witnessed al Qaeda scientists and technicians manufacturing nuclear weapons from radioactive isotopes—weapons that remain to be recovered.[41]

On February 11, 2003, bin Laden again made a guest appearance on Aljazeera to give his own sixteen-minute take on the "great battle" of Tora Bora:

> We were about three hundred mujahideen. We dug trenches that were spread in an area that does not exceed one square mile, one trench for every three brothers, so as to avoid the huge human losses resulting from the bombardment.
>
> Since the first hour of the U.S. campaign of 20 Rajab, 1422 [October 7, 2001], our centers were exposed to constant bombardment. And this bombardment continued until mid-Ramadan.
>
> On 17 Ramadan, a very fierce bombardment began, particularly after the U.S. command was informed that some of al Qaeda's leaders were still in Tora Bora, including the humble servant of God [referring to himself] and the brother *mujahad* Dr. Ayman al-Zawahiri.
>
> The bombardment was round the clock and the warplanes continued to fly over us day and night. The U.S. Pentagon, together with its allies, worked full-time on blowing up and destroying this small spot, as well as removing it entirely. Planes poured their lava on us, particularly after accomplishing their main mission in Afghanistan.
>
> The U.S. forces attacked us with smart bombs, bombs that weigh thousands of pounds, cluster bombs, and bunker blasters. Bombers, like the B-52, used to fly overhead for more than two hours and drop between twenty to thirty bombs at a time. The modified C-130 aircraft kept carpet-bombing us at night, using modern types of bombs.
>
> The U.S. dared not break into our positions, despite the unprecedented massive bombing and terrible propaganda targeting this completely besieged small area. This is in addition to the forces of hypocrites, whom they prodded to fight us for fifteen days nonstop. Every time they

attacked us, we forced them out of our area carrying their dead and wounded. Is there any clearer evidence of their cowardice, fear, and lies regarding their legends about their alleged power?

To sum it up, the battle resulted in the complete failure of the international alliance of evil, with all its forces, to overcome a small number of mujahideen—three hundred mujahideen—hunkered down in trenches spread over an area of one square mile under a temperature of minus ten degrees Celsius.

The battle resulted in the injury of 6 percent of personnel—we hope Allah will accept them as martyrs—and the damage of 2 percent of our trenches, praise be to Allah.

If all the world forces of evil could not achieve their goals on a one square mile of area against a small number of mujahideen with very limited capabilities, how can these evil forces triumph over the Muslim world? This is impossible, Allah willing, if people adhere to their religion and insist on jihad for its sake.[42]

President Bush had allowed bin Laden to "go away and come again another day" by relying on the double-minded Pakistani president Musharraf and failing to deploy U.S. troops to cut off the escape route to Pakistan. Bin Laden could have been contained to an area of several dozen miles rather than an area that snakes around forty thousand square miles.[43] The victory to the war was within Bush's grasp, but he had been too dumb to realize it. The president, with his natural tendency to delegate duties, had relied upon Donald Rumsfeld and Tommy Franks to direct the course of military operations and to make the key decisions. Few military commanders, including George B. McClellan and George Armstrong Custer, have been more inept or more adept at making disastrous military tactics than this pair of dunces.

MENDACITY AND A MISGUIDED MISSION

The blunders in Afghanistan would not end with Operation Enduring Freedom. They would continue with the next ill-fated offensive that was dubbed Operation Anaconda. It was a campaign that came from the CIA's bag of bad intelligence. The bad intelligence this time was provided by Badshah Khan Zadran, another Afghan warlord who milked millions from the great cash cow that George W. Bush had sent into his poverty ridden and war-scarred country. Zadran informed his CIA contacts that thousands of al Qaeda and Taliban soldiers—the very ones who had fled Tora Bora—had regrouped in the mountainous terrain of Shah-i-Kot in preparation for striking U.S. military bases and toppling the shaky interim government of Hamid Karzai.[44]

Only complete idiots (such as the men in black suits and shades with attaché cases stuffed with cash) would have received information from Zadran without some degree of suspicion. On December 20, 2001, Zadran triggered a missile attack on a convoy of Paktia elders that left sixty-five dead. The elders, as it turned out, were aligned neither to bin Laden nor Mullah Omar. They were Khan's political rivals who had resisted his attempt to add Gardez, the central city of Paktia, to his fiefdom.[45]

The plans for Operation Anaconda called for coalition forces to encircle the camps of al Qaeda and the Taliban like a huge snake in order to squeeze them to death. This would require the creation of a vast ring of military units that would encompass an area of seventy-two miles—an area that at one point reached an altitude of two thousand feet.

Things did not go as planned—at least, not as planned by the Pentagon. As soon as the operation began on March 2, 2002, U.S. military officials began receiving reports of unexpected, heavy resistance. One American soldier and four members of the Northern Alliance were killed. The fighting was said to be heaviest at Operation Position Ginger, where an advance unit of the Tenth Mountain Division was bogged down in mud under enemy fire. Original intelligence reports appeared to be wrong. Instead of a few hundred al Qaeda and Taliban forces at Shah-i-Kot, U.S. officials now believed that thousands had gathered to stage a massive counteroffensive.

Coalition ground forces summoned air support, and within the first twenty-four hours, more than two hundred bombs, including a two-thousand-pound thermobatic bomb, were dropped on Position Ginger. U.S. commanders were now convinced that the advance unit had stumbled into a hornet's nest, the last stronghold of enemy resistance. Of course, this appraisal lacked an ounce of common sense. It implied that two of the most-wanted groups of radical Islamists could wander into a war zone and set up shop within twenty miles of Gardez, a busy provincial city, under the nose of the most sophisticated military unit in the world.[46] But such matters defied analysis. Crazier things had happened—like bin Laden walking away free and clear with thousands of his soldiers from his besieged hideout at Tora Bora.

Simple Math Mistakes

By the sixth day of the great battle of Shah-i-Kot, the White House announced that al Qaeda and the Taliban were being systematically decimated and that more than eight hundred enemy bodies were strewn over the mountain terrain. Commenting on the high number of dead terrorists, Secretary of Defense Donald Rumsfeld modestly said that he did not want to get into the "numbers game" but could say with absolute certainty that "hundreds" had been killed during the opening days of the conflict.[47] Not to be outdone by Rumsfeld's remarks, Maj. Gen. Frank Hagenbeck, commander of the coalition force, said that "hundreds" were "confirmed dead" and that the actual number could not be stated, "because of the types of killing that went on—with laser guided bombs, for example."[48] Throughout the operation, the enemy death toll, as a reporter from the *New York Times* put it, came to rise and fall like "the fluctuations of a troubled currency: 100, 500, 200, 800, 300."[49]

As the fighting continued, megaton bombs were dropped at the increased rate of 260 a day. At a March 8, 2002, press conference, President Bush said: "These people evidently don't want to give up, and that's okay. If that's their attitude, we'll just have to adjust, and they'll have made a mistake."[50]

Victory Without Victims

Reports of the tenaciousness of the enemy now convinced President Bush and Rumsfeld that bin Laden and Mullah Omar had taken refuge in a bunker or a cave and that the terrorists were fighting to the last man in order to protect and defend them.[51]

It took ten days of fighting for the United States to gain the upper hand. By that time the coalition forces reported that eleven soldiers had been killed, eight of them American, and eighty-eight had been wounded. In the Pentagon, a growing sense of euphoria arose that a monumental battle had been won and that the tide of the war had been turned.

When the battle came to an end on March 12, 2002, Gen. Tommy Franks hailed Operation Anaconda as "an unqualified and absolute success."[52] Maj. Gen. Frank Hagenbeck added, "The world is a safer place than it was on the second of March when we inserted several thousand coalition forces—including soldiers, sailors, airmen, and marines—that put their lives on the line to confront al Qaeda and Taliban terrorists."[53]

All for Naught?

On March 18, the last day of maneuvers, coalition commanders were faced with a bewildering mystery. The resistance had been fierce. Hundreds of enemy soldiers had been confirmed dead. The escape route to Pakistan had been sealed. And yet only ten—that's right, ten—enemy soldiers were taken prisoner and, what's worse, fewer than twenty bodies were found in the battle zone. "There were no dead al Qaeda fighters," a USA Today reporter wrote from eastern Afghanistan. "There were no fresh graves. Just one macabre reminder stuck out: dried blood on a patch of dirt here in the village."[54]

The absence of hundreds of corpses and the scant number of prisoners gave rise to several theories: (1) the fighters had escaped before the start of the full military offensive, (2) the spotting of the bodies by military observers had been either hype or hallucination, or (3) the 3,250 bombs had been dropped on a site that was almost totally uninhabited.[55] General Franks bore the brunt of widespread criticism, with the British press saying that his reliance on Afghan warlords with ambiguous loyalties represented "the greatest error in the war."[56] But the general was reluctant to wipe the egg from his face. When the coffins of the dead soldiers from Operation Anaconda arrived in the United States for burial, Franks said, "Our thoughts and prayers go out to the families and friends of those who lost their lives in our ongoing operations in Vietnam."[57] He failed to acknowledge his error of mistaking Afghanistan for Vietnam, but few slips of the tongue from military commanders were more telling.

THE POPPY FIELDS

In truth, the greatest error in the war had yet to be committed. It occurred after the full-scale military operations came to a close in the spring of 2002 when the coalition forces surveyed the 30,750 hectares in the southern and eastern provinces that were flowering with poppies.[58] Each hectare would yield forty-one kilograms of opium—enough to fund the jihad for years to come.

Before bin Laden's return to Afghanistan in 1996, the Turkish *bubas* controlled the flow of drugs from Afghanistan through northern Iran and Turkey to Sofia, the Bulgarian capital, from which the Sicilian Mafia transported the product to Greece and Yugoslavia for shipment to Western Europe, the United States, and elsewhere. It was an incredibly lucrative enterprise. For decades, agents of such illustrious Sicilian dons as Luciano Liggio, Salvatore Runna, Bernardo Provenzano, Nitto Santapaola, and the Farrar brothers could be seen wheeling and dealing with the *bubas* in the opulent lobby of the Hotel Vitosha in Sofia.[59]

But those heady days were gone. The Sicilians began having serious difficulty in moving the shipments from Bulgaria because of the prolonged conflict in the Balkans. To compound matters, the key suppliers of the product—the Afghan warlords—had been driven from power by the Taliban.

As a result, ethnic Albanians (all of whom were Muslims) gained control of the drug trade by carving out a new smuggling route that bypassed the peninsula's war zones. Known as the Balkan route, it ran from Bulgaria through Kosovo and into Albania, Greece, and Yugoslavia. From Yugoslavia, the route continued to Western Europe.[60] In 1990 Hungarian police confiscated 14 pounds of heroin from Albania smugglers. By 1994 the amount confiscated from these same smugglers rose to 1,304 pounds.[61]

Like its counterpart in the United States, the Sicilian Mafia became a spent power, a thing of the past. Proof of this came with the ability of the Albanians to gain control of key branches of the Sicilian organization, including *Sacra Corona* in Corona, directly across the Otranto Canal from Albania,[62] and the fact that they took over the Italian prostitution operation in Italy before the once-great dons could utter a word of protest, let alone squeeze a trigger.[63] The same development occurred in America, where the Albanian Mafia gained ascendancy over La Cosa Nostra to become the chief perpetrator of such crimes as drug smuggling, counterfeiting, forgery, trafficking in human body parts, sex slavery, abduction, gun running, and murder.[64]

Bin Laden, on behalf of the Taliban and his fellow jihadists, forged a business alliance with the Turks and the Albanians during his visit to the Balkans in 1996. He ensured a continuous flow of narcotics from the golden crescent by establishing an alternative route (known as the Abkhaz drug route) from Afghanistan to the port city of Sukhumi in the breakaway Georgian province of Abhaz, where it would be loaded on ships, under the watchful eyes of the *bubas,* for transport to Famagusta in northern Cyprus. There the crystallized cakes would be broken down into small packets by the Albanians for worldwide distribution.[65]

Upon bin Laden's return to Afghanistan, heroin started to flow into Sofia and Famagusta at the rate of six metric tons a month.[66] The drug market quickly became saturated. Business boomed while prices dropped. By the end of 1996 prisons throughout Europe were filled with Muslim drug dealers from the Balkans. In Germany alone, more than eight hundred ethnic Albanians were cooling their heels behind bars for possession of an average of 124 grams of product.[67]

Since the greatest demand was for number-four heroin, bin Laden established sophisticated laboratories near Kabul and recruited chemists from China, Pakistan, and Russia to refine the raw paste into choice powder. Mullah Omar ordered Afghan farmers to produce "all the opium they could grow."[68] By 1997 the poppy harvest climbed to 3,276 tons, with the Taliban reaping annual profits in excess of five billion dollars.[69] In 1998 Yossef Bodansky, director of the U.S. Congressional Task Force on Terrorism and Unconventional Warfare, issued the following information: "The Afghans are selling 7 to 8 billion dollars of drugs in the West a year. Bin Laden oversees the export of drugs from Afghanistan. His people are involved in growing the crops, processing, and shipping. When Americans buy drugs, they fund the jihad."[70]

On July 27, 2000, Mullah Omar announced his decision to ban the growing of opium poppies within the Islamic emirate of Afghanistan. This news was greeted by cheers from the United Nations, who hailed the announcement as a major step in curtailing the sale and distribution of heroin. After the enactment of the prohibition, a handful of farmers were arrested and paraded before the press as testimony to the Taliban's resolve. But the prohibition was only a ploy by Mullah Omar to gain U.N. recognition for his rogue regime. Indeed, NATO satellite surveillance showed that more surface areas of farming throughout Afghanistan were devoted to growing opium poppies in 2000 than any previous year.[71]

THE BLIND EYE

Every intelligence official in the United States knew that the poppy fields were the central source of funding for the jihad and a primary source of crime throughout the world. So what happened to the fields during the occupation and the propping up of the government of former warlord Hamid Karzai? Were the fields firebombed and covered with lye? Were they sprayed with mycoherbicides (not genetically engineered but taken from nature) that could destroy the crops at the meager cost of forty thousand dollars? Were the laboratories for the processing of the heroin destroyed and the narco-chemists sent packing? Of course not. The heroin business after the U.S. invasion boomed as never before. By 2004, production had reached five thousand tons—an all-time high—when Congressman Mark Steven Kirk issued this statement to his colleagues: "The Afghans are selling 7 to 8 billion dollars of drugs in the West a year. Bin Laden oversees the export of drugs from Afghanistan. His people are involved in growing the crops, processing, and shipping. When Americans buy drugs, they fund the jihad."[72]

Even in the wake of Kirk's comments, the Bush administration adopted no measures to eradicate the opium poppies even though the fields of red flowers remained in full view of the U.S. troops and the location of the laboratories for the refinement of the opium paste was known by practically every peasant farmer and street peddler.

Think about it. In one move, George Bush and company could wipe out the source of funding for radical Islam and leave bin Laden and the mujahideen without the means to implement another full-scale attack. But this isn't likely to happen. Sure, the White House allocates seventy-five million dollars a year for opium destruction. But not a dime is spent to address the real source of the problem. Most is squandered by the formation of committees, including the Pakistani-Afghani-U.S. committee, which has its headquarters in Kabul.

Destruction of the poppy fields, as Bush and Rumsfeld well knew, would mean the financial collapse of a country in which opium production constitutes more than 60 percent of the GNP.[73] It would cause economic earthquakes and financial disaster for a host of other Islamic countries, including Albania, Chechnya, Pakistan, and Turkey. And no one in the White House is in a mood to annoy more Muslims (especially the warlords in Afghanistan, the mullahs in Pakistan, and the *bubas* in Turkey).

BLUNDER 9

Leaving Open the Back Door to America

While the vast majority of illegals from the Middle East are not terrorists, the fact that tens of thousands of people from that region—and millions more from the rest of the world—can settle in the U.S. illegally means that terrorists who wish to do so face few obstacles. We cannot protect ourselves from terrorism without dealing with illegal immigration.

Stephen A. Camarota, director of research, the
Center for Immigration Studies, November 2004

In the first place we should insist that if the immigrant who comes here in good faith becomes an American and assimilates himself to us, he shall be treated on an exact equality with everyone else, for it is an outrage to discriminate against any such man because of creed, or birthplace, or origin. But this is predicated upon the man's becoming in very fact an American and nothing but an American. . . . There can be no divided allegiance here. Any man who says he is an American, but something else also, isn't an American at all. We have room for but one flag, the American flag, and this excludes the red flag, which symbolizes all wars against liberty and civilization, just as much as it excludes any foreign flag of a nation to which we are hostile. . . . We have room for but one language here, and that is the English language . . . and we have room for but one sole loyalty, and that is a loyalty to the American people.

Theodore Roosevelt, 1907

B Y THE TIME OF the millennium, the Albanian Mafia—with ties to radical Islam—replaced La Cosa Nostra (LCN) as the "leading crime outfit in the United States."[1] This development was the result of the FBI's success in busting the Sicilian mob. By 2001 the number of LCN families in the United States shrank from twenty-four to nine. The crackdown resulted in the incarceration of more than one hundred leading dons and capos and six hundred of their associates. John Gotti of the Gambino family died of throat cancer in prison. Vincent Chin Giganti, the "Odd Father" and head of the Genovese crime family, was sentenced to hard time for murder and labor racketeering. Steven Crea, the Lucchese head, remained in a state penitentiary on charges of enterprise corruption. Alphonse "Allie Boy" Persico, the Colombo capo, was behind bars for gun possession and loan sharking. And Joseph Massino, the Bonnano boss, was facing charges regarding three gangland killings.

THE ISLAMIC MAFIA

The successful prosecution of these cases created a void in the crime industry that was quickly filled by the Albanians who had worked as enforcers and triggermen for the leading LCN families. Zef Mustafa, for example, had served as the chief "clipper" (assassin) for the Gambinos. His capacity for violence was only equaled by his capacity for booze. Zed drank from morning to night, consuming two or three bottles of vodka before falling into a stupor.[2] While serving a stint in prison, he used the resources of the Gambinos to organize a $650 million Internet and phone sex heist by the use of pornographic Web sites and 1-800 sex numbers. Zef was arrested in 2002, pleaded guilty to fraud, and was sentenced to five years in the big house.

Abedin "Dino" Kolbiba also served as a Gambino hired gun. He was so adept at executing a hit and the fine art of making a corpse disappear without a trace that his talents were in demand by the four other New York LCN families.[3] Dino himself performed a vanishing act as soon as his name appeared on the FBI's Most Wanted list.

The ruthlessness of the Albanians was well illustrated by Simon and Victor Deday, two brothers who worked cleanup for the Gambinos. On one occasion the Dedays pulled out their .357 magnums and shot a waiter at Brooklyn's Scores restaurant because they were dissatisfied with the service. For good measure, they also plugged the bouncer on their way to the parking lot.[4]

By 1990 radical Muslim émigrés from Albania became the new kings of the drug underworld on the East Coast. Skender Fici ran a travel agency in New York that served as a front for a billion-dollar business in narcotics. Fici was well served by his countrymen, including Is-mail Liva. Caught with a stash of $125 million in number-four heroin, Fici and Liva ordered a hit on the New York detectives who arrested them and the federal prosecutors who had managed to send them to prison.[5]

Daut Kadriovski, another member of the Albanian Mafia, escaped from a German lockup in 1993 to travel to America, where he established a drug business in the Bronx. By 1998 his business had become so lucrative that he set up branch offices in cities throughout the country, including Chicago, Detroit, Philadelphia, Richmond, Trenton, and Washington DC.[6]

Members of the LCN families and other ethnic crime groups freely admitted their fear of the Albanians. Speaking anonymously to a reporter from the *City Paper* in Philadelphia, a prominent member of the "Kielbasa Posse," an ethnic Polish mob, maintained that his organization was willing to conduct business with "just about anyone," including blacks, Asians, Hispanics, Russians, and even Chechens, but they refused to go anywhere near the Albanian Mafia. "They are too violent and unpredictable," he said.[7]

In addition to taking over the drug business, counterfeiting and forgery, prostitution and sex slavery rackets, illegal weapons and firearms sales, and the underground commerce in human body parts, the Albanians, like their LCN predecessors, gained control over major ports of entry into the United States. This development accounts for the fact that America has witnessed a 40 percent *increase* in the flow of drugs from the golden crescent wake of 9/11.

HOMELAND INSECURITY

Despite repeated high security alerts, America, at the close of 2005, continued to possess "zip-port security."[8] Stephen Flynn, senior fellow for national security studies at the U.S. Council of Foreign Affairs, observed: "The United States has 16,000 ships entering its ports every day. Adding in shipments entering by truck, train or air freight, the total number of import shipments to the United States is 21.4 million tons a year. You could put a nuclear or chemical weapon aboard a ship leaving Karachi, and that ship will land at Vancouver, Oakland, San Francisco, or the Gulf Coast, and we would never know the difference." Flynn went on to say that less that 3 percent of shipping containers ever get inspected—even the containers of ships arriving from the Middle East."[9] And many of the containers that are earmarked for inspection have been singled out by arrangement with the Albanian mob. The same situation exists at U.S. airports, where the Albanians have gained control of incoming cargo and where less than 25 percent of the freight from private planes is ever inspected.[10] Surely no country in history, not even ancient Rome when the barbarians were at the gates, has been so complacent in the midst of a time of war.

There are problems at other ports and places of entry as well, including the country's porous borders. This is hardly surprising. If George W. Bush and company were reluctant to deploy American troops to secure the border between Afghanistan and Pakistan at the height of Operation Enduring Freedom, why should anyone think they would closely monitor the illegal passageways between the United States and its friendly neighbors? This oversight, perhaps, represents the greatest blunder of all—a blunder that could be the cause of the greatest and most powerful nation on earth losing the war with the forces of Islam.

CIUDAD DEL ESTE: RED HOT GOODS

The problem with the southern border began in 1995 when Osama bin Laden traveled to South America to plant a cell of al Qaeda in the so-called Triangle of Argentina, Brazil, and Paraguay. The central city in the Triangle is Ciudad Del Este in Paraguay. At this writing, it continues to be a major base for the shipment of Bolivian cocaine via hidden landing strips that have been carved out of the rain forest. Within the stores and galleries of this dingy jungle city, one can purchase a bottle of the finest French champagne for ten bucks, Nike and Adidas gym shoes for five dollars, bootlegged CDs of favorite pop artists for a dollar, and even a Steinway piano for the price of a cut-rate concertina. Within Ciudad Del Este, a shopper can buy smuggled electronic goods from Miami and stolen sports cars from Brazil. A Mercedes E55 AMG with a sticker price of eighty-one thousand dollars can be driven away by anyone with seven thousand or eight thousand dollars in his pocket. It's small surprise that half of the 450,000 cars in Paraguay have been acquired illegally. Here one can also obtain rare and endangered animals, prescription drugs and packets of heroin, land mines, assault rifles, and antiaircraft guns.[11]

Despite its population of 240,000, Ciudad Del Estate boasts fifty-five banks and foreign exchange companies. U.S. officials believe that more than six billion dollars a year in illegal funds are laundered here, an amount equivalent to 50 percent of Paraguay's gross domestic product.[12]

Directly across the Parana River from Ciudad Del Estate is Foz do Iguaçu, Brazil, a city of 190,000. The golden domes and high minarets that rise from the mosques in this lush jungle setting appear as bizarre and incongruous as the sight of the magnificent Teatro Amazonas Opera House within the scruffy port town of Manaus. Muslims began to migrate to Foz do Iguaçu in 1975, at the outbreak of the civil war in Lebanon. By 2005 the Islamic population had swollen to 60,000.[13]

Day and night, the rusty iron Bridge of Friendship (*Puente de la Amistad*) that connects the two cities is packed with peddlers, merchants, and smugglers transporting boxes of stolen goods without the slightest scrutiny from any customs agent or law-enforcement official. The goods include plasma televisions, computers, iPods, American cigarettes, digital cameras, laser tools, designer jeans, and leather jackets. There are other goods as well, including choice Colombian marijuana, hashish, and cocaine for drug dealers to ship to Puerto Paranagua on Brazil's Atlantic coast.[14]

To reach Puerto Iguaçu, Argentina, the third city within the Triangle, a visiting mobster, criminal on the lam, or jihadist must cross the Tancredo Neves International Bridge from Foz do Iguaçu. This small city with a population of twenty-eight thousand is the perfect place to pick up a counterfeit passport from corrupt Argentine government officials for the measly sum of five thousand dollars.[15] Such passports, under the present visa waiver program, open the portals to the Magic Kingdom north of the Mexican border.

HEZBOLLAH DISCOVERS AMERICA

In 1983 Hezbollah (the Shi'ite "Party of God") became the first terrorist group to establish a base in the New World. Funded by the Iranian

Revolutionary Guard under Ayatollah Khomeini, the group was delighted to discover the lawless city of Foz do Iguaçu with its surrounding jungle to be an ideal place to train new recruits in guerrilla warfare and to raise money for the jihad to ward off Israeli and American forces in Lebanon.[16] Not only was the city remote from scrutiny by U.S. and Israeli intelligence, but also the Brazilian government was kind enough to recognize Hezbollah as a legitimate political party. Therefore, all contributions to the terrorist organization are in full accordance with the law.[17]

After setting up shop in Latin America, Hezbollah wasted no time in establishing business relations with the drug cartels from Colombia, Ecuador, Paraguay, and Uruguay and with paramilitary groups such as the Revolutionary Armed Forces of Colombia (FARC) and Peru's Shining Star (*Sendero Luminosos*).[18] The drug lords and the revolutionaries sought weapons that Hezbollah could provide, and Hezbollah sought cocaine that it could sell throughout the Middle East and Europe through its Sicilian connections.[19]

With money, munitions, and recruits flowing into its Brazilian cell, Hezbollah began to launch major attacks in Buenos Aires. One attack against the Israeli Embassy on March 17, 1992, killed 29 people and wounded 242; a second against the AMIA Jewish Center on July 18, 1994, killed 86 and wounded 250.[20]

Osama bin Laden arrived in the Triangle in 1995 after forming an alliance with Hezbollah. He spent three days visiting the mosques of Foz do Iguaçu, meeting with the local Hezbollah officials, and attending meetings with leaders of the various drug cartels in Ciudad Del Este. News of his visit was first reported by CNN,[21] but its significance remained beyond the comprehension of the international press.

In 2003, eight years after the visit, *Vega*, Brazil's leading weekly newspaper, published photographs from a twenty-eight-minute video that had been taken to commemorate the event. In the photographs, bin Laden appears in his traditional *shalwat kameez,* but he sports a rather well-trimmed goatee rather than the scruffy beard that he grew when he returned to Afghanistan in 1996.[22]

In recent years the municipal leaders of Foz do Iguaçu have attempted to capitalize on bin Laden's stay by running full-page ads in international newspapers with a photograph of the smiling terrorist chief and the caption: "When he's not blowing up the world, Osama bin

Laden enjoys himself. If bin Laden risked his neck to visit Foz do Iguaçu, it means it is worthwhile! Everyone wants to see it. Why haven't you come?"[23]

THE IMPLANTED AL QAEDA CELLS

Khalid Shaikh Mohammad, bin Laden's military operations chief, became the next al Qaeda official to visit the Triangle. He arrived on December 4, 1995, for a three-week stay in order to meet with local Hezbollah leaders to make plans for attacks on the United States and Canada. One plan called for a series of bombings in Ottawa "to undermine the Middle East peace process."[24] A second plot called for the bombing of the Los Angeles International Airport. Neither plan came to fruition, thanks largely to the arrest of Ahmed Ressam of Montreal, who was collared by border officials while trying to smuggle massive amounts of explosives from British Columbia into the United States.[25]

Despite the failure of the planned attacks to materialize, Khalid Mohammad's visit remained a resounding success. It resulted in the establishment of two Sunni terrorist cells in Foz do Iguaçu. The first was a branch of al-Gama'a al-Islamiyya, a sister agency of al Qaeda. This cell was headed by al-Said Ali Hassan Mokhles, who had been trained by the mujahideen for fifteen months in Afghanistan. From 1995 to 2002, Mokhles kept in close contact with the al Qaeda high command. Copies of his communiqués were discovered by U.S. intelligence officials with the arrest of Khalid Shaikh Mohammad in Karachi on March 2, 2003.[26]

The second cell was also a branch of al-Gama'a al-Islamiyya. It was placed under the command of Mohamed Ali Aboul-Ezz al-Mahdi Ibrahim Soliman, an Egyptian national and close friend of Ayman al-Zawahiri.

Eventually, the continuous communication between the al Qaeda high command in Afghanistan and the terrorist cells in the South American Triangle led to a seamless terrorist highway that ran from the Port of Iquique in Chile, through the Argentina-Brazil-Paraguay Triangle, north through the Brazilian jungle, then branched out to Colombia, Guyana, Honduras, Mexico, Panama, Surinam, and Venezuela. Within Mexico, the route led to a passageway through the Sierra Madre that emptied into Cochise County, Arizona.

OSAMA'S BABY BROTHER

A host of other al Qaeda luminaries eventually made their way to the Triangle, including Khalil bin Laden, Osama's younger brother, who owns a twenty-acre estate in Winter Garden, Florida. Khalil's visits usually included outings to Minas Gerias, the site of an al Qaeda training camp in the Brazilian outback, where he engaged in "suspicious business activities."[27] The younger bin Laden developed a close relationship with Brazilian officials, married a Brazilian, and became Brazil's honorary council in the Saudi Arabian city of Jeddah in 1998.[28]

As an honorary council, Khalil may have served in establishing close connections between Brazilian president Luiz Inácio Lula da Silva (affectionately known as Lula) and nuclear madman Abdul Qadeer Khan. Khan eventually sold his centrifuge technology and blueprints for a nuclear bomb to Lula, who supports anti-U.S. activities throughout the world. *Science* magazine predicts that Brazil will be capable of producing five to six nuclear warheads at its Resende facility by the end of 2006.[29]

On September 20, 2001, Khalil bin Laden, although named as a key terror suspect, received permission from the Bush administration to board a chartered jet from Saudi Arabia, along with fourteen other members of the bin Laden family, and depart the United States. U.S. intelligence officials have never questioned Osama's younger brother. And President Bush did not want to disturb his Saudi friends by subjecting members of the bin Laden clan to cold showers and straight-chair interrogations. In this way, the latest dunce in the White House prevented the CIA from obtaining information of strategic importance to the war against radical Islam.

An opportunity was lost that could not be recovered. Eighteen months after Bush waved good-bye to the bin Ladens at the airport, Bosnian police seized documents from the Muslim Benevolence International Foundation in Sarajevo. One document contained a list of the top twenty financial supporters of al Qaeda. Near the top of the list was Khalil bin Laden's name.[30]

THE CELLS METASTASIZE

The two cells that had been implanted by al Qaeda within the belly of

South America quickly metastasized so that the cancer of radical Islam spread to other places in Brazil and Paraguay. One such location was Pedro Juan Cabrallero on the northern border between the two countries—a jungle town renowned for its potent marijuana and its absence of law enforcement.[31] Another was the Brazilian village of Chui, near the Uruguayan border, with a population of fifteen hundred Muslims and a mayor who purportedly served as an agent for bin Laden.

Within Paraguay, officials of the Silvio Pettiriosi International Airport in Asunción reported regular arrivals of individuals from the Middle East with European passports. When questioned by immigration officials, the newcomers spoke fluent Arabic but were unable to communicate in the language of the land listed on their identification papers.[32]

By 2001 the cancer had spread to nearly every country in South America. The once sleepy town of Iquique in Chile became a center for money-laundering activities by Muslim terrorists. It was designated by the Bush administration as a "hot spot" for radical Islam south of the border, second only to the Triangle.[33]

Within a year, Peru loomed as a place of even greater concern after investigators discovered evidence that Vladimiro Montesinos, the former head of Peruvian intelligence, had allowed bin Laden to purchase a host of homes and apartment buildings to serve as safe havens for his terrorist network. In one of the secretly recorded conversations that led to Montesinos's arrest on charges of money laundering, bribery, and terrorism, Montesinos told the mayor of the Peruvian port city of Callao that "bin Laden's center of importance in Latin America is here in Lima."[34] He went on to explain that bin Laden's center in Lima had been established "to act against Americans in Argentina, Brazil, Chile, and the rest of South America."[35] By the close of 2001, Peruvian authorities realized that the corrupt spy chief had received millions for his assistance from al Qaeda cells throughout the country.[36]

The risk of Bolivia as a terror threat was elevated from low to moderate in 2002 when Bolivian officials arrested nine Bangladeshis in La Paz. As it turned out, they were involved in a plan to hijack a jumbo jet for an attack on an American target in Argentina. The Bangladeshis were members of a virulent al Qaeda cell with tentacles throughout Bolivia and ties to the country's illegal and highly lucrative drug trade.[37]

Ecuador, rated by the CIA as Latin America's second most corrupt country (superceded only by Paraguay), is also a haven for radical Islam. This was evidenced by the case of Lago Agrio, once a picturesque village in a tropical rain forest, now a fetid dump after years of oil drilling and exploration by the Chevron Texaco Corporation. From 1964 to 1992, Texaco reportedly spilled eighteen billion gallons of toxic by-products throughout the flora, fauna, and waterways.[38] The toxic village, with its rotting infrastructures and lack of law enforcement, no longer could attract oil speculators, international entrepreneurs, or wealthy American terrorism. But it represented an ideal breeding place for al Qaeda. Texaco terrorism gave way to Islamic terrorism as Lago Agrio, with its population of twenty-eight thousand, experienced an influx of hundreds of holy warriors from the Middle East. Overnight the village became a center for drug trafficking, arms dealing, smuggling, and money laundering—and with a murder rate in excess of one hundred a year—one of the most dangerous places on earth.[39]

In Colombia, according to Gen. Rosso Jose Cerraro, the country's former chief of police, hundreds of bin Laden's Arab Afghani comrades have relocated with false identification papers. They came to work with the drug lords to oversee the planting, cultivation, and harvesting of poppy fields (from the seeds they brought with them) and the establishment of laboratories for the refinement of the raw opium paste into number-four heroin. The poppy fields throughout the Colombian mountains bear an exact resemblance to the fields in Afghanistan, giving positive proof to the symbiotic relationship between international terrorism and organized crime.[40] Thanks to radical Islam, Colombia in recent years has become the third-largest exporter of heroin in the world.

ISLAMIC LATIN CONQUEST NEARS COMPLETION

Radical Islam also reared its hoary head in French Guiana, Guyana, Surinam, Tobago, and Trinidad. The case of Surinam, a small country—the size of the state of Georgia—with a population of 437,000, is particularly telling. By 2005, nearly 40 percent of the population was Muslim. Along with the minarets and mosques appeared cells of Shi'ite and Sunni terrorism, including an al Qaeda link to Jemaah Islamiyah, the group responsible for the 2002 Bali bombing. The Chechen Mafia, thanks to an invitation from bin Laden, also set up operations in Surinam, where the price of an AK-47 became one kilogram of cocaine.[41]

But no place in the Western Hemisphere proved to be more worrisome than Venezuela. On January 5, 2003, Venezuelan air force Maj. Juan Diaz Castillo, the personal pilot of Venezuela's President Hugo Chavez, blurted out that Chavez had awarded al Qaeda a gift of one million dollars from the national treasury in the wake of 9/11. The gift was conveyed to bin Laden through Walter Marquez, the Venezuelan ambassador to India.[42] This news was not surprising to observers of Latin America. On September 12, 2001, Chavez supporters celebrated the terrorist attack by burning an American flag in Caracas's Plaza Bolivar.[43] When U.S.-led forces invaded Afghanistan, Chavez decried them as "terrorists."[44] In 2002 Chavez and Fidel Castro visited such radical Muslim nations as Iran, Iraq, and Libya, where Chavez signed a cooperative agreement while Castro told the cheering throngs, "Together we will bring America to its knees."[45]

Reports about Venezuela kept getting worse. On February 13, 2004, a Muslim extremist with ties to al Qaeda was arrested at London's Gatwick Airport after a grenade was found in his luggage. His ticket showed that he had flown to London from Colombia. British officials later learned that he was a Venezuelan who had been trained at an al Qaeda cell on Venezuela's Margarita Island, a place that had served as a haven for American tourists.[46] Bin Laden's agents were alive and well and less than a three-hour flight from the United States.

In the wake of the arrest, British MI5 agents were sent to Venezuela to prevent the al Qaeda cell from running guns and cocaine into the United Kingdom. The agents discovered that shipments of highly sophisticated weapons were arriving for FARC and the Muslim terrorists on fishing boats off the virtually unguarded Venezuelan coastline.[47] The weapons, including surface-to-air missiles, were coming from North Korea.

Developments in South America show that radical Islam is pressing ever northward, closer and closer to the U.S. border. In December 2003 Canadian intelligence officials and Interpol informed Mexico that al Qaeda had established a series of cells within the country to mount the next 9/11. "The alert has been sounded," Jose Luis Santiago Vasconcelos, Mexico's top anticrime prosecutor, told the Associated Press.[48]

In May 2004, Honduran security minister Oscar Alvarez announced that police within his country had uncovered evidence that al Qaeda had infested Honduras and were recruiting men for the next attack on American soil.[49] "This is very serious," Alvarez said. "We are talking of Honduran citizens being prepared to commit terrorist acts. We understand that the recruits undergo a kind of 'brainwashing' in order to become Muslim followers and possible martyrs in attacks against civilians."[50]

THE NEXT MOHAMMED ATTA

In July 2004, Adnan el Shukrijumah, the al Qaeda operative who has been commissioned to spearhead the next 9/11, was spotted at an Internet café in Tegucigalpa, the capital of Honduras with members of Mara Salvatrucha, Latin America's most violent street gang.[51]

Adnan was born in Guyana, South America, on August 2, 1975—the firstborn of Gulshair el Shukrijumah, a forty-four-year-old radical Muslim cleric, and his sixteen-year-old wife. In 1985 Gulshair gathered his family and migrated to the United States, where he assumed duties as the imam of the infamous Al-Farouq Mosque (see chapter 1). In 1995 the Shukrijumah clan migrated to Miramar, Florida, where Gulshair became the spiritual leader of Majid al-Hijah, another radical mosque, and where Adnan made new friends, including Jose Padilla, who later launched a plan to detonate a radiological bomb in midtown Manhattan, and Mandhai Jokhan, who attempted to blow up several nuclear power plants in southern Florida.[52]

The aspiring terrorist attended flight schools in Florida and Norman, Oklahoma, with Mohammad Atta and the other 9/11 hijackers. He became an accomplished commercial jet pilot, although he never applied for a license with the Federal Aviation Administration.[53]

In April 2004 Adnan spent his spring break from Broward Community College in Panama, where he met with al Qaeda officials to assist in the plans for the next 9/11. He also found time for side trips to Guyana and Trinidad. The following month he received an associate degree in computer engineering—his education had been subsidized by the good citizens of southern Florida.[54]

In addition to collecting his degree, Adnan amassed passports from such places as Canada, Guyana, Saudi Arabia, Trinidad, and the United States. He also began to assume a number of aliases, including Abu

Arifi, Jafar al-Tayyar, and Mohammad Sher Mohammad Khan (the name that originally appeared on his FBI file).[55] He traveled to Saudi Arabia and Pakistan, where he met with Khalid Shaikh Mohammad, Ramzi Binalshign, and other members of al Qaeda's *shura* (planning council).[56] He also spent weeks in a training camp in Afghanistan where he mastered the knack of detonating explosives.[57]

The Nuclear Mission

Following the success of 9/11, Adnan el Shukrijumah received his commission to serve as the field commander for the next attack on U.S. soil—the so-called American Hiroshima. In preparation for this mission, he—along with fellow al Qaeda agents Anas al-Liby, Jaber A. Elbaneh, and Amer el-Maati—was sent to McMaster University in Hamilton, Ontario, a facility that housed a five-megawatt nuclear research reactor, the largest reactor of any educational facility in Canada.[58]

At McMaster University, where the al Qaeda agents may have registered under fictitious names, Shukrijumah and friends wasted no time in gaining access to the nuclear reactor and stealing more than 180 pounds of nuclear material for the creation of radiological bombs.[59]

In the course of Operation Enduring Freedom, U.S. military officials discovered the reoccurrence of Shukrijumah's name among "pocket litter"—documents and scraps of paper taken from prisoners and dead enemy soldiers.[60] The name failed to set off alarms until the arrest of Khalid Shaikh Mohammad in Karachi. From Mohammad's laptop the CIA obtained information concerning bin Laden's plan to create a "nuclear hell storm" throughout the United States. Unlike other attacks, the chain of command for this attack, Khalid Mohammad later told interrogators, answered directly to bin Laden, al-Zawahiri, and a mysterious scientist referred to as "Dr. X" (later identified as Dr. Abdul Qadeer Khan).[61] He also confessed that the commander for the next attack (an event he called the "American Hiroshima") was a naturalized American citizen named Jaafar Al-Tayyar ("Jafer the Pilot").[62]

A Chicken Sandwich in Colorado

The CIA soon learned that Jafer the Pilot was an alias for Adnan el

Shukrijumah, who had been sent by al Qaeda to study at McMaster with several other sleeper agents. By the time Canadian officials received word of the situation, it was too late—Shukrijumah and the other agents had hightailed it across the border into Buffalo, New York, where they remained sheltered by members of a local mosque.[63]

On March 21, 2004, Attorney General John Ashcroft and FBI director Robert Mueller issued a BOLO ("be on the lookout") for Shukrijumah, Amer el-Maati, and Abderraouf Jdey, the leader of the al Qaeda cell in Toronto.[64] Several days later, Shukrijumah and Jdey were spotted at a Denny's restaurant in Avon, Colorado, where one ordered a chicken sandwich and a salad. The restaurant manager described them as "demanding, rude, and obnoxious."[65]

One month later, the five-foot-four-inch Shukrijumah resurfaced at a terrorist summit in the lawless Waziristan Province of Pakistan. The meeting was described by the FBI as a "pivotal planning session" in much the same manner as a 2000 meeting in Kuala Lumpur was for the 9/11 attacks. In attendance at the meeting were Mohammed Junaid Babar, who has since been charged with buying materials to build bombs for attacks in England, and Abu Issa al-Hindi, a Pakistani technician whose computer contained plans for attacks at financial institutions in New York, New Jersey, and Washington DC.[66]

Shukrijumah was next spotted at an Internet café in Honduras. From Tegucigalpa, he made his way north to Belize, and from there to Mexico's Quintana Roo state, south of Cancun.[67]

The Missing Plane

The man in charge of the next 9/11 remained in Mexico for much of the summer. In late August he was spotted in the northern region of Sonora near the U.S. border.[68] Alberto Chapetti of the U.S. Consulate in Nogales issued warnings of the presence of the terrorist in the area and posted a five-million-dollar reward for tips leading to his arrest.[69]

Concerns about Shukrijumah's extended vacation in Mexico were heightened by the arrest in Pakistan of Sharif al-Masri in November 2004. Al-Masri, an Egyptian national with close ties to Ayman al-Zawahiri, informed his CIA interrogators that al Qaeda had made arrangements to smuggle nuclear weapons into Mexico. From Mexico, the weapons were to be transported across the border by members of Mara Salvatrucha, the gang that Shukrijumah had trekked across the North American continent to meet with in a small, nondescript Honduran café.[70]

In response to this information, U.S. border patrol members began to monitor all heavy trucks crossing the border, and Mexican officials pledged to keep a close watch on flight schools and aviation facilities. But the cat was already out of the bag. On November 1, 2004, a Piper PA Pawnee crop duster was stolen from Ejido Queretaro near Mexicali. The plane's tail number was XBCYP. The thieves, Mexican police surmised, were either drug dealers or al Qaeda operatives, and one was clearly a trained pilot.[71]

THE ALIEN INVASION

Despite this development, the Bush administration paid little heed to these events. What was happening at the Rio Grande and other points of entry might just as well have been taking place in Middle Earth or a colony on the moon. George W. Bush was not about to lower an iron curtain at the border—not when the open passageway offered farmers, businessmen, and industrialists a continuous, steady supply of cheap labor for agricultural concerns, meatpacking plants, fast-food restaurants, sweatshops, and factories. "It's the economy, stupid," was the message that had been delivered to George H. W. Bush by Bill Clinton, and despite the fact that America might be on the brink of a nuclear holocaust, this was the one message that George W. Bush was not willing to forget.

And so the illegal immigration continued at an incredible rate throughout Bush's tenure. Every day he sat in the White House, more than four thousand illegals entered the United States through the back door—enough to fill sixty jumbo jetliners. This amounted to a total of more than three million a year.[72] Almost two hundred thousand were dubbed OTMs (other than Mexicans) by immigration officials.

The Muslim Migrants

In addition to the OTMs, thousands of others—known as SIAs (special interest aliens) also made their way into the country. SIAs came from terror-sponsoring countries that posed high national security concerns. These included Afghanistan, Egypt, Iran, Iraq, Jordan, Lebanon, Pakistan, Saudi Arabia, Somalia, Syria, and Yemen. The illegal passageways into the United States were littered with discarded Muslim prayer blankets, pages from the Koran, Arabic newspapers, and beverage boxes with Arabic letters.[73] Among the litter, one border guard in Texas discovered a jacket with an Arabic military badge that depicted a jet headed toward a tower with the words "Midnight Mission."[74]

Between October 1, 2002, and June 30, 2003, the Department of Homeland Security reported 4,226 SIAs had been apprehended at the Mexican and Canadian borders. By June 30, 2004, that number rose to 6,025, an increase of 42 percent.[75] Commenting on this development, Colorado Congressman Tom Tancredo observed: "One must take into account that, even by the most conservative estimates, the number of folks getting by the Border Patrol are two or three times the number caught. If so, at least 18,000 SIAs have entered America just in the first nine months of 2004."[76] By December 2005, Homeland Security confirmed that fifty-one terror suspects from various Middle Eastern countries had been nabbed at the border on a wide variety of charges that included smuggling weapons and illegally wiring large sums of money into the country.[77]

Catch and Release

Since space in detention cells remained at a premium, with thousands of illegals pouring over the border every day, the newly collared SIAs, along with Mexicans and OTMs, were released from custody as soon as they received hearing dates from immigration judges. Few local law-enforcement officials expressed surprise that 95 percent of the detainees failed to appear at their scheduled hearings.[78]

When complaints were raised about the wholesale release of SIAs, federal officials insisted that such detainees must be treated in the same way as illegals from countries that did not harbor or support terrorism. Asa Hutchinson, the undersecretary of Homeland Security in 2004, pointed out that the arrest of illegal migrants who appeared to come from the Middle East smacked of egregious insensitivity and betrayed an odious attitude of racial profiling.[79]

And so the crazy practice of catch and release continued day after day as code yellow gave way to code orange. More alarms were raised. Texas Congressman Solomon P. Ortiz, the highest-ranking Democrat on the House Armed Services Subcommittee on Readiness, confirmed that Middle Easterners with possible ties to al Qaeda were being arrested on a regular basis and then released for lack of jail space. "It's true," Ortiz said. "It is very reliable information from the horse's mouth, and it's happening all over the place. It's very, very scary, and members of Congress know about this. We have contacted several agencies, and I have talked to some people, but I can't say who."[80]

Such talk, no doubt, fell on deaf ears in Washington's corridors of power. The Bush administration allowed the situation to continue even after the arrest in April 2004 of Mohammed Junaid Babar, a leading al Qaeda operative, upon his return to Queens, New York, from the terrorist summit in Waziristan with Adnan el Shukrijumah. Babar, who was born and raised in Queens, had been commissioned to conduct a bombing campaign in London on the model of the 1995 attack on the Murrah Federal Building in Oklahoma City. Faced with seventy years in prison, Babar agreed to talk in exchange for admission into a witness protection program. He said that a spectacular attack on American soil—a nuclear 9/11—was planned for the near future and that key agents and nuclear materials were being smuggled into the country from Mexico.[81] This same information was confirmed by Sharif al-Masri several months later. But the Bush administration opted to pay scant attention to such reports. *It's the economy, stupid!* That message was foremost on the administration's agenda. What is a nuclear blast or two compared to an economic recession?

In June 2004 patrol guards from Willcox, Arizona, arrested seventy-seven individuals "of Middle Eastern descent." They were trekking through the Chiricahua Mountains with a caravan of hundreds of Mexican migrant workers. "These guys didn't speak English," a field agent explained, "and they were speaking to each other in Arabic. It's ridiculous we don't take this more seriously. We're told not to say a thing to the media." Another field agent added, "All the men had brand-new clothing and the exact same cut of mustache."[82]

By this time, Sheriff D'Wayne Jernigan of Del Rio, Texas, had a belly full of the catch-and-release program and expressed his frustration to the press:

> Are they criminals? Are they terrorists? We don't know who they are. The agency officials at this level here locally, I truly believe, are just as much against these releases as I am. They feel betrayed. They're thinking, "We work hard to apprehend these people, and then the next day someone at the Washington level orders their release." Why are we apprehending them in the first place? They turn these people loose with a piece of paper that tells them to report to an immigration hearing at an unknown time and place, and there's no way for an agency to get in touch with them again. Are they going to show up at those hearings? Will the agency ever be able to find them? Let's be realistic. It's ridiculous! A war on terrorism? Homeland security? Ha![83]

Asa Hutchinson responded to Sheriff Jernigan's outcry by insisting that the American people lack the "will" to "tell our law enforcement people to go out there and uproot those 8 million here—some of whom might have been here 8 to 12 years, who got kids here that are American citizens—and to send them out of the country."[84]

THE TALKING MULE

Maybe Americans have lost their will to fight, if not survive. Certainly the case of Farida Goolam Mohamed Ahmed should have raised an alarm throughout the country. But few cries were even raised within the hallowed halls of Congress. Ahmed, a Muslim woman, was arrested at the airport in McAllen, Texas, on July 28, 2004, when customs and border protection agents noticed that her South African passport was missing pages and lacked a stamp of official entry into the United States. Ahmed immediately confessed: "I did come illegally. I came through the bush."[85]

Ahmed was a terrorist courier who provided information and instruction from the mujahideen in the Middle East to an al Qaeda cell in New York. Several of her communiqués concerned plans for a major bombing operation in Midtown Manhattan. What's more, Ahmed had managed to sneak into the country not just once or twice but more than 250 times before she was finally collared.[86]

Fortunately, like Francis in the old movie series, Ahmed was not only a faithful mule but also a talking mule. Her interrogation led to the arrests of several al Qaeda agents in Mexico. These agents, along with Ahmed, were transported to one of the CIA's clandestine terrorist detention facilities.

BLUNDER 10

Failing to Declare War Against Radical Islam

For all the atrocities the Axis perpetrated against civilians, and they were many, it was the peace-loving Anglo-Americans—once their blood lust was up—who proved to be utterly implacable in dealing destruction and death to the homes, wives, and children of the men they faced in battle. This was the route to which the President gave his powerful assent. The choice of it led a long way, longer perhaps than any other choice the Allies made. Their political objectives were implicit in the way they chose to fight. . . . That is, the total defeat of their enemies came first and determined the strategies employed to that end.

> *Eric Larrabee,* Commander-in-Chief: Franklin Delano Roosevelt, His Lieutenants, and Their War

Acquiring [nuclear] weapons for the defense of Muslims is a religious duty. If I have indeed acquired these weapons, then I thank God for enabling me to do so. And if I seek to acquire these weapons, I am carrying out a duty. It would be a sin for Muslims not to try to possess the weapons that would prevent the infidels from inflicting harm on Muslims.

> *Osama bin Laden, December 1999,*
> *Interview with* Time

THE LESSON THAT THE American people should learn from the border comes from the story of the three little pigs. The report has been sounded that the big, bad wolf is coming to blow the house down. However, many of the little pigs are not taking heed.

HOUSE OF STRAW

One group of pigs (the Democrats in Congress who have opposed the Patriot Act) have opted to build a house of straw—permitting radical

Muslims to plan the next 9/11 within the sanctity of their own mosques and Islamic Centers—upon the rationale that any attempt to stop them from blowing up America would constitute a violation of their constitutional rights and liberties (even though most of them are not U.S. citizens). They also oppose effective interrogation procedures and believe that terrorist prisoners should be treated to milk and cookies along with constant, twenty-four-hour exposure to MTV and HBO within their cell-blocks so that they will truly come to understand that the United States is totally decadent and worthy of destruction. This group, headed by its own version of Napoleon Pig (Massachusetts Senator Ted Kennedy), calls for immigration reform that would expand the guest-worker program. This legislation would allow legal immigration to increase by 400,000 and make it easy for the 11 million illegal immigrants to take their first steps toward full citizenship by filling out a form and paying a fine (in recognition of their wrongdoing).[1]

This group of pigs fails to realize that such a bill would also make it much easier for the terrorists to enter the country, since many special interest aliens already possess bogus immigration papers—which they obtained from corrupt officials in such countries as Argentina, Brazil, and Paraguay—that will permit them to enter and stay without a visa. Most Democrats fail to realize that their policy represents almost total amnesty for millions who not only have broken the law but also have displayed little desire to assimilate within American society.

While building this house of straw, Kennedy and friends (including Republican Arizona Senator John McCain) believe that border security can be tightened by more government reports to more government committees. They fiddle and dance day after day in the nation's capital without the slightest concern that the wolf is at the door and ready to huff and puff and blow the house down.

HOUSE OF STICKS

The second group of little pigs (the Republican neo-cons and moderates) has opted to build a house of sticks. Headed by their own version of Snowball (George W. Bush), this group has drafted initiatives for immigration reform that call for a guest-worker program that would enable illegal immigrants to work at slave wages for six years before being sent home. Of course, these pigs fail to say how the government intends to round up the millions for deportation when their work licenses expire. Would they utilize cattle cars, lease fleets of moving vans, or make use of decommissioned cargo planes?

Still and all, this proposal is better than Kennedy's, since it provides no means for the illegal immigrants to become citizens at the end of their stay. President Bush believes security can be increased by hiring more border guards, installing electronic surveillance equipment, and creating two thousand new beds for the detention facilities.[2] He and his supporters refuse to realize that such measures would only serve to give more illegal immigrants a good night's rest before they go on their merry way to the heartland.

NIX TO BRICKS

The third group (the Democrats and Republicans on Capitol Hill who remain truly concerned about national security) would like to build a house of bricks by shutting down the borders, deporting the illegal immigrants, and amending the constitutional law that grants children born on U.S. soil immediate citizenship. Some members of this group (including Colorado Congressman Tom Tancredo) call not only for more border control officials but also for the use of hundreds of troops and deputized citizens to secure the 1,820-mile border between the United States and Canada.[3] Others (such as Texas Congressman Sam Johnson) have sponsored a bill that would make illegal immigration a felony, a measure that would subject millions to deportation or extended stays in detention camps.[4] They know that the big, bad wolf is on the way, and they remain determined to keep the American people safe and secure from his clutches. Unfortunately, such officials are in the minority, constituting only one quarter of the House and Senate.[5]

TWEEDLEDEE, TWEEDLEDUM, HALF A TRILLION, QUITE A SUM

The solution to the problem at the border and most of the other problems outlined in this book rests with the executive office. Presently, White House officials can't decide whether to bomb or build nations. For this reason, they have opted to do both at a cost that soon will hit half a trillion dollars, making the so-called war on terror the most expensive undertaking in human history.[6]

The Bush administration vacillates over just about everything. It remains reluctant to firebomb the poppy fields in Afghanistan and to ferret out the mujahideen (including Osama Bin Laden and Ayman al-Zawahiri) in Pakistan. The administration has been unwilling to address the seditious situation within U.S. mosques and the problem of radical Islam within the federal prison system. It has shelled out tens of millions in aid for the Muslim victims of tsunamis and earthquakes in Indonesia and Pakistan but there's little recognition for the three million Bengali Hindu, Buddhists, and Christian victims of Islamic genocide in Bangladesh.[7]

According to the Constitution, Congress possesses the sole right "to declare war [and] grant letters of marque and reprisal." But the United States has not officially declared war against any enemy since December 7, 1941. The military conflicts in which America has been engaged over the past sixty years (including Korea, Vietnam, Panama, Grenada, the Gulf War, Haiti, Somalia, and Kosovo) have been unofficial wars or "police actions." This refusal to call a war a war accounts for the fact that most American military engagements in recent years have been halfhearted ventures without clear-cut objectives or decisive results.

Moreover, these conflicts have given rise to interminable and enervating legal disputes that remain to be settled. Harry S. Truman, Lyndon B. Johnson, Richard M. Nixon, Jimmy Carter, Ronald Reagan, George H. W. Bush, Bill Clinton, and George W. Bush have justified their decisions to deploy troops for combat on the basis that the president of the United States, in accordance with article 2, section 2 of the Constitution, is "the Commander in Chief of the Army and Navy." As such, these presidents have upheld their power to command the army and the navy into action without the consent of Congress.[8]

Congress tried to settle this argument with the War Powers Resolution of 1973 that was about as clear and straightforward as an information packet from the Internal Revenue Service. The resolution was an attempt to avoid another Vietnam by granting the president a mere ninety days to obtain congressional approval after ordering troops into combat. It solved nothing. Subsequent presidents simply ignored the resolution on the grounds of the power granted to them by article 2 of the Constitution or by maintaining that the conflicts did not represent acts of war but rather attempts to "restore international peace and security."[9] Such duplicitous tactics have failed to produce meaningful and lasting results in the past and, no doubt, will fail to effect a final determination of events (the end of Islamic terrorism) and a measure of real stability for the future.

To achieve victory, the president must remove the velvet glove, toss down the metal gauntlet, and demand from Congress a formal declaration of war against radical Islam in all its militant manifestations. Securing such a declaration should not be a Herculean task. War against America is being proclaimed from thousands of minarets throughout the Muslim world. It has been officially sanctioned by fatwas from al Qaeda and hundreds of other terrorist groups, both Sunni and Shi'ite. It has been actualized by militant acts of aggression against American holdings overseas and a full-scale assault on U.S. soil that produced more casualties on 9/11 than any other day in American history. The offensive war against America has been heightened by attacks on U.S. troops in Afghanistan and Iraq and by the stated objective of radical Islam to kill millions of Americans, including two million children, for the sake of parity.[10]

The Smith Act

By obtaining such a declaration, as Tony Blankley points out in *The West's Last Chance,* the president will be able to address the situation with a force and determination that hasn't been displayed since World War II. He will be entitled to make use of existing laws without apology and with impunity. One such law is the Alien Registration Act of 1940, known as the Smith Act. This legislation makes it illegal for any group to advocate the overthrow or the destruction of the government. Anyone who violates this act faces twenty years in a federal slammer. Certainly, this bit of legislation can be brought to bear against the hundreds of radical mosques and seditious Islamic societies that have popped up in every major metropolitan area across the country.

The Smith Act also requires all aliens to register with the federal government. During World War II, this resulted in the first complete inventory of noncitizens. Five million aliens were registered. Of these,

600,000 were Italians, 260,000 Germans nationals, and 40,000 Japanese.[11] They were listed as "enemy aliens" in accordance with the Alien Enemies Act of 1798. This meant that they could be apprehended, detained, or deported at the whim of federal prosecutors.

Eventually, the FBI interrogated every individual on the enemy alien list, and the most dangerous were taken into custody. This came to 5,100 Japanese nationals, 3,250 Germans, and 650 Italians. After official hearings were conducted, 4,989 of the 9,000 were paroled or released. Those who were proven to be a threat to national security were sent to federal prisons and detention camps. Several of these camps were established on converted racetracks and fair grounds. Many detainees were forced to live in crowded horse stalls with few sanitary facilities. The compounds were placed under armed guard and surrounded with electrified barbed wire.[12]

The Supreme Court, in *Dennis v. the United States* (1948), upheld the constitutionality of the Smith Act. The Court ruled that an individual could be convicted and sent to prison for advocating the violent overthrow of the government even though he had never acted on that advocacy, never bought a gun, and never committed a criminal act.[13] In his concurring opinion, Chief Justice Frederick Moore Vinson wrote: "Overthrow of the Government by force and violence is certainly a substantial enough interest for the Government to limit speech: indeed, this is the ultimate value of any society, for if a society cannot protect its very structure from armed internal attack, it must follow that no subordinate value can be protected."[14]

In *Johnson v. Eisentrager* (1950), the Supreme Court ruled that the internment or deportation of noncitizens because of their race or nationality is permissible whenever Congress has declared a state of war. The decision reads:

> Executive power over enemy aliens, un-delayed and unhampered by litigation, has been deemed, throughout our history, essential to wartime security. This is in keeping with the practice of the most enlightened of nations and has resulted in treatment of alien enemies more considerate than that which has prevailed among any of our enemies and some of our allies. This statue was enacted or suffered to continue by men who helped found the Republic and formulate the Bill of

Rights, and although it obviously denies enemy aliens the constitutional immunities of citizens, it seems not then to have been supposed that a nation's obligations to its foes could ever be put on a parity with those of its defenders. The resident enemy alien is constitutionally subject to summary arrest, internment and deportation whenever a "declared war" exists.[15]

Surely, the enforcement of the Smith Act would do much to settle the problem of Muslim aliens—including imams and college professors, who support the jihad or express virulent anti-American sentiments—and of special interest aliens who poured into the United States from Latin America. Detention camps, modeled after the World War II prototypes, would be ideal places to house such troublesome factions of the present population for an indeterminate time.

The president could also bring the Voorhis Act of 1941 into play. This legislation requires all organizations that have as their goal the overthrow and destruction of the U.S. government to register with the federal government.[16] In terms of the present conflict, the Voorhis Act means that all Muslim groups that call for the imposition of *shariah* (Islamic law) on American citizens and engagement in a political struggle that will result in the Day of Islam could be listed as suspect, subjected to intense scrutiny, and incarcerated.

WAR POWERS ACT: CENSORSHIP AND PROPAGANDA

More important, an official declaration of war would reinstate the War Powers Act of December 18, 1941. This would give the executive office the power to crush the exponents of radical Islam like bedbugs. By this act, the president could impose censorship on the mass media in order to suppress all negative information regarding the war effort (say goodbye to Michael Moore) or give aid and comfort to the enemy (such as the *New York Times* accounts of Abu Ghraib).

During World War II, the Office of Censorship black-lined twenty-six stories a day, opened a half million private letters, and intercepted thousands of telegrams. The *Militant,* the newspaper of the Socialist Workers Party, was banned, along with seventy additional publications. Anti-Semitic Catholic priest Father Charles Coughlin was prevented from broadcasting his weekly radio program. Even the annual share-holders' report of U.S. Steel was censored to show production of "00,000 thousand tons" for 1941.[17]

The War Powers Act would provide authorization for a propaganda campaign that could serve the war effort by informing the public of Muslim atrocities that have taken place since the time of the Prophet (including the recent roasting alive of eleven members of the same family in Banshkhali[18] and the torture, rape, and slaughter of hundreds of villagers in Purba Delua[19]). Such propaganda would serve as a necessary corrective to such wrongheaded and subversive films as *Syriana, The Kingdom of Heaven,* and *Fahrenheit 9-11.*

During World War II, great movies were made to aid the war effort by such great patriotic directors as Frank Capra, John Ford, Howard Hawks, John Huston, and George Stevens. In today's America, there are filmmakers, including Mel Gibson and Clint Eastwood, equal to this important task.

In Defense of Internment and Racial Profiling

In accordance with the War Powers Act, Franklin D. Roosevelt issued Executive Order #9066 in 1942, granting the right for the army to designate military areas from which "any or all persons may be excluded." Although the words Japanese or Japanese Americans never appeared on the order, it represented authorization for the installation of additional detention camps for people who should be racially profiled because of their ethnic or religious ties to the enemy. In compliance with this directive, 120,000 Americans of Japanese descent were ordered to leave their homes in Arizona, California, Oregon, and Washington and to be placed in newly created detention camps where they remained for the duration of the war.[20] Surely these measures were unfair to many Japanese Americans—the majority of whom were patriotic, law-abiding citizens. But such measures would not be unfair for American Muslims who have pledged their allegiance to radical Islam and who seek the destruction of the American way of life.

With the case of *Karematsu v. U.S.,* the Supreme Court ruled that the government had the constitutional right during times of warfare to intern prisoners without hearings and without adjudicative determination that they were seditious or had done anything wrong. The order was set forth as follows:

> We are not unmindful of the hardships imposed upon a large group of American citizens. But hardships are part of war, and war is an aggregation of hardships. Karematsu was not excluded from the West Coast because of his race, but because the military authorities decided that the urgency of the situation demanded that all citizens of Japanese ancestry be segregated from the area. We cannot—by availing ourselves of the calm perspective of hindsight—say that their actions were unjustified.

Racial profiling for the sake of national security has been sanctioned. It was approved and upheld in 1944 by the highest court in the land.

The Limits of Religious Freedom

Nor after war has been declared can American Muslims, who support the jihad, hide under the freedom of religion provision of the Constitution. In *Ft. Minersville School District v. Gobitis,* the Supreme Court ruled that the right of government in times of war overrides the rights of religion, dissent, and conscience. In expressing the majority opinion, Justice Felix Frankfurter wrote: "To affirm that the freedom to follow conscience has itself no limits in the life of society would deny that very plurality which, as a matter of history, underlies protection of religious toleration."[21] Frankfurter added: "National unity is the basis of national security. To deny the legislature the right to elect appropriate means for its attainment presents a totally different order of problem from that of the propriety of subordinating the possible ugliness of littered streets to the free expression of opinion through distributing handbills."[22]

ONCE A DUNCE

These measures could enable the American people to prevail over the enemy. But there remains one problem—a problem that is almost insurmountable. A dunce is always a dunce. Scripture says, "As a dog returns to his own vomit, so a fool repeats his folly" (Proverbs 26:11, NKJV).

In Miss O'Malley's classroom, Bernie Vahunis never completed a homework assignment despite the fact that he was obliged to sit on a high stool with a dunce cap on his head throughout the school year. And I never ceased and desisted from writing essays that were destined to arouse widespread ire and result in a stay within a critical pillory.

President George W. Bush has established himself to be a dunce—no less than Clinton, Reagan, Carter, and his father (the apple *really* doesn't fall far from the tree). He has allowed the greatest alien invasion in history to occur on his watch. He has led U.S. and Allied forces into a quagmire in Iraq that has resulted in the deaths (thus far) of more than twenty-one hundred American soldiers who were killed to prop up a government that has established an alliance with Iran. He has neglected to apply pressure on Pakistani president Pervez Musharraf to obtain the right for CIA interrogators to question Drs. Abdul Qadeer Khan, Sultan Bashiruddin Mahmood, Chaudhry Abdul Majeed, and the other Pakistani nuclear scientists and technicians who were working with al Qaeda to create a "nuclear hell storm" through America. President Bush has agreed with fellow dunderhead Arizona Senator John McCain that the terrorist prisoners must be treated like incarcerated southern gentlemen. He has allowed the poppy fields of Afghanistan to remain in full bloom before the U.S. forces. He has turned a blind eye to the situations in Latin and Central America. He has expressed his lack of support for racial profiling by saying: "Airline travelers have experienced harassment and delay because of their ethnic heritage. Such indiscriminate use of passenger profiling is wrong and must be stopped."[23] He has opposed the use of secret documentation—classified intelligence evidence—to deport suspected Muslim terrorists by complaining: "Arab Americans are racially profiled in what's called secret evidence. People are stopped, and we got to do something about that. My friend, Senator Spencer Abraham of Michigan, is pushing a law to make sure that, you know, Arab Americans are treated with respect."[24] He has sheltered the Wahhabists of Saudi Arabia from the war on terrorism, in part, because of his close business relationship with the oil-rich sheikhs—a relationship that resulted in $1.477 billion flowing from the Saudi royal family to individuals and business entities closely connected to the Bush family.[25] And he continues, despite daily evidence to the contrary, to insist that Islam means peace and that the majority of Muslims throughout the world salute his efforts and blanch with horror at the mere mention of 9/11. Giving increased power to George W. Bush is tantamount to giving a schoolboy a loaded revolver.

A SOUR NOTE

A book like this is not supposed to end with a downbeat. It is supposed to conclude on a high note, or at least a pleasing chord. These last pages are reserved for authors to wax poetic over the inevitable triumph of good over evil, to utter platitudes about the indomitable spirit of the American people, or to sound the clarion call for the emergence of a new Siegfried from the halls of Congress or the Pentagon.

But no Siegfried appears to be waiting in the wings to lead the American people to victory (only Hillary Clinton, John McCain, John Kerry, Condoleezza Rice, and a flock of political predators). The country appears to have lost its fighting spirit and is manifesting telltale signs of enervating decadence—a "sickness unto death" (as Friedrich Nietzsche would have it) by its inability to evacuate its own waste. And as the evil forces have begun to pour through the gates, they have encountered little or no resistance.

The situation is dire. Osama bin Laden began amassing nuclear weapons in 1992, when he was in Sudan. His first purchase was of highly enriched uranium that had been stolen from Valendaba, a nuclear manufacturing facility near Pretoria in South Africa.[26] When bin Laden returned to Afghanistan in 1996, he purchased off-the-shelf nukes from Chechnya, China, Kazakhstan, Russia, Turkmenistan, and the Ukraine.[27] By 2001 Osama had begun working with scientists and technicians from the Abdul Qadeer Khan Research Laboratory in Pakistan, who removed the active uranium and plutonium from ready-made devices so they could be processed and placed in backpacks, small lead-lined containers, and suitcases for easier transportation and little chance of detection.[28] The Pakistani scientists also developed new weapons, which included nukes shaped like artillery shells that could be fired from recoilless rifles. Several of these weapons were deployed to the United States from Karachi in cargo containers.[29] Investigative reporter Daniel Pearl was executed by ISI (Pakistan's Inter-Service Intelligence agency) while investigating the trafficking of nuclear blueprints and materials from

Khan's research laboratory near Islamabad to al Qaeda cells in the Northwest Frontier Province of Pakistan.[30]

The al Qaeda nuclear arsenal is not a matter of speculation but of substantiated fact. In October 2001 an al Qaeda agent was arrested while trying to enter Israel at the Ramallah checkpoint. He was carrying a tactical nuclear bomb in his rucksack. Israeli intelligence confirmed that the agent could have activated the plutonium-implosion device.[31] The previous year, as noted earlier, two British agents infiltrated an al Qaeda training camp in Afghanistan by posing as recruits from a London mosque. After completing the training and taking the oath of allegiance, they were sent to Herat in western Afghanistan for special training. On the outskirts of this city, they visited an al Qaeda nuclear laboratory where scientists and technicians were putting the finishing touches on weapons manufactured from radioactive isotopes.[32] The whereabouts of these weapons remain unknown.

CRIES OF ALARM

Few military and intelligence officials question bin Laden's ability to launch a nuclear attack on America. Gen. Eugene Habiger, former executive chief of U.S. Strategic Weapons at the Pentagon, maintains that an event of nuclear megaterrorism within the United States is "not a matter of if, but when."[33] The Robb-Silberman Commission concluded in its report to the Bush White House: "The U.S. intelligence community has assessed that al Qaeda was capable of fabricating at least a crude nuclear device."[34]

During the 2004 presidential debates, President Bush and Senator John Kerry agreed that nuclear weapons in the hands of the terrorists represent the "single most serious threat to U.S. national security." And Vice President Dick Cheney, on the campaign trail, admitted that a nuclear attack by al Qaeda appears to be imminent.[35] Upon leaving office, Attorney General John Ashcroft and Homeland Security director Tom Ridge both voiced their belief that bin Laden's plan for an American Hiroshima soon might come to fruition.[36]

From the business sector, billionaire Warren Buffet, who establishes odds against cataclysmic events for major insurance companies, concluded that a nuclear nightmare within the very near future is "virtually a certainty."[37]

From the academic community, Graham T. Allison, director of Harvard University's Belfer Center for Science and International Affairs, proclaimed: "Is nuclear terrorism inevitable? Harvard professors are known for being subtle or ambiguous, but I'll try to be clear. 'Is the worst yet to come?' My answer: Bet on it. Yes."[38]

The national media has largely ignored such warnings. This is particularly surprising in light of a think piece about the seriousness of the nuclear threat that was penned by Bill Keller, editor of the *New York Times*. He wrote that the only reason to believe the terrorists will not launch a nuclear attack on American soil is because "it hasn't happened yet"—adding that such a conclusion represents "terrible logic."[39]

Any lingering doubts about what the future holds should have been put to rest by Michael Scheuer, the CIA agent who had been in charge of the bin Laden file (code-named Alec). On November 14, 2004, Scheuer appeared on CBS's *60 Minutes* to warn the American people that a nuclear attack by al Qaeda "is pretty close to being inevitable."[40]

THE FINAL FATWA

When the United States invaded Iraq, Sheikh Nasir bin Hamid al Fahd issued a fatwa on behalf of the Wahhabi clerics of Saudi Arabia that granted Osama bin Laden and al Qaeda permission to use nuclear weapons in the jihad against the United States. In the ruling, titled "A Treatise on the Legal Status of Using Weapons of Mass Destruction Against Infidels," Fahd maintains that international law must not be taken into account when deciding if the United States should be nuked. Islamic law, he writes, overrides all man-made laws.

To the question of whether a nuclear attack would violate the Islamic teaching that "the basic rule in killing is to do it in a good manner," Fahd states that this teaching means that one should only kill in a good manner (such as decapitation) "when one can." He further rules that it is permissible to kill women, children, the elderly, and even fellow Muslims for the sake of jihad.[41]

The Saudi cleric justifies the fact that millions of Americans would be killed by a major nuclear attack by arguing that an estimate of the number of Muslims killed by Americans by the sanctions against Muslim peoples and the invasion of Muslim lands in recent years would total "almost 10 million." He writes: "If a bomb killed 10 million of them [Americans] and burned as much of their land as they have burned the lands of Muslims, it would be permissible, with no need to mention any further argument."[42]

Fahd's fatwa, despite its incredible importance, has not been published in part or in its entirety by any leading American newspaper or media outlet that broadcasts news 24/7. This shows that the dunces of doomsday are not only among the inhabitants of the Oval Office but also among the pasty-faced and beady-eyed reporters who occupy cubicles in crowded newsrooms and the well-tanned and bright-eyed news boobies who face the cameras in the studios at ABC, CBS, CNN, Fox, MSNBC, and NBC.

Osama bin Laden did not seek this fatwa to keep it in a desk drawer. He did not obtain nuclear weapons to store them in a cave. And he did not declare war without the intent to achieve victory.

Sure, deployed weapons require maintenance. The "triggers," which emit large quantities of neutrons at high speeds, decay rapidly and have short half lives. The nuclear cores also are subject to decay, and over the course of several years, these will fall below the critical mass threshold. But bin Laden doesn't fret over such matters. Adnan el Shukrijumah and the commanders of the next 9/11 have been trained as nuclear technicians.

The attack—the American Hiroshima—is scheduled to take place simultaneously in Chicago, Houston, Las Vegas, Los Angeles, Miami, New York, and Washington DC. It will occur when conditions become propitious for complete success. Bin Laden is not a backward Bedouin warrior with little knowledge of nuclear physics and sophisticated weaponry. He is a highly trained engineer and one of the most gifted tacticians in military history. He will not waste billions in expenditures, years of planning, and his coveted "crown jewels" on an operation that is poorly planned, ill-timed, and carelessly coordinated.

Moreover, a cardinal virtue of all faithful Muslims is patience. The Koran teaches, "Only the patient will be paid back (in the hereafter); their reward in full without measure" (39:10). And bin Laden, who waited eight years between his first and second attacks on American soil, is a man of almost infinite patience. He can launch the next attack in his own good time. He knows that he is dealing with dunces.

Appendix

Al Qaeda's Weapons of Mass Destruction Activities

DATE	TYPE	INCIDENT	SOURCE
Unspecified	Nuclear	Bin Laden paid more than two million British pounds to a middleman in Kazakhstan for a suitcase bomb.	Marie Colvin, "Holy War with US in His Sights," *Times* (London), August 16, 1998
Unspecified	Nuclear	Bin Laden paid a group of Chechens $30 million in cash and two tons of opium in exchange for approximately twenty nuclear warheads.	Riyad 'Alam al-Din, "Report Links Bin Laden, Nuclear Weapons," *Al-Watan al-Arabi*, November 23, 1998; Emil Torabi, "Bin Laden's Nuclear Weapons," *Muslim Magazine* (Winter 1998)
Unspecified	Biological	Al Qaeda operatives bought anthrax and plague from arms dealers in Kazakhstan.	Paul Daley, "Report Says UBL-Linked Terrorist Groups Possess 'Deadly' Anthrax, Plague Viruses," *Melbourne Age*, June 4, 2000
Unspecified	Nuclear/ Radiological	Bin Laden dispatched envoys to several eastern European countries to purchase enriched uranium.	"Arab Security Sources Speak of a New Scenario for Afghanistan: Secret Roaming Networks That Exchange Nuclear Weapons for Drugs," *Al-Sharq al-Awsat*, December 24, 2004
Unspecified	Nuclear/ Radiological	Bin Laden purchased seven enriched-uranium rods from Ukrainian arms dealer Semion Mogilevich.	Uthman Tizghart, "Does Bin Laden Really Possess Weapons of Mass Destruction? Tale of Russian Mafia Boss Semion Mogilevich Who Supplied Bin Laden with the Nuclear 'Dirty Bomb,'" *Al-Majallah* (London), November 25, 2005
Unspecified	Biological	U.S. officials discovered documents concerning the aerial dispersal of anthrax via balloon within the Kabul office of Pakistani scientist Dr. Bashiruddin Mahmood.	"Sketches of Anthrax Bomb Found in Pakistani Scientist's Office," *Rediff.com*, November 28, 2001
Unspecified	Chemical/ Biological	Al Qaeda's five-thousand-page *Encyclopedia of Jihad* is devoted to construction of CBW (chemical and biological weapons).	"Osama Bin Laden's Bid to Acquire Weapons of Mass Destruction Represents the Greatest Threat That Western Civilization Has Faced," *Mail on Sunday* (London), June 23, 2002

SOURCE: Kimberly McCloud, Gary A. Ackerman and Jeffrey M. Bale, "Chart Al Qaeda's WMD Activities," Center for Nonproliferation Studies, Monterey Institute of International Studies, January 21, 2003. Revised and enlarged by Paul L. Williams.

Appendix

DATE	TYPE	INCIDENT	SOURCE
Unspecified	Chemical	CNN correspondent Mike Boettcher reports that U.S. intelligence agencies discovered evidence of recent purchases of cyanide by al Qaeda operatives.	*Wolf Blitzer Reports,* CNN, July 31, 2002
Unspecified	Nuclear/ Biological/ Chemical	Two Pakistani scientists shared nuclear, biological, and chemical weapons information with bin Laden, who said that the nuclear material had been provided by the Islamic Movement of Uzbekistan.	Toby Harnden, "Rogue Scientists Gave Bin Laden Nuclear Secrets," *Daily Telegraph* (London) December 13, 2001; Peter Baker, "Pakistani Scientist Who Met Bin Laden Failed Polygraphs, Renewing Suspicions," *Washington Post,* March 3, 2002; Susan B. Glasser and Kamra Khan, "Pakistan Continues Probe of Nuclear Scientists," *Washington Post,* November 14, 2001
1993–94	Nuclear/ Radiological	Jamal al-Fadl claimed that, on behalf of Bin Laden, he had made arrangements for the purchase of uranium for nuclear weapons.	Kimberly McCloud and Matthew Osborne, "WMD Terrorism and Usama Bin Laden," CNS Report, November 20, 2001
1996–98	Chemical	Bin Laden bought CW (chemical weapons) over a two-year period prior to 1998 from European states and the former Soviet Union. This information comes from the testimony of a jihad leader arrested on August 20, 1998, in Baku Azerbaijan.	Muhammad Salah, "Bin Laden Front Reportedly Bought CBW from E. Europe," *Al-Hayah,* April 20, 1999; Muhammad Salah, "US Said Interrogating Jihadist over CBW," *Al-Hayah,* April 21, 1999
1997–98	Chemical/ Biological	Islamic extremists, including al Qaeda operatives, were trained in secret camps near Baghdad in the use of CW and BW (biological weapons) by instructors from Iraq's secret military intelligence Unit 999.	Gwynne Roberts, "Militia Defector Claims Baghdad Trained Al-Qaeda Fighters in Chemical Warfare," *Sunday Times* (London), July 14, 2002
October 1997	Chemical/ Biological	A meeting was held in Sudan between bin Laden, Ayman al-Zawahiri, and Hasan al-Turabi, leader of Sudan's National Islamic Front regime, about the construction of a CBW factory.	Jihad Salim, "Report on Bin Laden, Zawahiri, Afghans," *Al-Watan al-Arabi,* February 16, 2001
1998	Nuclear/ Radiological	Russian intelligence blocked an attempt by bin Laden to purchase Soviet-origin uranium.	Earl Lane and Knut Royce, "Nuclear Aspirations? Sources: Bin Laden Tried to Obtain Enriched Uranium," *Newsday,* September 19, 2001
1998	Chemical/ Biological	From looters in Kabul a reporter obtained two computers that had been found in an abandoned al Qaeda safe house. One of the computers contained a file describing "plans to launch a chemical and biological weapons program." Bin Laden's deputy al-Zawahiri reportedly created the documents describing his CW and BW program, code-named "Curdled Milk." The document included work on a pesticide—nerve agent that was tested on rabbits and dogs. Al-Zawahiri was assisted by Midhat Mursi (a.k.a. Abu Khabbab), a chemical engineer.	Alan Culluson and Andrew Higgins, "Computer in Kabul Holds Chilling Memos," *Wall Street Journal,* December 31, 2001; "Report: Al Qaeda Computer Had Plans for Bio-Weapons," Reuters, December 21, 2001
May 1998	Chemical/ Biological	Al Qaeda purchased three CBW factories in the former Yugoslavia and hired a number of Ukrainian chemists and biologists to train its members.	Guido Olimpio, "Islamic Group Said Preparing Chemical Warfare on the West," *Corriere della Sera,* July 8, 1998; Yossef Bodansky, *Bin Laden: The Man Who Declared War on America* (New York: Prima, 2001), 326

DATE	TYPE	INCIDENT	SOURCE
August 1998	Chemical	The CIA discovered that bin Laden had attempted to acquire unspecified CW for use against U.S. troops stationed in the Persian Gulf.	Barry Schweid, "US Suggests Iraq Got Weapons from Sudan," *Record* (New Jersey), August 27, 1998
September 1998	Nuclear/ Radiological	Mamdouh Mahmud Salim, an al Qaeda operative, was arrested in Munich, Germany, for trying to purchase nuclear material, including highly enriched uranium.	Benjamin Weiser, "US Says Bin Laden Aide Tried to Get Nuclear Weapons," *New York Times*, September 26, 1998
September 1998	Chemical	Wadi al-Hajj, a Lebanese national, is arrested in Arlington TX for perjury. The FBI contends that he had lied about his affiliation with bin Laden and that he was involved in procuring WMD for al Qaeda.	CNN, December 20, 1998
December 1998	Chemical/ Nuclear	In an interview with *Time* magazine, bin Laden said that acquiring weapons of any type, including chemical and nuclear, is a Muslim "religious duty."	"Interview with bin Laden," *Time*, December 24, 1998
1999	Chemical	Afghan sources maintained that bin Laden made use of a plant in Charassiab, a district south of Kabul, to produce CW.	"Afghan Alliance—UBL Trying to Make Chemical Weapons," *Parwan Payam-e Mojahed*, December 23, 1999
April 1999	Biological	Bin Laden obtained BW substances through the mail from former Soviet Union republics (the Ebola virus and salmonella bacterium), from East Asia (anthrax-causing bacteria), and from the Czech Republic (botulinum toxin).	Al J. Venter, "Elements Loyal to Bin Laden Acquire Biological Agents 'Through the Mail,'" *Jane's Intelligence Review* (August 1999); Khalid Sharaf al-Din, "Bin Laden Men Reportedly Possess Biological Weapons," *Al-Sharq al-Awsat*, March 6, 1999
July 1999	Chemical/ Biological	An Islamist lawyer testified that al Qaeda has CBW and will likely use such weapons against the United States.	"Islamist Lawyer on Bin Laden, Groups," *Al-Sharq al-Awsat*, July 12, 1999
February 2000	Chemical	Italian police foil a plot by nine Moroccans, with ties to al Qaeda, to poison the water supply of the U.S. Embassy in Rome with a cyanide compound.	Eric Croddy et al., "Chemical Terrorist Plot in Rome?" *CNS Research Story*, March 11, 2002
Late 2000	Nuclear	The intelligence agency of an unnamed European country intercepted a shipment—originating in Kazakhstan, Russia, Turkmenistan and the Ukraine—of approximately twenty nuclear warheads intended for bin Laden and the Taliban regime of Afghanistan.	"Arab Security Sources Speak of a New Scenario for Afghanistan: Secret Roaming Networks That Exchange Nuclear Weapons for Drugs," *Al-Sharq al-Awsat*, December 24, 2000
2001	Biological	Various sources confirmed that Muhammad Atta, the leader of the September 11 hijackers, was provided with a vial of anthrax by an Iraqi intelligence agent at a meeting in Prague.	Kreindler and Kriendler 9/11 lawsuit; "Prague Discounts an Iraqi Meeting," *New York Times*, October 21, 2001; "Czechs Retract Iraq Terror Link," United Press International, October 20, 2001
2001	Biological	Ahmed Ressam, arrested in a plot to bomb LA International Airport, testified that bin Laden is interested in using low-flying aircraft to dispense BW agents over major U.S. metropolitan areas.	"Bin Laden's Biological Threat," BBC, October 28, 2001
2001	Biological	Documents found in Afghanistan revealed that al Qaeda was conducting research on using botulinum toxin to kill two thousand people.	"Al Qaeda Tested Germ Weapons," Reuters, January 1, 2002

Appendix

DATE	TYPE	INCIDENT	SOURCE
2001	Chemical	Ahmed Ressam claimed to witness the gassing of a dog with cyanide in an al Qaeda training camp.	Pamela Hess, "Al-Qaeda May Have Chemical Weapons," United Press International, August 19, 2002
February 2001	Chemical	After receiving warnings from an Arab embassy in Islamabad, Pakistan, the United States aborted a planned air strike against Afghanistan for fear of a chemical attack by al Qaeda.	Sa'id al-Qaysi, "US Said Aborted Planned Attack on Bin Laden for Fear of 'Chemical Strike,'" Al-Watan al-Arabi, February 16, 2001
February 2001	Chemical	Bin Laden's elite 055 Brigade reorganized under the leadership of Midhat Mursi, a.k.a. Abu Khabab, an Egyptian and expert in sarin gas production.	Sa'id al-Qaysi, "US Said Aborted Planned Attack on Bin Laden for Fear of 'Chemical Strike,'" Al-Watan al-Arabi, February 16, 2001
April 2001	Nuclear/ Radiological	Ivan Ivanov claimed to have met with bin Laden in China to discuss the establishment of a company to buy nuclear waste. Ivanov was then approached by a Pakistani chemical engineer interested in buying nuclear fuel rods from the Bulgarian Kozlodui reactor.	Adam Nathan and David Leppard, "Al-Qaeda's Men Held Secret Meetings to Build 'Dirty Bomb,'" Sunday Times (London), October 14, 2001
Since Summer 2001	Chemical/ Biological/ Nuclear	Iraqi military instructors provided training to 150–250 al Qaeda operatives in northern Iraq in the use of CBW and the handling of nuclear devices.	"Abu Nidal's Nemesis," DEBKA File (Jerusalem), August 20, 2002
Before September 11, 2001	Nuclear	Bin Laden purchased forty-eight suitcase nukes from the Russian Mafia.	"Al-Majallah Obtains Serious Information on Al-Qaeda's Attempt to Acquire Nuclear Arms," Al-Majallah (London-based Saudi weekly), September 8, 2002
October 2001	Nuclear	Mossad arrested an al Qaeda operative with backpack containing a tactical nuclear weapon at the checkpoint in Ramallah.	United Press International, December 21, 2001. First reports spoke of a radiological bomb.
Before November 2001	Chemical	CNN releases al Qaeda videotapes that show dogs being killed by unidentified toxic chemicals, which experts believe could be either a crude nerve agent or hydrogen cyanide gas.	Insight, CNN, August 19, 2002
November 2001	Chemical/ Nuclear	In an interview bin Laden declared: "We have chemical and nuclear weapons as a deterrent, and if America uses them against us, we reserve the right to use them."	Hamid Mir, "Osama Claims He Has Nukes: If US Uses N-Arms It Will Get Same Response," Dawn (Pakistan), November 10, 2001
November 2001	Nuclear	Evidence obtained from the offices of Ummah Tameer E-Nau of Kabul shows that a nuclear weapon may have been shipped to the United States from Karachi in a cargo container.	Arnaud de Borchgrave, "Al Qaeda's Nuclear Agenda Verified," Washington Times, December 10, 2001
November 2001	Nuclear	Bin Laden acquired a Russian-made suitcase nuclear weapon from central Asian sources. The weapon was reported to weigh 8 kg and to possess at least 2 kg of fissionable uranium and plutonium. The report said the device, with serial number 9999 and a manufacturing date of October 1998, could be set off by a mobile-phone signal. This weapon, according to sources, had been forward-deployed to the United States.	"N-weapons May Be in US Already," Daily Telegraph (Sydney, Australia), November 14, 2001

DATE	TYPE	INCIDENT	SOURCE
November 2001	Nuclear	A *Times* (London) reporter discovered a blueprint for a "Nagasaki bomb" in an abandoned al Qaeda house in Kabul.	"Nuke Plans Found; Brit Paper Discovers Details of Weapons in Kabul Safe House," *Toronto Sun*, November 15, 2001; Hugh Dougherty, "Afghan Nuclear Weapons Papers 'May Be Internet Spoofs,'" *Press Association*, November 19, 2001
November 2001	Nuclear	A "superbomb" manual that addresses the physics of nuclear weapons and dirty bombs was discovered in a safe house in Afghanistan.	"Osama Bin Laden's Bid to Acquire Weapons of Mass Destruction Represents the Greatest Threat That Western Civilization Has Faced," *Mail On Sunday* (London) June 23, 2002
December 2001	Radiological	Uranium-235 was found in a lead-lined canister in Kandahar.	Barbie Dutterand Ben Fenton, "Uranium and Cyanide Found In Drums at Bin Laden's Base," *Daily Telegraph* (London), December 24, 2001
Late 2001	Biological	U.S. intelligence agents uncovered evidence in Afghanistan that one or more Russian scientists were helping al Qaeda develop biological weapons, including anthrax.	Jeffrey Bartholet, "Terrorist Sleeper Cells," *Newsweek*, December 9, 2001
Late 2001	Biological	Al-Zawahiri's home in Kabul tested positive for traces of anthrax, as did five of nineteen al Qaeda labs in Afghanistan.	"Al-Qaeda: Anthrax found in Al-Qaeda Home," Global Security Newswire, December 10, 2001; Judith Miller, "Labs Suggest Al Qaeda Planned to Build Arms, Officials Say," *New York Times*, September 14, 2002
Late 2001	Biological	John Walker Lindh told interrogators that a biological attack was expected to be part of a "second wave" of al Qaeda attacks.	"Walker Lindh: Al Qaeda Planned More Attacks," CNN, October 3, 2002
2002	Chemical	The facility of Ansar al-Islam, a radical Islamist group operating in northern Iraq with ties to al-Qaeda, produced a form of cyanide cream that kills on contact.	William Safire, "Tying Saddam to Terrorist Organizations," *New York Times*, August 25, 2002
January–June 2002	Biological	Ansar al-Islam had conducted experiments with ricin, a deadly toxin, on at least one human subject.	"US Knew of Bio-Terror Tests in Iraq," BBC News, August 20, 2002; "US Monitors Kurdish Extremists," Fox News, August 21, 2002; Isma'il Zayir, "Ansar al-Islam Group Accuses [Jalal] Talabani of Spreading Rumors About Its Cooperation with Al-Qaeda," *Al Hayah*, August 22, 2002
January 2002	Nuclear	Diagrams of U.S. nuclear power plants were discovered in abandoned al Qaeda camps and facilities in Afghanistan.	Bill Gertz, "Nuclear Plants Targeted," *Washington Times*, January 31, 2002; John J. Lumpkin, "Diagrams Show Interest in Nuke Plants," Associated Press, January 30, 2002
February 2, 2002	Chemical/ Biological	CIA director George Tenet informed the Senate that bin Laden has displayed a strong interest in CW and that his operatives have been "trained to conduct attacks with toxic chemicals or biological toxins."	Pamela Hess, "Al Qaeda May Have Chemical Weapons," United Press International, August 19, 2002
Before March 2002	Biological	U.S. forces discovered a BW laboratory under construction near Kandahar. It had been abandoned by al Qaeda. The laboratory was being built to produce anthrax.	Dominic Evans, "Us Troops Found Afghan Biological Lab," Reuters, March 22, 2002; Michael R. Gordon, "US Says It Found Al Qaeda Lab Being Built to Produce Anthrax," *New York Times*, March 23, 2002

Appendix

DATE	TYPE	INCIDENT	SOURCE
April 2002	Radiological	Abu Zubayda said that al Qaeda possesses the ability to produce a radiological weapon and already has one in the United States.	Jamie McIntyre, "Zubayda: al Qaeda Had 'Dirty Bomb' Know-How," CNN, April 22, 2002; "Al-Qaeda Claims 'Dirty Bomb' Know-How" BBC, April 23, 2002
May 2002	Radiological	U.S. citizen Abdullah al-Muhaji (formerly Jose Padilla) was arrested in Chicago. He had been involved with al Qaeda in a plan for a radiological bomb attack on the United States.	Dan Eggen and Susan Schmidt, "'Dirty Bomb' Plot Uncovered, US Says: Suspected Al Qaeda Operative Held as 'Enemy Combatant,'" *Washington Post*, June 11, 2002
May 2002	Chemical	During the arrest of Sami Uthman, a Lebanese national who moved to the United States and became an imam at an Islamic mosque in Seattle, police officials found papers by London-based al Qaeda recruiter Shaykh Abu Hamza al-Masri, firearms, military manuals, and "instructions on poisoning water sources."	Patrick J. McDonnell and Josh Meyer, "Links to Terrorism Probed in Northwest," *Los Angeles Times*, July 13, 2002
June 3, 2002	Radiological	Bin Laden tried to acquire eleven pounds of radioactive thallium from measuring devices on decommissioned Russian submarines, but Russia's Federal Security Service claimed to have blocked the sale.	"Insider Notes," United Press International, June 3, 2002
July 18, 2002	Biological	Stephen Younger, director of the Defense Threat Reduction Agency, testified that al Qaeda's interest in BW focused mainly on anthrax.	"Weapons Worries," CBS News, July 18, 2002
September 13, 2002	Chemical/ Biological	Lab equipment found near Kandahar supports the assessment that al Qaeda has acquired the necessary ingredients for "a very limited production of biological and chemical agents."	Judith Miller, "Lab Suggests Al Qaeda Planned to Build Arms, Officials Say," *New York Times*, September 14, 2002
October or November 2002	Chemical	The Islamist group Asbat al-Ansar, a Lebanon-based Sunni group affiliated with al Qaeda, obtained the nerve agent VX from Iraq.	Barton Gellman, "US Suspects Al Qaeda Got Nerve Gas Agent from Iraqis," *Washington Post*, December 12, 2002
November 9, 2002	Chemical	British security officials arrested three agents of al Qaeda who were planning a cyanide attack on the London subway.	Hala Jaber and Nicholas Rufford, "MI5 Foils Poison-Gas Attack on Tube," *Sunday Times* (London), November 17, 2002
March 3, 2004	Nuclear	In an interview with Pakistani journalist Hamid Mir, Ayman al-Zawahiri claimed that al Qaeda possessed nuclear weapons. Zawahiri told Mir that al Qaeda agents had been sent to "Moscow, Tashkent, and other countries in Central Asia" to buy portable nukes.	Max Delany, "Under Attack from Al Qaeda," *Moscow News*, March 3, 2004
September 2004	Radiological	Midhat Mursi, an al Qaeda affiliate, managed chemical laboratories in Afghanistan for the manufacturing of radiological bombs. Musri used the alias "Abu Khabab" and remained in contact with Ayman al-Zawahiri.	Muhammad Wajdi Qandyl, "Secret Weapons of Mass Destruction and al Qaeda," *Al-Akhbar* (Cairo), January 18, 2004
November 2004	Nuclear	Sharif al-Masri, a key al Qaeda operative, informed authorities that bin Laden has arranged to smuggle nuclear supplies and tactical weapons into Mexico.	"Al Qaeda Wants to Smuggle N-Material to US," *Nation*, November 17, 2004

DATE	TYPE	INCIDENT	SOURCE
February 17, 2005	Nuclear	CIA director Porter Goss said that it remains only a matter of time before al Qaeda attempts to use weapons of mass destruction, including tactical nuclear bombs, against the United States. His remarks were upheld by FBI director Robert Mueller.	CNN, February 17, 2005
April 20, 2005	Nuclear	Intelligence agents confirmed that Abu Musab Zarqawi has obtained a nuclear devise or is preparing a radiological explosive for an attack. The nuclear devise/dirty nuke is being stored in Afghanistan.	Bill Gertz, "Reports Reveal Zarqawi's Nuclear Threat," *Washington Times*, April 20, 2005

Notes

BLUNDER 1: REFUSING TO IDENTIFY THE ENEMY

1. Yaroslav Trofimov, *Faith at War: A Journey on the Frontiers of Islam from Baghdad to Timbuktu* (New York: Henry Holt, 2005), 1–21.
2. Sulaiman Abu Ghaith, "Why We Fight America?" in Paul L. Williams, *The Al-Qaeda Connection: International Terrorism, Organized Crime, and the Coming Apocalypse* (Amherst, NY: Prometheus Books, 2005), 21. Abu Ghaith's statement first appeared on an official al-Qaeda Web site from which it was downloaded and verified as authentic by the FBI.
3. Paul L. Williams, *Osama's Revenge: The Next 9-11* (Amherst, NY: Prometheus Books, 2004), 100. Paul Sperry, *Infiltration: How Muslim Spies and Subversives Have Penetrated Washington* (Nashville, TN: Nelson Current, 2005), 45.
4. Jane Corbin, *Al-Qaeda: In Search of the Terror Network That Threatens the World* (New York: Thunder Mouth's Press/Nation Books, 2003), 255.
5. Peter L. Bergen, *Holy War, Inc.: Inside the Secret World of Osama bin Laden* (New York: Free Press, 2002), 231.
6. "Islamic Extremism: Common Concern for Muslim and Western Publics," Pew Global Attitude Project, Princeton, NJ, Pew Research Center, July 14, 2005.
7. "A Year After Iraq War: Mistrust of America in Europe Ever Higher, Muslim Anger Persists," Pew Global Attitude Project, Princeton, NJ: Pew Research Center, March 16, 2004.
8. Ibid.
9. Walter M. Weiss, *Islam* (Koln, Germany: DuMont Buchwerlag GmbH und Co., 1999), 131–33.

10. William A. Mayer and Beila Rabinowitz, "President Bush Sending WH Representative Karen Hughes to Radical ICNA Conference," *Militant Islam Monitor,* August 29, 2005, http://www.militantislammonitor.org/article/id/1027.

11. Symptoms of Islamophobia outlined in Robert Spencer, *The Politically Incorrect Guide to Islam (and the Crusades)* (Washington DC: Regnery, 2005), 197.

12. Ibid., 198–99.

13. Testimony of Dr. Ali Suna, Joint Inquiry into Intelligence Community Activities Before and After the Terrorist Attacks of September 9, 2001, U.S. Senate Select Committee on Intelligence and U.S. House Permanent Select Committee on Intelligence, December 2002.

14. Kroft's interrogation of Secretary Norman Mineta in Michelle Malkin, *In Defense of Internment* (Washington DC: Regnery, 2004), 22. See also Tony Blankley, *The West's Last Chance* (Washington DC: Regnery, 2005), 168–69.

15. Daniel Pipes, "The FBI Fumbles," *New York Post,* March 14, 2003.

16. Ibid.

17. Mark Flessner, quoted in "The Story of Gamal Abdel-Hafiz: Former Special Agent in the FBI's International Terror Squad," *Frontline,* Public Broadcasting System (PBS), September 11, 2002.

18. Ibid.

19. "FBI Charges Florida Professor with Terrorist Activities," CNN, February 20, 2003.

20. Michael Fechter, "FBI Agent Who Refused to Tape al-Arian Is Suspended," *Tampa Tribune,* March 3, 2003.

21. Harvey Kushner with Bart Davis, *Holy War on the Homefront* (New York: Sentinel, 2004), 17.

22. Ibid.

23. Michael Isikoff and Mark Hosenball, "Reinstated," *Newsweek,* February 25, 2004.

24. Ibid.

25. Pipes, "The FBI Fumbles."

26. Isikoff and Hosenball, "Reinstated."

27. Marlena Telvick, "The Story of Gamal Abdel-Hafiz: Former Agent in the FBI's International Terror Squad," *Frontline,* Public Broadcasting System (PBS), September 11, 2002.

28. Isikoff and Hosenball, "Reinstated."

29. Ibid.

30. Paul Sperry, *Infiltration,* 3.

31. Ibid.

32. Ibid., 9.
33. Ibid., 4.
34. Ibid.
35. Daniel Pipes, "A Slick Islamist Heads to Jail," *New York Sun*, August 3, 2004.
36. Sperry, *Infiltration*, 27.
37. "Abdurahman Alamoudi Sentenced to Jail in Terrorism Financing Case," The U.S. Department of Justice, Press Release, October 15, 2004.
38. Douglas J. Hagman, "U.S. Treasury Department: Abdurahman Alamloudi Raised Money for al-Qaeda in U.S.—Revelation Called 'Stunning,'" Northeast Intelligence Network, July 18, 2005, http://www.homelandsecurityus.com/alamoudi.asp.
39. Pipes, "A Slick Islamist Heads for Jail"; see also Sperry, *Infiltration*, 26.
40. Pepe Escobar, "The Shadow Iraqi Government," *Middle East News*, April 25, 2005.
41. Robert Wright, "Iraq Winners Allied with Iran Are the Opposite of U.S. Vision," *Washington Post*, February 14, 2005.
42. Ibid.
43. Ibid.
44. "Iranian Official on Landmark Iraq Visit," *Aljazeera*, May 17, 2005.
45. Escobar, "The Shadow Iraqi Government."
46. Trofimov, *Faith at War*, 184.
47. Ibid., 183.
48. Pepe Escobar, "The Shadow Iraqi Government."
49. See Daniel Pipes, *Militant Islam Reaches America* (New York: Norton, 2003), 137.
50. Dave Eberhart, "Muslim Moderate Kabbani Firm on Terrorist Nuclear Threat," United Press International, *Newsmax.com*, November 19, 2001, http//www.newsmax.com/archives/article?ARTICLE_ID=29100.
51. Mark Clayton, "How Are Mosques Fighting Terror?" *Christian Science Monitor*, August 12, 2002.
52. Paul Sperry, "I.S.—Saudi Oil Imports Fund American Mosques," *World Net Daily*, April 22, 2002, http://www.worldnetdaily.com/news/article/asp?ARTICLE_ID=27327.
53. Ibid.
54. Many of these mosques are discussed by Sperry, *Infiltration*, 100–118.
55. Paul L. Williams, *Al-Qaeda: Brotherhood of Terror* (Indianapolis: Alpha Books, 2002), 10.
56. Carl Limbacher, "Mosque Linked to '93 World Trade Center Bombing Funded Bin Laden," *Newsmax*, November 26, 2003.

57. Peter Lance, *100 Years of Revenge* (New York: Regan Books, 2003), 38–42.
58. Quoted in Peter L. Bergen, *Holy War, Inc.: Inside the Secret World of Osama bin Laden* (New York: Free Press, 2002), 136.
59. Pipes, *Militant Islam Reaches America*, 137.
60. Ibid.
61. Bergen, *Holy War, Inc.*, 138.
62. Simon Reeve, *The New Jackals: Ramzi Yousef, Osama Bin Laden, and the Future of Terrorism* (Boston: Northeastern University Press, 2002), 24.
63. Daniel Benjamin and Steven Simon, *The Age of Sacred Terror* (New York: Random House, 2002), 7.
64. Ibid., 18.
65. Joe Kaufman and Beila Rabinowitz, "Father Knows Terror Best," *Front Page,* October 27, 2003, http://www.frontpagemag.com/articles/ReadArticle .asp?ID=10517.
66. Sperry, *Infiltration*, 109.
67. Ibid.
68. Kaufman and Rabinowitz, "Father Knows Terror Best."
69. Benjamin and Simon, *The Age of Sacred Terror,* 5.
70. John Miller, "A Decade of Warnings: Did Rabbi's 1990 Assassination Mark Birth of Islamic Terror in America?" *20/20,* ABC News, August 16, 2002.
71. Jason Williams and Andrew Brent, "The World Comes to Atlantic Avenue," *Street Level,* New York University School of Journalism, July 15, 2003, http://www.journalism.nyu.edu/publiczone/streetlevel/atlanticave /world/money.html.
72. Serge Trifkovic, "Sword of the Prophet," *Wall Street Journal,* February 5, 2003.

BLUNDER 2: BELIEVING ISLAM IS A RELIGION OF PEACE AND TOLERANCE AND THAT MUHAMMAD WAS A KIND AND MERCIFUL PROPHET

1. "'Islam Is Peace,' Says President," Remarks by the President at Islamic Center of Washington DC, September 12, 2001.
2. Ibid.
3. Ibid.
4. Robert Spencer, *The Politically Incorrect Guide to Islam (and the Crusades)* (Washington DC: Regnery, 2005), 84–85.
5. Bernard Lewis, *The Political Language of Islam* (Chicago: University of Chicago Press, 1988), 73.
6. Ibid.
7. Ari Fleischer, September 17, 2001, http://www.whitehousegov/news /releases/2001/09/20010917-8.html.

8. Colin Powell, *Dateline*, September 12, 2001. See also Daniel Pipes, "The United States Government: Patron of Islam?" *Middle East Quarterly*, January 2002, http://www.danielpipes.org/article/90.

9. "President Bush's Statement on the First Anniversary of 9-11," Afghanistan Embassy, Washington DC, September 10, 2002.

10. "President Clinton's Ramadan Message," November 27, 2001, http://pdg .state.gov/scripts/cpcgi.exe/@pdqtest.1.env.

11. President Clinton's Remarks on Islam, U.S. Information Agency, December 22, 2000, http://pdq.state.gov.

12. Hillary Clinton, "First Lady Hosts Annual Eid Celebration," WSIA, January 22, 1999.

13. Madeleine Albright, "Learning More About Islam," *State Magazine*, September 2000.

14. Sir John Glubb, *The Life and Times of Muhammad* (New York: Cooper Square Press, 1998), 69–70.

15. Edward Rice, *Captain Sir Richard Francis Burton* (New York: Harper-Collins, 1990), 263–89.

16. Paul Fregosi, *Jihad in the West: Muslim Conquests from the 7th to the 21st Centuries* (New York: Prometheus Books, 1998), 34.

17. Hafiz Ghulam Savuav, *Muhammad, the Holy Prophet* (Pakistan: M. Ashraf, 1969), 18–19.

18. Karen Armstrong, *Muhammad: A Biography of the Prophet* (San Francisco: HarperCollins, 1993), 64.

19. W. Montgomery Water, *The History of Al Tabari: Mohammad at Mecca* (Binghamton: State University of New York Press, 1988), 26–45.

20. Will Durant, *The Age of Faith*, vol. 5, *The Story of Civilization* (New York: Simon & Schuster, 1950), 161.

21. Ibid., 162.

22. Glubb, *The Life and Times of Muhammad*, 72.

23. Durant, *The Age of Faith*, 162.

24. William L. Cleveland, *A History of the Modern Middle East*, 3rd ed. (Boulder, CO: Perseus Book Group, 2004), 15–18.

25. Mohammad Ibn Ishaq, *Sirat Rasul Allah* (*The Life of Mohammad*), trans. A. Guillaume (Oxford: Oxford University Press, 1955), 106.

26. Armstrong, *Muhammad*, 83–84.

27. Walter Weiss, *Islam* (New York: Barron's, 2000), 15.

28. *Islamic Dictionary*, http://muttaguin.com/dictionary3.html; Thomas P. Hughes, *A Dictionary of Islam* (London: W. H. Allen, 1896), 289.

29. Ibid., 16.

30. Fregosi, *Jihad*, 32.

31. Ibn Ishaq, *Sirat Rasul Allah,* 287.

32. Ibid., 289–313.

33. Ibid., 305.

34. Fregosi, *Jihad,* 43; Ishaq, *Sirat Rasul Allah,* 309–14.

35. Fregosi, *Jihad,* 63.

36. Ahmad ibn Naqib al-Misri, *Reliance of the Traveler,* trans. Nuh Ha Mim Keller (Beltsville, MD: Amana Publications, 1994), 600.

37. Ibn Ishaq, *Sirat Rasul Allah,* 675.

38. Fregosi, *Jihad,* 44.

39. Ibn Ishaq, *Sirat Rasul Allah,* 676.

40. Ibid., 367.

41. Ibid.

42. Ibid., 369.

43. Ibid.

44. Ayatollah Ja'far Subhani, *The Message* (Karachi, Pakistan: Islamic Seminary Publications, n.d.), chap. 31, "The Dangerous Designs of the Jews." http://al-islam.org/message/32.htm.

45. Fregosi, *Jihad,* 59.

46. *Sahih al-Muslim,* 8:3371, trans. Abdul Hamid Siddiqui, Muslim Student Association, University of Southern California, 2001, http://www.usc.edu/dept/MSA/fundamentals/hadithsunnah/muslim/.

47. Ibid.

48. Ibn Ishaq, *Sirat Rasul Allah,* 665.

49. Ibid., 515.

50. Ibid., 258–59.

51. Ibid.

52. Durant, *The Age of Faith,* 171.

53. *Sahih Bukhari,* 1:268, trans. M. Muhsin Khan, Muslim Student Association, University of Southern California, 2001, http://www.usc.edu/dept/MSA/fundamentals/hadithsunnah/bukhari/.

54. Ibn Ishaq, *Sirat Rasul Allah,* 525–26.

55. *Sahih Bukhari,* 5:235.

56. Ibid., 8:151, 5:234.

57. Ibid., 5:62, 64.

58. Ibid., 5:58, 236.

59. Ibid., 8:151.

60. Ibid., 1:270, 3:36, 7:6, 3:148, 3:149, 3:150, 7:142.

61. *Hadith of Bukhari,* trans. by Muhammad Assad, http://www.sacred-texts.com/isl/bukhari/index.htm.

62. Ayatollah Ruhollah Khomeini, *Tahrirolvasyleh*, vol. 4 (Gom, Iran: Darol Elm, 1990), 186.
63. Ibn Ishaq, *Sirat Rasul Allah*, 678.
64. Ibid., 681.
65. *Sahih Bukhari*, 5:716.
66. Fregosi, *Jihad*, 116–21.
67. Paul L. Williams, *The Complete Idiot's Guide to the Crusades* (New York: Macmillan, 2001).
68. Fregosi, *Jihad*, 347–48.
69. Spencer, *Politically Incorrect Guide to Islam*, 114–15.
70. *Sahih al-Muslim*, 26:5430.
71. Paul Sperry, "Airline Denied Atta Paradise Wedding Suit," *World Net Daily*, September 11, 2002, http://www.worldnetdaily.com/news/article.asp?ARTICLE_ID=28904.
72. *Sahih al-Muslim*, 4:2127.
73. David Fielding and Anja Shortland, "An Eye for an Eye, a Tooth for a Tooth: A Study of Political Violence," University of Otago, Economic Discussion Paper, no. 0507, May 2005.
74. Khalid Dawaud, "Light at the End of the Tunnel?" *Al-Ahram Weekly*, April 1, 1999.
75. Tony Blankley, *The West's Last Chance* (Washington DC: Regnery, 2005), 73.
76. World Islamic Statement, "Jihad Against Jews and Crusaders, February 28, 1998," in Paul L. Williams, *Osama's Revenge: The Next 9/11* (New York: Prometheus Books, 2004), 215–18.
77. Osama bin Laden, "Declaration of War Against the Americans Occupying the Land of the Two Holy Places," August 23, 1996, in Williams, *Osama's Revenge*, 179–213.
78. Sulaiman Abu Ghaith, "Why We Fight America," in Paul L. Williams, *The Al-Qaeda Connection: International Terrorism, Organized Crime and the Coming Apocalypse* (New York: Prometheus Books, 2005), 15–21.
79. "Sheikh Nasir bin Hamid al Fah's fatwa, 'A Treatise on the Legal Status of Using Weapons of Mass Destruction Against Infidels,'" cited in *Osama bin Laden's Mandate for Nuclear Terror*, Jewish Institute for National Security Affairs, December 10, 2004.

BLUNDER 3: ELECTING A PEANUT FARMER AS PRESIDENT

1. Victor Lasky, *Jimmy Carter: The Man and the Myth* (New York: Richard Marek Publishers, 1979), 78.

2. Lewis L. Gould, *The Modern American Presidency* (Lawrence: University of Kansas Press, 2003), 18.

3. Allen Rostron, "Mr. Carter Goes to Washington," *The Journal of Film and Television* (Summer 1997).

4. "Gerald Rashsoon: Exit Interview," conducted by Davis Alsobrook of the Presidential Papers Staff, September 12, 1979, http://webstorage2.mcpa .virginia.edu/library/nara/jec/oral history/exit/jec_rafshoon_gerald.pdf.

5. Lasky, *Carter,* 240–42.

6. Jack Anderson with Daryl Gibson, *Peace, War, and Politics* (New York: Forge, 1999), 307–8.

7. Klaus Rohrich, "The Trouble with Jimmy Carter," Canada Free Press, August 5, 2005, http://www.canadafreepress.com/2005/Klaus080505.htm.

8. Paul Johnson, *Modern Times: The World from the Twenties to the Nineties,* rev. ed. (New York: HarperCollins, 1992), 673.

9. Matthew M. Ojos, "Jimmy Carter and Salt II: The Path to Frustration," *American Diplomacy,* July 1979.

10. "Research: Latin America," Heritage Foundation, Washington DC, 2005, http://www.heritage.org/Research/LatinAmerica/BG1579.cgm

11. Johnson, *Modern Times,* 673.

12. Ibid.

13. Jamie Glazov, "Remembering Sandinista Genocide," *Front Page Magazine,* June 2, 2002, http://www.frontpagemag.com/Articles/ReadArticle.osp? ID=180.

14. Stephen Kinzer, *All the Shah's Men: An American Coup and the Roots of the Middle East Terror* (Hoboken, NJ: John Wiley and Sons, 2003), 45.

15. Ibid., 43–61.

16. Ibid., 195–96.

17. Johnson, *Modern Times,* 711.

18. Robin Wright, *The Last Great Revolution: Turmoil and Transformation in Iran* (New York: Knopf, 2000), 46.

19. "Ayatollah Khomeini," Iran Chamber Society, November 1, 2005, http:// www.irancamber.com/history/rkkhomeini/ayatollah_khomeini.php.

20. Ayatollah Ruhollah Khomeini, *Islam and Revolution: Writings and Declarations of Imam Khomeini,* trans. Hamid Algar (Berkeley, CA: Mizan Press, 1981), 374.

21. Bernard Lewis, *From Babel to Dragomans: Interpreting the Middle East* (New York: Oxford University Press, 2004), 306.

22. Ibid., 310.

23. William L. Cleveland, *A History of the Modern Middle East,* 3rd ed. (Boulder, CO: Perseus Books, 2004), 427.

24. Ibid.
25. Lewis, *From Babel to Dragomans,* 310.
26. Johnson, *Modern Times,* 711.
27. Grace Goodell, "How the Shah De-Stabilized Himself," *Policy Review* (Spring 1981).
28. Shaul Bakhash, "The Islamic Revolution," in *The World's Hot Spots: Iran* (Farmington Hills, MI: Greenhaven Press, 2005), 20.
29. Cheuch Morse and Abavat Torah, "Carter Sold Out Iran," American Freedom Network, Johnstown Foundation, Washington DC, http://www.americannewsnet.com/cmtrs/cmtrs.04.htm.
30. Quoted in Lasky, *Carter,* 380.
31. Morse and Torah, "Carter Sold Out Iran."
32. Bakhash, "The Islamic Revolution," 24.
33. Ibid.
34. Ibid.
35. "Ayatollah Khomeini: Holy Terror," Arts and Entertainment Television Network, New York, Time/Warner, airdate October 3, 2003.
36. Alan Peters, "Role of US Former President Carter Emerging in Illegal Financial Demands on Shah of Iran," *Defense and Foreign Affairs Daily,* March 15, 2004, http://rescueattempt.tripod.com/id24.html.
37. Ibid.
38. Ibid.
39. Ibid.
40. Quoted in Clark R. Mollenhoff, *The President Who Failed: Carter Out of Control* (New York: Macmillan, 1980), 228.
41. Morse and Torah, "Carter Sold Out Iran."
42. Bernard Lewis, *The Political Language of Islam* (Chicago: University of Chicago Press, 1988), 57.
43. Cleveland, *A History of the Modern Middle East,* 440.
44. Bakhash, "The Islamic Revolution," 26.
45. Johnson, *Modern Times,* 713.
46. Ibid.
47. Lowell Ponte, "Carter's Appease Prize," *Front Page Magazine,* October 16, 2002, http://frontpagemag.com/articles/Printable.asp?ID=3843.
48. Mitchell Bard, *The Complete Idiot's Guide to the Middle East Conflict* (Indianapolis: Alpha Books, 1999), 288.
49. "Jimmy Carter," *The American Experience,* Public Broadcasting System (PBS), http://www.pbs.org/wqbh/amex/carter/peopleeventse_hostage.html.
50. Ibid.
51. Jimmy Carter, "Crisis of Confidence Speech," July 15, 1979, Jimmy

Carter: Primary Sources, Public Broadcasting System (PBS), http://www
.pbs.org/wgbh/amex/carter/filmmore/ps_crisis.html.

52. Quoted in Johnson, *Modern Times,* 674.

53. Quoted in Ibid.

54. Bard, *Middle East Conflict,* 292.

55. Ibid.

56. Ibid.

57. Ibid.

58. David Harris, *The President, the Prophet, and the Shah* (New York: Little, Brown: 2004).

59. Paul L. Williams, *The Al-Qaeda Connection: International Terrorism, Organized Crime, and the Coming Apocalypse* (New York: Prometheus Books, 2005), 34–35.

60. Johnson, *Modern Times,* 713.

BLUNDER 4: PLAYING BOTH SIDES AGAINST THE MIDDLE AND GIVING HUSSEIN THE SCREWS

1. William L. Cleveland, *A History of the Modern Middle East,* 3rd ed. (Boulder, CO: Perseus Books, 2004), 437.

2. Mark Danner, "Taking Stock of the Forever War," *New York Times Magazine,* September 11, 2005.

3. Stephen Schwartz, *The Two Faces of Islam: Saudi Fundamentalism and Its Role in Terrorism* (New York: Random House, 2003), 162.

4. Paul Johnson, *Modern Times: The World from the Twenties to the Nineties,* 3rd ed. (New York: Harper Collins, 1992), 713.

5. Gary Sick, "The Iran-Iraq War," in *Iran: The World's Hot Spot,* ed. Mikko Canini (San Diego: Greenhaven Press, 2005), 34.

6. Johnson, *Modern Times,* 713.

7. McNair Paper Number 41, "Radical Responses to Radical Regimes: Evaluating Pre-Emptive Counter-Proliferation," Washington DC, Institute for National Strategic Studies, May 1995.

8. Ibid.

9. Johnson, *Modern Times,* 715.

10. Schwartz, *The Two Faces of Islam,* 162.

11. Ibid., 714.

12. Danner, "Taking Stock of the Forever War."

13. Ibid.

14. Johnson, *Modern Times,* 715.

15. Julie Wolf, "The Iran-Contra Affair," *The American Experience,* Public

Broadcasting System (PBS), WGBU, 1999, http://www.pbs.org/wgbh/amex/reagan/peopleevents/pande08.html.

16. Ibid.

17. Casper Weinberger to Lt. Gen. Colin Powell, Document 61, in the *Iran-Contra Scandal: The Declassified History,* ed. Peter Kornbluh and Malcolm Byrne (New York: New Press, 1993), 228.

18. Ibid., 214

19. Ibid.

20. Ibid.

21. Robert McFarlane, "Memorandum for George Shultz," July 13, 1986, in ibid., 255.

22. Kornbluh and Byrne, *Iran-Contra Scandal,* 214.

23. Ibid.

24. *United States of America v. Oliver L. North,* U.S. District Court for the District of Columbia, May 5, 1989.

25. Caspar Weinberger, testimony in Joint Hearings before the Select Committees on the Iran-Contra Investigation, July 31, 1987.

26. *Iran-Contra Scandal,* 217.

27. Ibid.

28. George Shultz, testimony in Joint Hearings before the Select Committees on the Iran-Contra Investigation, July 23, 1987.

29. Wolf, "The Iran-Contra Affair."

30. Ibid.

31. Ibid.

32. Cleveland, *History of the Modern Middle East,* 418.

33. Ted Koppel, "The USS *Vincennes*: Public War, Secret War," *Nightline,* ABC News, July 1, 1992.

34. Cleveland, *A History of the Modern Middle East,* 418.

35. Sick, "The Iran-Iraq War," 40.

BLUNDER 5: SPREADING DEATH AND DESTRUCTION TO PROTECT SAUDI OIL

1. William L. Cleveland, *A History of the Modern Middle East,* 3rd ed. (Boulder, CO: Perseus Books, 2004), 479.

2. Ibid.

3. Ibid.

4. Ibid.

5. Daniel Pipes, "Heroes and Knaves of the Kuwait Crisis," in *A Restless Mind: Essays in Honor of Amos Perlmutter,* ed. Benjamin Frankel (London

and Portland, OR: F. Cass, 1996). The material here comes from the pre-published version of Pipes's article, which can be found at http://www.danielpipes.org/article/985.

6. April Glaspie, quoted in "Excerpt from Iraqi Document on Meeting with U.S. Envoy," *New York Times*, September 23, 1990.

7. Paul Johnson, *Modern Times: The World from the Twenties to the Nineties*, rev. ed. (New York: Harper Collins, 1992), 769.

8. Ibid., 768–69.

9. Mark Danner, "Taking Stock of the Forever War," *New York Times Magazine*, September 11, 2005.

10. Yossef Bodansky, *Bin Laden: The Man Who Declared War on America* (New York: Random House, 1999), 29.

11. Phil Gasper, "Afghanistan, the CIA, bin Laden, and the Taliban," *International Socialist Review*, November-December 2001, http://www.thirdworldtraveler.com/Afghanistan/Afghanistan_CIA_Taliban.html.

12. "Prince Sultan Air Base," GlobalSecurity.org, http://www.globalsecurity.org/military facility/princesiltan.htm.

13. Ibid.

14. Paul L. Williams, *The Al-Qaeda Connection: International Terrorism, Organized Crime, and the Coming Apocalypse* (New York: Prometheus Books, 2005), 42.

15. Osama bin Laden, "Jihad Against Jews and Christians," World Islamic Statement, appendix B, cited in Paul L. Williams, *Osama's Revenge: The Next 9/11: What the Media and the Government Haven't Told You* (New York: Prometheus Books, 2004), 215.

16. Daniel Benjamin and Steven Simon, *The Age of Sacred Terror* (New York: Random House, 2002), 107–8.

17. Simon Reeve, *The New Jackals: Ramzi Yousef, Osama bin Laden, and the Future of Terrorism* (Boston: Northern University Press, 2002), 172.

18. Peter Bergen, *Holy War, Inc.: Inside the Secret World of Osama Bin Laden* (New York: Simon & Schuster, 2002), 86–87.

19. Yaroslav Trofimov, *Faith at War: A Journey on the Frontlines of Islam from Baghdad to Timbuktu* (New York: Henry Holt, 2005), 13–14.

20. Ibid.

21. Craig Unger, *House of Bush, House of Saud* (New York: Scribner, 2004), 136.

22. Ibid.

23. James Baker, quoted in David Hoffman, "Gulf Crisis Tests Baker as Diplomat," *Washington Post*, November 2, 1990.

24. George H. W. Bush, quoted in Unger, *House of Bush, House of Saud*, 135.

25. Ibid., 135.
26. Ibid., 136–37.
27. Ibid., 137.
28. George H. W. Bush, quoted in ibid.
29. Ibid.
30. Ibid., 117–28.
31. Mitchell Bard, *The Complete Idiot's Guide to the Middle East Conflict* (Indianapolis: Alpha Books, 1990), 341.
32. Johnson, *Modern Times*, 771.
33. Ibid., 773.
34. Robert Young Pelton, *The World's Most Dangerous Places*, 4th ed. (New York: HarperCollins, 2000), 574.
35. Ibid.
36. Johnson, *Modern Times*, 774.
37. Cleveland, *A History of the Modern Middle East*, 486–87.
38. Ibid.
39. Martti Ahtisaari, U.N. undersecretary for administration and management, *Report to the General Assembly*, March 20, 1991.
40. Felicity Arbuthnot, "Cradle to Grave: The Impact of the UN Embargo," *New Internationalist Magazine* (January-February 2005), http://www.thirdworldtraveler.com/Iraq/CradleGrave_IraqEmbargo.html.
41. Ibid.
42. George Bush and Brent Scowcroft, *A World Transformed* (New York: Vintage Books, 1998), 489.

BLUNDER 6: IGNORING THE BOOMING NUCLEAR BLACK MARKET

1. Graham Allison, *Nuclear Terrorism: The Ultimate Preventable Catastrophe* (New York: Henry Holt, 2004), 69.
2. Robert Young Pelton, *The World's Most Dangerous Places*, 4th ed. (New York: Harper Resource, 2000), 783.
3. Ibid.
4. Ibid. See also Paul L. Williams, *The Al-Qaeda Connection: International Terrorism, Organized Crime, and the Coming Apocalypse* (New York: Prometheus Books, 2005), 82–83.
5. Patrick J. Buchanan, *The Death of the West: How Dying Populations and Immigrant Invasions Imperil Our Country and Civilization* (New York: St. Martin's Press, 2000), 102.
6. Allison, *Nuclear Terrorism*, 70.
7. Pelton, *The World's Most Dangerous Places*, 783.

8. Allison, *Nuclear Terrorism*, 70.

9. Williams, *The Al-Qaeda Connection*, 83.

10. Pelton, *The World's Most Dangerous Places*, 784.

11. Phil Williams and Paul Woessner, "The Real Threat of Nuclear Smuggling," *Scientific American* (January 1996).

12. "Chechnya's Special Weapons," Global Security, October 2001, http://www.globalsecurity.org/wmd/wond/chechnya/.

13. Ibid.

14. Mark Riebling and R. Eddy, "Jihad@Work," *National Review*, October 24, 2002, http://www.nationalreview.com/comment/comment-riebling102402.asp.

15. Bill Nichols, Mimi Hall, and Peter Eisler, "Dirty Bomb Threatens U.S. with Next Terror Attack," *USA Today*, June 11, 2002.

16. Ibid.

17. "Dirty Bombs: Response to a Threat," Public Information Report, *Journal of the Federation of American Scientists* (March–April 2002).

18. Andrew Cockburn and Scott Cockburn, *One Point Safe* (New York: Doubleday, 1997), 101–3.

19. Barry Farber, "The Case of Keith Idema," *Newsmax.com*, July 22, 2004, http://www.newsmax.com/archives/2004/7/22/105010.shtml. Idema's exploits are chronicled in Robin Moore, *The Hunt for Bin Laden* (New York: Random House, 2003).

20. David Smigielski, "A Review of the Nuclear Suitcase Bomb Controversy," Policy Update, Russian-American Nuclear Security Council (RANSAC), September 2003, http://www.ransac.org/Documents/suitcasenukes/090103.pdf.

21. Nimrod Raphaeli, "Ayman Muhammed Rabi al-Zawahiri: The Making of an Arch Terrorist," *Terrorism and Political Violence* (Winter 2002): 1–22.

22. Williams, *The Al-Qaeda Connection*, 92.

23. Ibid., 93.

24. Scott Parish, "Are Suitcase Nukes on the Loose? The Story Behind the Controversy," Center for Nonproliferation Studies, Monterey Institute of International Studies, Monterey, California, November 1997.

25. Ibid.

26. Ibid.

27. "Osama's Nukes Traced to Soviet General," *Newsmax.com*, July 18, 2004, http:www.newsmax.com/archives/articles/2004/7/18/213209.shtml.

28. Allison, *Nuclear Terrorism*, 48–49.

29. Michael Barletta and Erik Jorgensen, "Weapons of Mass Destruction in the Middle East," Center for Nuclear Nonproliferation Studies, Monterey Institute for International Affairs, Monterey, California, April 1999.

30. Indictment of Mahmouh Mahmud Salim, U.S. Attorney General's Office, Southern District of New York, January 6, 1999.

31. Jane Corbin, *Al-Qaeda: In Search of the Terror Network That Threatens the World* (New York: Thunder's Mouth Press/Nation Books, 2002), 59.

32. "Bin Laden Endorses 'The Nuclear Bomb of Islam,'" *Fact Sheet: The Charges Against Osama bin Laden,* U.S. Department of State, December 15, 1999. Also see "Interview with bin Laden," *Time,* December 23, 1998.

33. Simon Reeve, *The New Jackals: Ramzi Yousez, Osama bin Laden, and the Future of Terrorism* (Boston: Northeastern University Press, 2002), 186–87.

34. "Al-Majallah Obtains Serious Information on Al-Qaeda's Attempt to Acquire Nuclear Arms," *Al-Majallah* (London-based Saudi weekly), September 8, 2002.

35. "N-weapons May Be in US Already," *Daily Telegraph,* Sydney, Australia, November 14, 2001.

36. Ryan Mauro, "Terrorist Possession of Weapons of Mass Destruction," *World Threats,* Monthly Analysis, February 2003, http:www.worldthreats .com/monthly%20Analysis/MA%202003.htm. Also see Robert Friedman, "The Most Dangerous Mobster in the World," *Village Voice,* May 22, 1998.

37. Mauro, "Terrorist Possession of Weapons of Mass Destruction."

38. "Bin Laden's Nuclear Weapons," *Insight,* November 2, 2001.

39. Ryan Mauro, "The Next Attack on America," *World Threats,* November 27, 2003, http://www.freepublic.com/focus/f-news/1020690/posts. Also see "Bin Laden Buys Nuclear Materials," *World Net Daily,* November 26, 2003.

40. Testimony of Col. Stanislav Lunev, National Security Committee, Hearings on Russian Threats, January 2000.

41. Ibid.

42. Yossef Bodansky, *Bin Laden: The Man Who Declared War on America* (New York: Random House, 1999), 330.

43. "Bin Laden's Nuclear Weapons."

44. Richard Sale, "Feds Look for Smuggled Nukes in the United States," United Press International, *Newsmax,* December 21, 2001, http://www .newsmax.com/archives/articles/2001/12/20/181037.shtml. See also *Insight,* December 21, 2001.

BLUNDER 7: SIDING WITH THE ENEMY

1. "Ibrahim Rugova: Pacifist at the Crossroads," BBC, May 5, 1999, http:// news.bbc.ci.uk/1/hi/special_report/1998/kosovo/110821.stm.

2. Marcia Christoff Kurop, "Al-Qaeda's Balkan Links," *Wall Street Journal,* November 1, 2001.

3. Ibid.

4. Peter Wolf, "The Assassination of Ahmad Shah Massoud," Center for Research and Globalization, September 14, 2003, http://www.globalresearch.co/articles/wol409A.html.

5. Tom Walker and Aiden Laverty, "CIA Aided Kosovo Guerrilla Army," *Sunday Times* (London), March 12, 2000.

6. Ibid.

7. Milan Pavolic, "Chronology of KLA's Terrorism," *Nedeljni Telegraph* (the Belgrade daily newspaper), http://members.tripod.com/Balkania/resources/terrorism/kla_chronology_96-98.html.

8. Jon Silberman, "Racak Massacre Haunts Milosevic Trial," BBC, February 12, 2002.

9. "Kosovo: Obscure Areas of a Massacre," *Le Figaro* (Paris), January 20, 1999; "Were the Racak Dead Really Massacred?" *Le Monde* (Paris), January 20, 1999.

10. Daniel Pearl and Robert Block, "Despite Tales, the War in Kosovo Was Savage, but Wasn't Genocide," *Wall Street Journal,* December 31, 1999.

11. "Ibrahim Rugova: Pacifist at the Crossroads."

12. William Cohen, quoted in Jonathan Steele, "Serb Killings 'Exaggerated' by West," *Manchester Guardian,* August 18, 2000, http://www.guardian.co.uk/Archive/Archive/0,4273,4052755,00.html.

13. Paul L. Williams, *The Al-Qaeda Connection: International Terrorism, Organized Crime, and the Coming Apocalypse* (New York: Prometheus Books, 2005), 69.

14. "Kosovo Fact-Finding Mission," A White Paper of the Religious Freedom Coalition, August 2004, http://www.serbianunity.net/bydate/2004/October9/file/1096632196_3t3qqcixix.sksovowhitepaper.html.

15. Ibid.

16. Robert Fisk, "Serbs Murdered by the Hundreds," *Independent,* November 24, 1999.

17. David Lynch, "Serbs Fear They Will Be Eliminated from Kosovo," *USA Today,* March 27, 2000.

18. Pearl and Block, "Despite Tales."

19. Juan Lopez Palafox, quoted in "Where Are Kosovo's Killing Fields?" Center for Peace in the Balkans, October 17, 1999, http://www.balkanpeace.org/monitor/mgen21.html.

20. Pearl and Block, "Despite Tales."

21. "At a Glance: The Hague Tribunal," BBC, June 10, 2005, http://news.bbc.co.uk/1/world/europe/1418304.stm

22. Paul Mitchell, "Milosevic Trial Sets Precedent: US Granted Right to Censor Evidence," International Committee of the Fourth International, December 31, 2002, http://www.wsws.org/articles/2003/dec2003/cens-d31 .shtml.
23. Michael Grunwald, "CIA Helps Thwart Bomb Plot Against Embassy in Uganda," *Seattle Times*, September 25, 1998.
24. Rohan Gunaratna, *Inside Al-Qaeda: Global Network of Terror* (New York: Berkeley Books, 2002), 63.
25. Bill Clinton, quoted in Peter L. Bergen, *Holy War, Inc.: Inside the Secret World of Osama Bin Laden* (New York: Simon & Schuster, 2002), 125.
26. Ibid.
27. Ibid.
28. Mauvi Fazlur Rehman Khalil, quoted in Yossef Bodansky, *Bin Laden: The Man Who Declared War on America* (New York: Random House, 1999), 284–85.
29. Rahimullah Yusufzai, quoted in ibid., 295.
30. Hassan Abdullah al-Turabi, quoted in ibid.
31. Bergen, *Holy War,* 166.
32. Ibid., 167.
33. Tim Werner, "Terror Suspect Said to Anger Afghan Hosts," *New York Times*, March 4, 1999.
34. William C. Rempel, "Saudi Tells of Deal to Arrest Terror Suspect: Afghans Back-Pedaled on Hand-Over of bin Laden After U.S. Embassy Blasts," *Los Angeles Times*, August 8, 1999.
35. Prince Turki bin Faisal ibn Abdul Aziz Al Saud, quoted in Jane Corbin, *Al-Qaeda: In Search of the Terrorist Network That Threatens the World* (New York: Thunder's Mouth Press, 2003), 69–70.
36. Larry Goodson, quoted in Ed Warner, "The Taliban and al-Qaeda at Odds Before 1998 Bombing," *Voice of America*, August 7, 2002, http://www. why-war.com/news/2002/08/07/taliban.html.
37. Matthew Levitt, "The Network of Terrorist Funding," *Washington Institute*, August 15, 2002.
38. Steve Miller, "Oregon Group Thrives Despite al-Qaeda Ties," *Washington Times*, September 3, 2003.
39. Levitt, "The Network of Terrorist Funding."
40. Corbin, *Al-Qaeda*, 95.
41. Richard Miniter, *Losing Bin Laden: How Bill Clinton's Failures Unleashed Global Terror* (Washington DC: Regnery, 2003), 224.
42. Ibid.

43. Ibid., 224–26.

44. Ibid., 226–27

45. Bin Laden's poem in ibid., 228.

BLUNDER 8: INITIATING OPERATION ENDURING FOREVER

1. Alan Wood and Paul Thompson, "An Interesting Day: President Bush's Movements and Actions on 9/11," The Center for Cooperative Research, May 9, 2003, http://www.cooperativeresearch.net/timeline/main/essayaninterestingday.html.

2. Dan Balz and Bob Woodward, "America's Chaotic Race to War: Bush's Global Strategy Began to Take Shape in First Frantic Hours After Attack," *Washington Post*, January 21, 2002.

3. Michael Johnson, "They Had a Plan," *Time*, August 4, 2002.

4. Susan Taylor Martin, "The Man Who Would Have Led Afghanistan," *St. Petersburg (FL) Times*, September 1, 2002.

5. Wood and Thompson, "An Interesting Day."

6. Mike Allen, "Bush Reacts to Attacks, Moves to Nebraska," *Washington Post,* September 12, 2001.

7. Jean Heller, "In Chaos, TIA Tower Controlled 9/11 Skies," *St. Petersburg Times*, September 7, 2002.

8. William Langley, "Revealed: What Really Went on During Bush's 'Missing Hours,'" *London Daily Telegraph,* December 16, 2001.

9. "The President's Story," *60 Minutes II,* CBS News, September 11, 2002.

10. Richard Benedetto and Susan Page, "Bush's Job Approval Lowest Since 9/11," *USA Today,* January 13, 2003.

11. "Presidential Address to the Nation," October 7, 2001, White House Press Service, Washington DC.

12. "Infinite Justice Out—Enduring Freedom In," BBC News, September 25, 2001.

13. Ibid.

14. "President's Address to the Nation," September 11, 2001, White House Press Service, Washington, DC.

15. Rohan Gunaratna, *Inside al-Qaeda: Global Network of Terror* (New York: Berkeley Books, 2002), 102.

16. Jane Corbin, *Al-Qaeda: In Search of the Terror Network That Threatens the World* (New York: Thunder's Mouth Press/Nation Books, 2003), 248.

17. Peter L. Bergen, *Holy War, Inc.: Inside the Secret World of Osama bin Laden* (New York: Simon & Schuster, 2002), 231.

18. Luke Harding and Jason Burke, "U.S. Blamed for 100 Missile Deaths,"

Manchester Guardian, October 12, 2002.

19. Paul L. Williams, *Osama's Revenge: The Next 9/11* (New York: Prometheus Books, 2004), 69.

20. Bin Laden, quoted in Corbin, *Al-Qaeda*, 260.

21. Ibid.

22. During the first week of Operation Enduring Freedom, M. Sgt. Evander Earl Andrews was killed in a heavy equipment accident that occurred in the Arabian Peninsula. Although Andrews was not killed in combat, he is often listed as the first casualty of the offensive.

23. Richard Lloyd Parry, "Al-Qaeda's Almost Immune from Attack," *Independent* (London), November 27, 2001.

24. Ibid.

25. Corbin, *Al-Qaeda*, 267.

26. "Bin Laden 'Heard' in Tora Bora," BBC, December 16, 2001.

27. Gen. Richard Myers, quoted in Mark Barker, "Anti-Taliban Troops Launch Offensive on Tora Bora," Radio Free Europe, December 10, 2001, http://www.rferl.org/features/2001/12/10122001075819.asp.

28. "Bin Laden Men to Surrender," BBC, December 11, 2001.

29. David Ensor, "Close In on al-Qaeda," CNN, December 21, 2001.

30. Ibid.

31. Ibid.

32. Mary Anne Weaver, "Lost at Tora Bora," *New York Times Magazine*, September 11, 2005.

33. Ibid.

34. Corbin, *Al-Qaeda*, 257.

35. Pir Baksh Bardiwal, quoted in ibid., 270.

36. Weaver, "Lost at Tora Bora."

37. Ilene R. Prusher and Philip Smucker, "Al-Qaeda Quietly Slipping into Iran, Pakistan," *Christian Science Monitor*, November 23, 2003.

38. Aamir Latif, "Al-Qaeda Said to Have Migrated to Iran," *Washington Times*, July 20, 2003.

39. Osama bin Laden, text of speech in *Washington Post*, December 27, 2001.

40. Williams, *Osama's Revenge*, 75.

41. "Al-Qaeda's Nuclear Plans Confirmed," BBC, November 16, 2001.

42. Osama bin Laden, address on Aljazeera, February 11, 2003.

43. Weaver, "Lost at Tora Bora."

44. Corbin, *Al-Qaeda*, 293.

45. Global Intelligence Company, "Operation Anaconda: Questionable Outcomes for the United States," March 11, 2002, http://www.stratfor.com/fib/fib_view.php?ID=203443.

46. John F. Burns, "U.S. Planes Pound Enemy as Troops Face Tough Fight," *New York Times,* March 4, 2002.

47. Global Intelligence, "Operation Anaconda."

48. Maj. Gen. Frank Hagenbeck, quoted in "U.S. Army 'On Top' in Afghan War," *Guardian* (Islamabad), March 6, 2002.

49. Barry Bearak, "Details of Victory Are Unclear, But It Is Celebrated, Nonetheless," *New York Times,* March 14, 2002.

50. President George W. Bush, quoted in Mushahid Hussein, "Operation Anaconda: Win-Win, Lose-Lose," *Asia Times,* March 22, 2002.

51. Corbin, *Al-Qaeda,* 298-99.

52. Gen. Tommy Franks, quoted in "U.S. Ends Operation Anaconda," *Online News Hour,* March 18, 2002, http://www.pbs.org/newshour/update/afghan_3-18-02.html.

53. Gen. Frank Hagenbeck, quoted in "Operation Anaconda Ends in Eastern Afghanistan," CNN, March 19, 2002, http://www.cnn.com/2002/WORLD/asispcf/central/03/19/ret.afghanistan.anaconda/index.html.

54. Vivienne Wait, "No Bodies Where Battle Began," *USA Today,* March 14, 2002.

55. Barry Bearak, "Details of Victory Are Unclear."

56. Julian Borger and Richard Norton-Taylor, "U.S. Blunder Let bin Laden Escape," *Guardian* (Islamabad), April 18, 2002.

57. Gen. Tommy Franks, quoted in Corbin, *Al-Qaeda,* 299.

58. Robert Young Pelton, *The World's Most Dangerous Places,* 5th ed. (New York: Harper Collins, 2004), 159.

59. Claire Sterling, *Octopus: How the Long Reach of the Sicilian Mafia Controls the Global Narcotics Trade* (New York: Simon & Schuster, 1990), 162.

60. Umberto Pascali, "KLA and Drugs: The 'New Colombia of Europe' Grows in the Balkans," *Executive Intelligence Review,* June 22, 2001.

61. Stella L. Jatras, "The Crimes of the KLA: Who Will Pay?" *Anti-War News,* March 14, 2002, http://www.antiwar.com/article/php?articleid=1499.

62. Ibid.

63. Ibid.

64. Terry Frieden, "FBI: Albanian Mobsters 'New Mafia,'" CNN, August 19, 2004.

65. Paul L. Williams, *The Al-Qaeda Connection: International Terrorism, Organized Crime, and the Coming Apocalypse* (New York: Prometheus Books, 2005), 64.

66. Research Analysis, Centre of Peace in the Balkans, May 2000, http://www.balkanpeaceorg/our/out02.shtml.

67. Ibid.

68. Jason Burke, "Afghanistan: Heroin in the Holy War," *New Delhi Observer,* December 6, 1998.

69. Paul L. Williams, *Osama's Revenge,* 75. See also "Bin Laden Sought on Christmas," United Press International, December 24, 2001, http://www .newsmax.com/archives/articles/2001/12/24/202348.shtml.

70. Yossef Bodansky, quoted in Paul L. Williams, *The Al-Qaeda Connection,* 57.

71. Roland Jacquard, *In the Name of Osama Bin Laden: Global Terrorism and the Bin Laden Brotherhood* (Durham, NC: Duke University Press, 2002), 138.

72. Congressman Mark Steven Kirk, quoted in Paul L. Williams, *The Al-Qaeda Connection,* 57.

73. Rachel Ehrenfeld, "Osama: The Heroin Pusher," *Front Page Magazine,* January 3, 2005, http://www.frontpagemag.com/Articles/Printable.asp ?ID=16510.

BLUNDER 9: LEAVING OPEN THE BACK DOOR TO AMERICA

1. Terry Frieden, "FBI: Albanian Mobsters 'New Mafia,'" CNN, August 19, 2004.

2. Jerry Capeci, "Zef's Got Staying Power Too," *Gangland,* September 4, 2003, http://www.ganglandnews.com/column346.html#zef.

3. Guy Xhudo, "Men of Purpose: The Growth of Albanian Criminal Activity," Ridgeway Center for International Security Studies, University of Pittsburgh, Spring 1996.

4. M. Bozinovich, "The New Islamic Mafia," *Serbianna,* February 21, 2005, http://www.serbianna.com/columns/mb/.028.shtml.

5. Anthony M. DeStefano, "The Balkan Connection," *Wall Street Journal,* September 9, 1985.

6. Ibid.

7. Bozinovich, "The New Islamic Mafia."

8. Richard Sale, "Feds Look for Smuggled Nukes in the United States," United Press International, *Newsmax.com,* December 21, 2001, http:// www.newsmax.com/archives/articles/2001/12/20/181037.shtml.

9. Stephen Flynn, quoted in ibid

10. Ibid.

11. Peter Hudson, "There Are No Terrorists Here," *Newsweek,* November 19, 2001.

12. Philip K. Abbot, "Terrorist Threat in the Tri-Border Area, *Military Review* (September–October 2004).

13. Mark S. Steinitz, "Middle East Terror Activities in Latin America," *Policy Papers on the Americas,* vol. 14, study 7 (July 2003).

14. William W. Mendel, "Paraguay's Ciudad Del Este and the New Centers of Gravity," *Military News* (March–April 2002).

15. Robert Young Pelton, *The World's Most Dangerous Places*, 5th ed. (New York: Harper Collins, 2004), 389.

16. Martin Edwin Andersen, "Al-Qaeda Across America," *Insight*, November 2, 2001.

17. Henry Chu, "Terrorist Suspicions Persist at Border Town in Brazil," *Los Angeles Times*, December 26, 2004.

18. Rohan Gunaratna, *Inside Al-Qaeda: Global Network of Terror* (New York: Berkeley Books, 2002), 221.

19. Ibid.

20. Harris Whitbeck and Ingrid Arneson, "Terrorists Find Haven in South America," CNN, November 7, 2001; Jeffrey Goldberg, "In the Party of God," *New Yorker*, October 10, 2001.

21. Marc Perelman, "Brazil Connection Links Terrorist Groups," *Forward*, March 21, 2003.

22. Henry Orrego, "Bin Laden Trail Grows Cold on South America's Triple Frontier," Aljazeera, May 20, 2003.

23. Sebastian Junger, "Terrorism's New Geography," *Vanity Fair* (December 2002).

24. Jim Bronskill, "Terrorists Eyed Ottawa Targets," *Ottawa Citizen*, February 8, 2004.

25. Ibid.

26. Paul L. Williams, *The Al-Qaeda Connection: International Terrorism, Organized Crime, and the Coming Apocalypse* (New York: Prometheus Books, 2005), 133.

27. Craig Unger, "Saving the Saudis," *Vanity Fair* (October 2003).

28. David Kalish, "Charming and Well-Connected, Bin Laden Family Spans the Globe," Associated Press, October 4, 2001.

29. George Jahn, "Brazil Has Tentatively Agreed to Let U.N. Atomic Watchdog View Parts of Its Equipment to Enrich Uranium," Associated Press, October 6, 2004.

30. Andersen, "Al-Qaeda Across America."

31. Hudson, "There Are No Terrorists Here."

32. Joseph Farah, "Al-Qaeda South of the Border," *G-2 Bulletin*, February 18, 2004, http:www.worldnetdaily.com/news/article.asp?Article_ID=37133.

33. Marc Perelman, "Feds Call Chile Resort a Terror Hot Spot," *Forward*, January 2, 2003.

34. Martin Arostegui, "Search for Bin Laden Looks South," United Press International, October 12, 2001.

35. Ibid.
36. "Narco-News Editorial on Citigroup and White Collar Terrorism," *Narco News*, October 12, 2001, http://www.narconews.com/issue14 /whitecollarterror1.html.
37. "Report Evaluates Al-Qaeda Risks World-Wide," *USA Today*, November 11, 2003.
38. "Texaco Faces $1 Billion Lawsuit," BBC, October 22, 2003.
39. "U.S. Lawyers Say Chevron Texaco Fears Lawsuit," *San Jose (CA) Mercury News*, October 24, 2003.
40. Arostegui, "Search for Bin Laden Looks South."
41. "Latin America Security Challenges," Newport Papers, Naval War College, New Port, RI, 2004.
42. Ivan G. Osorio, "Chavez's Bombshell," *National Review*, January 8, 2003.
43. Ibid.
44. Dale Hurd, "Terrorism's Western Ally," Christian Broadcasting Network, April 22, 2003.
45. Arostegui, "Search for Bin Laden Looks South."
46. Dale Hurd, "Terrorism's Western Ally."
47. Gordon Thomas, "The Secret War," *Sunday Express* (London), November 9, 2003.
48. "Latin America on Alert for Terror," *USA Today*, August 21, 2004.
49. "Al-Qaeda Said to Recruit in Latin America," *Newsmax.com*, August 23, 2004, http://www.newsmax.com/archives/2004/8/22/13453.shtml.
50. Honduran minister Oscar Alvarez, quoted in Julio Medino Murillo, "Analysis: Al-Qaeda Recruiting Hondurans?" *Insight*, January 17, 2005, http://www.insightmag.com/news/2004/05/11World/Analysis.AlQaeda .RecruitingHondurans.html.
51. Ibid.
52. Daniel Eggen and Manuel Roig-Franzia, "FBI on Global Hunt for Al-Qaeda Suspect," *Washington Post*, March 21, 2003.
53. Kelli Arena and Kevin Bohn, "Link Between Wanted Saudi Man and 'Dirty Bomb' Suspect," CNN, March 22, 2003.
54. Elaine Shannon and Tim McGirk, "What Is This Man Planning?" *Time*, August 23, 2004.
55. FBI Alert, March 20, 2003.
56. David Kidwell, "Broward Man Sought as Terror Suspect," *Miami Herald*, March 21, 2003.
57. "FBI Manhunt Targets Al-Qaeda Suspects," CBS News, March 26, 2004.
58. Bill Gertz, "Al-Qaeda Pursued a 'Dirty Bomb,'" *Washington Times*, October 7, 2003; "State Department Offers $5 Million Reward for Al-Qaeda Dirty

Bomb Plotter Who Attempted to Enter U.S.," *Nuclear Threat Initiative*, October 5, 2004.

59. Gertz, "Al-Qaeda Pursued a 'Dirty Bomb.'" Also see John Loftus, "180 Pounds of Nuclear Material Missing in Canada," WABC, November 7, 2003.

60. "Most Wanted: The Next Atta," *60 Minutes*, CBS News, March 26, 2004.

61. James Gordon Meek, "Officials Fear Al-Qaeda Nuclear Attack," *New York Daily News*, March 14, 2003.

62. Ibid. See also, Elaine Shannon and Michael Weisskopf, "Khalid Shaikh Muhammad Names Names," *Time*, March 24, 2003.

63. Meek, "Officials Fear Al-Qaeda Nuclear Attack."

64. "FBI Seeking Public Assistance in Locating Individuals Suspected of Terrorist Activities," FBI National Press Office, March 20, 2004.

65. Jim Kirksey, "Two Suspected Al-Qaeda Agents Dropped in for Meal, Says Denny's Manager," *Denver Post*, May 28, 2004.

66. Shannoon and McGirk, "What Is This Man Planning?"

67. "Border Breach Stirs Fears," *Dallas Morning News*, August 14, 2004.

68. Michael Marizco, "Sonora on Alert for #1 Al Qaida Suspect," *Arizona Daily Star*, August 18, 2004.

69. Luke Turf, "Al Qaida Leader May Try to Cross Border," *Tucson Citizen*, August 18, 2004.

70. "Al-Qaeda Wants to Smuggle N-Materials to US," *Nation*, November 17, 2004.

71. Anna Clearley and Ornell R. Soto, "Reason for Plane Theft Worrisome," *San Diego Union Tribune*, November 7, 2004.

72. Donald Bartlett and James Steele, "Who Left the Door Open?" *Time*, September 20, 2004.

73. Investigators on Eyewitness News 4, "Terrorist Alley: Illegals from Terrorist Nations Are Crossing the Border into Arizona," KVOA-TV, Tucson, Arizona, aired August 13, 2004.

74. Jon Dougherty, "Al Qaida Evidence Along U.S. Border?" *World Net Daily*, November 26, 2005, http://www.wnd.com/news/printer-friendly.asp?ARTICLE_ID=47589.

75. "Newly Obtained OTM and Special Interest Alien Information," Press Release, Office of Congressman Tom Tancredo, Colorado's Sixth District, August 10, 2004.

76. Congressman Tom Tancredo, quoted in "Al-Qaeda Coming Through," *National Review*, August 24, 2005.

77. "51 Terror Suspects Nabbed Trying to Enter U.S. Illegally," *World Net Daily*, December 15, 2005, http://www.wnd.com/news/printer-friendly.asp?ARTICLE_ID=47914.

78. Emma Perez-Trevino, "Potential Terrorists Released Due to Lack of Jail Space, Congressman Says," *Brownsville (TX) Herald,* June 23, 2004.

79. Jerry Seper, "Sensitivities 'Key in Future Arrests,'" *Washington Times,* July 4, 2004.

80. Congressman Solomon Ortiz, quoted in Perez-Trevino, "Potential Terrorists Released Due to Lack of Jail Space."

81. Keach Hagey, "Jamaica Man Pleads Guilty to Giving Al-Qaeda Money and Supplies," *Queens Chronicle,* August 19, 2004. Also see, Shannon and McGirk, "What Is This Man Planning?"

82. Julian Coman, *Daily Telegraph* (London), August 15, 2004.

83. Sheriff D'Wayne Jernigan, quoted in Karen Gleason, "Sheriff's Protest Delays Release," *Del Rio (TX) News Herald,* July 12, 2004.

84. Asa Hutchinson, quoted in Jerry Seper, "Rounding Up Illegals 'Not Realistic,'" *Washington Times,* September 10, 2004.

85. "Woman with Altered Passport Detained," CNN, July 28, 2004.

86. Michelle Malkin, "Homeland Insecurity Files," August 1, 2004, http:// michellemalkin.com/archives/00325.htm.

BLUNDER 10: FAILING TO DECLARE WAR AGAINST RADICAL ISLAM

1. Michael A. Fletcher and Darryl Fears, "Bush Pushes Guest-Worker Program," *Washington Post,* November 29, 2005.

2. Darryl Fears, "Little Support for Bush Immigration Plan," *Washington Post,* October 22, 2005.

3. Fletcher and Fears, "Bush Pushes Guest-Worker Program."

4. Dave Montgomery, "GOP Officials Urge President to Target Illegal Immigration," *Fort Worth Star-Telegram,* November 6, 2005.

5. Linda Feldman, "The Fractious Politics of Immigration," *Christian Science Monitor,* December 1, 2005.

6. Liz Sidotti, "War Costs May Hit Half a Trillion," Associated Press, December 14, 2005, http://aolsvc.news.aol.com/news/article.adp?id= 20051214013809990031.

7. *Bangladesh: A Portrait of Covert Genocide* (Woodhaven, NY: Bangladesh Hindu, Buddhist, & Christian Unity Council, 2004), i-xxiii.

8. Dahlia Lithwick, "What War Powers Does the President Have?" *Washington Times,* September 13, 2001, http://www.slate.com/toolbar.aspx?action =print&id=1008290.

9. Albert E. Jenner, "Fixing the War Powers Act," Heritage Lecture #529, Washington DC, The Heritage Foundation, May 22, 1995, http://www .heritage.org/Research/NationalSecurity/hl529.cfm.

10. Sulaiman Abu Ghaith, "Why We Fight America," in Paul L. Williams, *The Al-Qaeda Connection: International Terrorism, Organized Crime, and the Coming Apocalypse* (New York: Prometheus Books, 2005), 26.

11. Geoffrey R. Stone, *Perilous Times: Free Speech in Wartime* (New York: Norton, 2004), 285.

12. Ibid.

13. Tony Blankley, *The West's Last Chance* (Washington DC: Regnery, 2005), 128.

14. Chief Justice Frederick Moore Vinston, quoted in ibid.

15. *Johnson v. Eisentrager,* cited in ibid., 119.

16. Stone, *Perilous Times,* 617.

17. Ibid., 116–17.

18. "11 of the Same Family Roasted in Banshkhali," *Bangladesh Observer,* November 20, 2003.

19. John Vidal, "Rape and Torture Empties Village," *Manchester Guardian,* July 21, 2003.

20. Stone, *Perilous Times,* 286–87.

21. Justice Felix Frankfurter, quoted in Blankley, *The West's Last Chance,* 124.

22. Ibid.

23. President George W. Bush, quoted in Paul Sperry, *Infiltration: How Muslim Spies and Subversives Have Penetrated Washington* (New York: Nelson Current, 2005), 280.

24. Ibid.

25. Craig Unger, *House of Bush, House of Saud: The Secret Relationship Between the World's Two Most Powerful Dynasties* (New York: Scribner, 2004), 307–10.

26. Gordon Thomas, "Los Malerines de Osama," *El Mundo,* September 23, 2001; Williams, *The Al-Qaeda Connection,* 28. Testimony concerning bin Laden's acquisition of nuclear weapons and materials while living in Sudan was provided by former al Qaeda operatives in *United States v. Usama bin Laden, et al.,* S (10) 98 Cr. (LBS), Southern District of New York, 2001.

27. "Bin Laden's Nuclear Weapons," *Insight,* November 21, 2001.

28. Ibid.

29. Arnaud de Borchgrave, "Al-Qaeda Nuclear Agenda Verified," *Washington Times,* December 10, 2001.

30. Bernard Henri-Levy, "Pakistan Must Provide Proof of Reforming the ISI," *South Asia Tribune,* September 14, 2003.

31. Richard Sale, "Feds Look for Smuggled Nukes in the United States," United Press International, *Newsmax,* December 21, 2001, http://www

.newsmax.com/archives/articles/2001/12/20/181037.shtml. Sales is not only a UPI correspondent but also a former CIA agent. He is recognized as a leading authority on counterterrorism.

32. "Al-Qaeda's Nuclear Plans Confirmed," *BBC*, November 16, 2001, http://news.bbc.co.uk/1/hi/world/south_asia/1657901.stm.

33. Gen. Eugene Habiger, quoted in Graham Allison, *Nuclear Terrorism: The Ultimate Preventable Catastrophe* (New York: Times Books/Henry Holt, 2004), 6.

34. "The al-Qaida Nuke Terror Threat," *World Net Daily,* August 11, 2005, http://www.worldnetdaily.com/news/printer-friendly.asp?ARTICLE_ID =45717.

35. "Chemical, Nuclear Arms Still a Major Threat, Cheney Says," *Washington Post,* December 17, 2003; James Carroll, "For Nuclear Safety, the Choice Is Clear," *Boston Globe,* October 26, 2004.

36. "Ashcroft: Nuclear Bombs Biggest Threat in Terror War," *Columbia (MO) Daily Tribune,* January 28, 2005. Also see Tom Ridge, in Allison, *Nuclear Terrorism,* 6.

37. "Warren Buffet Warns of Terror Risks," BBC News, May 6, 2002.

38. Graham Allison, "Could the Worst Be Yet to Come?" *Economist,* November 1, 2001.

39. Bill Keller, "Nuclear Nightmares," *New York Times Magazine,* May 26, 2002.

40. "Interview with Michael Scheuer," *60 Minutes,* CBS News, November 14, 2004.

41. "Osama bin Laden's Mandate for Nuclear Terror," Jewish Institute for National Security Affairs, December 10, 2004, http://www.jinsa.rg/article /view.html?documentid=2762.

42. Ibid.

Index

227

Index

Index